Prairie State Books

In conjunction with the Illinois Center for the Book,
the University of Illinois Press is reissuing in paperback works
of fiction and nonfiction that are, by virtue of authorship
and/or subject matter, of particular interest to
the general reader in the state of Illinois.

Publication of this book and others in the Prairie State Books
program was supported in part by a generous grant from Carl A. Kroch.

BLOODY WILLIAMSON

BLOODY WILLIAMSON

A Chapter in
American Lawlessness

PAUL M. ANGLE

Introduction by John Y. Simon

University of Illinois Press
Urbana and Chicago

All of the photographs in this book, some from *Life and Exploits of
S. Glenn Young* (1989) and some from his private collection, are
used courtesy of Gordon Pruett, Crossfire Press, P.O. Box 365,
Herrin, Illinois 62948.

This book is printed on acid-free paper.

Library of Congress Cataloging-in-Publication Data

Angle, Paul M. (Paul McClelland), 1900–1975.
Bloody Williamson : a chapter in American lawlessness /
Paul M. Angle : with an introduction by John Y. Simon.
p.   cm. — (Prairie state books)
Originally published: New York : Alfred A. Knopf, 1952.
Includes bibliographical references.
ISBN 978-0-252-06233-9 (alk. paper)
1. Crime—Illinois—Williamson County—History. 2. Violence—Illinois—
Williamson County—History. 3. Coal miners—Illinois—Williamson County—
History. 4. Strikes and lockouts—Coal mining—Illinois—Williamson
County—History. 5. Vendetta—Illinois—Williamson County—History. 6.
Williamson County (Ill.)—History.
I. Title. II. Series
HV6795.W54A54   1992
331.89'28334'09773993—dc20   92-9721
                                                    CIP

Socialism, communism, and other doctrines have played no part in the violence and murder which have brought such ill fame to this "queen of Egypt." The issues are strictly American, and the wrongs done are the native products of the United States.

William L. Chenery in *The Century,*
December 1924.

INTRODUCTION

PAUL M. ANGLE's *Bloody Williamson* has sold briskly for forty years and never disappointed readers. This riveting chronicle of violence and crime in a southern Illinois county inspires revulsion and outrage overshadowed by horrified fascination. A master storyteller and skilled writer, both historian and journalist, Angle enlivened local history with drama and insight into human nature. A recent bibliographical essay, which emphasizes the book's value to historians, praises the "beautiful prose" of "a classic in Illinois literature."[1] Despite Angle's prominence as an authority on Abraham Lincoln, *Bloody Williamson* has become his best-known and most enduring work.

Born on Christmas Day 1900 in Mansfield, Ohio, the sixth of seven children in a grocer's family, Angle attended Oberlin College and graduated from Miami University of Ohio, where he worked his way through college, joined a fraternity, lettered in football, and earned a Phi Beta Kappa key. After eight months of an unsatisfactory stint selling life insurance, he enrolled at the University of Illinois, receiving an M.A. in history in 1924. He then became a salesman for the American Book Company, which he found as rewarding as selling insurance. One year later, offered both a teaching post at Miami and the position of executive secretary of the Lincoln Centennial Association, he chose the latter because it paid more.[2]

Angle single-handedly transformed a sleepy commemorative association (renamed the Abraham Lincoln Association) into a research center and propelled himself into the top ranks of Lincoln scholars. Before he turned thirty, Angle had chronicled

Lincoln's daily activities from 1854 to his inauguration as president in 1861, published a collection of newly gathered Lincoln letters, and won national recognition for exposing fraudulent Lincoln documents printed in the *Atlantic Monthly*. In 1932 he collaborated with Carl Sandburg on an unusual book about Mary Lincoln in which the first half displayed Sandburg's flamboyant prose and the second contained Angle's skillful editing of Mary Lincoln documents and letters.[3]

Also in 1932 he left the Lincoln Association to become Illinois state historian and director of the Illinois State Historical Library because he believed, incorrectly as it turned out, that a state agency could better ride out the depression than a private organization.[4] In the same year, however, Illinois elected Governor Henry Horner, a Chicagoan lonely in Springfield and an avid Lincoln collector, who relished Angle's intellectual companionship and collaborated in building the library's collections and prestige. When an eccentric descendant of Civil War general John A. McClernand offered to sell his ancestor's papers to the Historical Library at a bargain price if he could receive payment the same day, Horner himself approved bypassing state bureaucracy to acquire a major collection.[5] Horner capped this collaboration by bequeathing the library his superb collection of printed Lincolniana. In 1945 Angle moved to the Chicago Historical Society, where he served as director for twenty years, and his association with the society continued until his death ten years later. In 1946 he published *A Shelf of Lincoln Books*, a guide to the indispensable literature about Lincoln, an unusually readable and charming series of bibliographical essays. His 1947 *Lincoln Reader*, a composite biography consisting of selections from sixty-five authors skillfully woven into one narrative, a Book-of-the-Month Club selection, enhanced his reputation as a Lincoln scholar.[6]

With a few minor exceptions attributable to his connections to the Illinois State Historical Library and Chicago Historical Society, Angle's scholarship and writing had concentrated on

Lincoln. For more than a quarter century, however, he had been fascinated by the tragedies of Williamson County, especially the Herrin Massacre, which had occurred the year he graduated from college, and the continuing violence of the 1920s, still in progress when he arrived in Springfield. For years he expected someone in southern Illinois to examine and explain these dramatic incidents but nobody did. Meanwhile the events of the 1920s recurrently furnished grist for sensational and inaccurate journalism. Political and economic spokesmen for Williamson County hoped to attract business and industry by beautifying the gamy past. Concerned that truth would expire crushed between exploitation and repression, Angle decided to tackle the subject himself. Angle could heartily endorse the commandment of W. H. Auden: "Thou shalt not sit / With statisticians nor commit / A social science."[7] *Bloody Williamson* sails proudly between the shoals of sensationalism and sociology.

Angle maintained an ambivalent attitude toward other historians. "I never taught a minute in my life and never regretted the lack, and some of these academic historians don't think you're a *professional* historian unless you do teach in a university and have the union card—the Ph.D." Academic historians, "enamored of computers, statistical methods, the combination of disciplines," he grumbled, had "gotten away from one of the primary appeals of history, which is to tell a story."[8] The enthusiastic acclaim that reviewers gave *Bloody Williamson* came from journalists rather than academics.[9]

As director of historical agencies in Springfield and Chicago, Angle wrote much that was required by his occupation. He launched a sprightly journal, *Chicago History*, producing much of the graceful content himself. He also wrote for promotional and commercial purposes. His last book, an adulatory biography of Philip K. Wrigley, who had inherited a chewing gum company and a National League baseball franchise, carried an opening disclaimer. "I undertook this work of my own volition, unprompted by anyone. . . . The Wrigleys have read the manuscript in its final form and have made some corrections and clarified certain passages. They have not objected to any of my own interpretations, although with some I suspect they are not wholly in agreement. The book has not been subsidized in any way." [10] Such a disclaimer, of course, contributes to the embarrassment of Angle's admirers.

Certain indignities still rankled as Angle reviewed his career as public historian: herding children to the Lincoln shrines of Springfield for the Abraham Lincoln Association, tolerating patronage appointments and political chores as state historian, and pampering wealthy trustees of the Chicago Historical Society. Once required to add his signature as state historian to papers providing patronage appointments to supervisory positions in the WPA Federal Writers' Project, Angle complained in the presence of Governor Horner.

> "You talk as if all politicians are crooks," the governor snapped. I apologized as well as I could and scribbled for five minutes in silence. Then the governor spoke again. "You're damned near right."

Even Horner's staunch support of the library carried a price: Angle was "drafted" to prepare radio scripts for the governor's 1936 reelection campaign. [11]

Satisfaction and dissatisfaction still contended in Angle as he neared the end of his distinguished career. *Bloody Williamson*, however, occupied a special position on the shelf of Angle books. It was "as good a book as I am capable of writing," he had stated in his foreword and more than twenty years later explained why he considered it "the best book I ever wrote."

> I suppose that book came closer to achieving what I really set out to do than any other. That's my own opinion of it, and I suppose that's why it's my favorite. And I think it's my favorite because I devised a style that was new to me, which I'd never attempted before. And I believe I pulled it off. I would call it the staccato style. Short sentences, short paragraphs, keeping the story moving. I'm inclined to write more discursively

than I did in the book, but I thought that the situation called for a different kind of literary approach.[12]

Striving to achieve literary grace, Angle struggled equally for meticulous accuracy. He tried to keep faith with Williamson County friends, especially Oldham Paisley of the *Marion Republican* and Hal W. Trovillion of the *Herrin News*, who had so generously furnished information and assistance with the hope that the troubled past would receive fair treatment. If Angle's pen slipped in even minor matters of fact or interpretation concerning events thirty years or less in the past and remembered clearly by living witnesses, Williamson County critics would attempt to discredit the entire book. He provided no such opportunity. Forty years later the book stands alone, sui generis, as an authoritative account.

Angle had one predecessor. In 1876 Milo Erwin of Marion had published *The History of Williamson County, Illinois*, devoting more than half its pages to a catalog of crime in which the Bloody Vendetta received detailed coverage. A twenty-nine-year-old Williamson County native and a defense attorney in the vendetta cases, Erwin presented an account substantially accurate, though considerably overwritten and passionate. Whatever local embarrassment the controversial book caused, neighbors twice elected Erwin to the state legislature.[13] Angle began his book with an account of the 1922 Herrin Massacre, the single most dramatic and appalling event in Williamson County's past. He followed this with a flashback to the Bloody Vendetta of the 1870s, based to a considerable extent on Erwin, supplemented with a rich array of contemporary newspaper sources.

While drawing on Erwin's vivid account, Angle ignored implications that the family feud, triggered by trivial incidents, had roots in Williamson County's bitter division of allegiances during the Civil War. The opening shots at Fort Sumter found Williamson County filled with sympathy for the South based on the origins of a preponderance of the population in the upland

South, reinforced by decades of adherence to the pro-southern wing of the Democratic party and strong Negrophobic beliefs. Congressman John A. Logan, who had recently established residence in Marion, received the passionate loyalty of his constituents during the first two months of the war, when his own views on North and South were unformulated or concealed. Many assumed that his sympathies lay with secession. Marion residents passed resolutions of support for the Confederacy, mounted a foray to cut the vital Illinois Central Railroad in neighboring Jackson County, and even raised a company that marched south to join Confederate forces in Kentucky.[14]

After two months of silence, Logan announced his support for the Union, returned to Marion to begin recruiting a regiment, and commenced the political metamorphosis that would make him a staunch Republican when the war ended. Not all in southern Illinois followed him, however, and the effect of the Emancipation Proclamation in transforming a war for the Union into a war against slavery aroused such bitterness in Williamson County that one locally raised regiment disintegrated. After five months and before the unit marched beyond Illinois, desertion had trimmed the rolls of the 128th Illinois Volunteers from 860 to 161 men. Disgusted officials discharged most of the officers and transferred the remaining men to another regiment.[15] Many deserters returned home to live as outlaws, drawing on the sympathies of county residents to elude the provost forces sent to arrest them. They had "declared that they would lie in the woods until the moss grew on their backs rather than help free the slaves."[16]

In June 1863 Provost Marshal Isaac N. Phillips reported that citizens of Williamson County refused to assist in enrolling men for the draft because deserters and "rebel sympathizers" threatened their lives and property.[17] Backed by 240 cavalrymen and 40 infantry, Phillips imposed martial law on Marion. His action, he explained, might appear unwarrantable to those unaware of "the dreadful and stupendous opposition to the Government that exists among the people of Marion—as well as their hatred to all officers of the Government."[18] While enforcing the draft, soldiers dispersed some 130 deserters and their allies from a fortified camp on the Big Muddy River.[19] Most likely this was the band—led by George Aiken, former quartermaster of the 128th Illinois—believed responsible for robbery and murder in Franklin and Williamson counties.[20]

After the war ended, a group of thirteen men, including George W. Sisney, recently discharged as a Union captain, met in the rear of a Marion drugstore to organize a Williamson County Republican Party a decade after the party's establishment elsewhere in the state. Carrying the county in their first appearance, Republicans soon elected Sisney sheriff.[21] Local political division exacerbated tensions between wartime loyalists and disloyalists in the county. During the Bloody Vendetta, the Sisney faction was identified with the Republicans, although both feuding factions contained Union veterans.[22] While the vendetta raged, a local Ku Klux Klan flourished, only loosely connected to its southern counterpart. These local vigilantes, whose true motivations remain obscure, terrorized Egypt in the name of morality.[23] The Bloody Vendetta had increased potential for escalation because it arose in a county already divided between Unionists and disloyalists, Democrats and Republicans, Klansmen and their foes. Reflecting the views of their constituents, local authorities often favored a faction at the expense of preserving order.

As Angle moved to the opening of the coal-mining era, his narrative achieved tighter structure and greater dramatic power. Too many have remembered the title but ignored the subtitle: *A Chapter in American Lawlessness*. Attentive readers could note the parallels and examples Angle emphasized.

> The resort to violence may take the form of a Boston Tea Party or a Whiskey Rebellion and become a matter of national pride; it may assume the shape of a Civil War draft riot or a reprisal crusade of the Molly Maguires and go down in oblo-

quy; it may manifest itself in Frank and Jesse James or the Hatfields and McCoys and become a legend; it may materialize at Cripple Creek or the Haymarket, and appear as a blaze of tragic glory to some and a dark stain to others. It may erupt in the latest lynching or the Cicero race riot of 1951. Its forms are as diverse as the emotions of our people, and its power to break through conventional barriers, and to thrive on itself, has been demonstrated in every part of the country at every period in our history.[24]

Williamson County offered an opportunity to examine an endemic American propensity to violence in a compact setting that possessed all the necessary ingredients: "family hatreds, labor strife, religious bigotry, nativistic narrowness, a desire for money and to hell with the rules."[25] Even so, Angle included a chapter on Joseph Leiter's battle with the United Mine Workers at Zeigler, five miles north of Williamson County in Franklin County, and might appropriately have included another on the 1920 West Frankfort riot, also in Franklin County. Citizens infuriated by murders attributed to the so-called Black Hand Society retaliated with arson, assault, and murder directed against all Italians. Labeling the violence a "race" riot, the mayor and sheriff asked the governor to send troops. Some 1,000 soldiers—including a machine gun company—eventually quieted West Frankfort.[26] Enlarging upon Angle's research by following coal seams rather than county lines, a historian studied mining towns in four adjacent counties including Williamson. He concluded that as the prosperity of the region dissolved in the 1920s so also did social systems, with similar results throughout the region.[27]

Far from Williamson County, and lacking a few of the combustible elements Angle enumerated, lies "Bloody Harlan" County, Kentucky, also rich in coal and violence. "Coal has always cursed the land in which it lies," concluded Harry Caudill, the impassioned spokesman for the land and people of ravaged eastern Kentucky.[28] Counties rich in coal enriched owners living far from the mines. Yet an unstable mining economy sustained communities without alternate resources. Labor violence threatened all social and economic structures. Williamson County editors, who denounced exaggerated reports of the Herrin Massacre in other newspapers, moderated their own accounts. Oldham Paisley witnessed, but did not report, the crowds of men and women spitting on corpses of strike-breakers in the Herrin morgue.[29] Crusading country editors, however stereotypical, remain rare, especially where a single industry dominates the community.

When S. Glenn Young achieved power in Williamson County, the Ku Klux Klan had enrolled two million members nationwide, dominated some state elections, and enlisted the sympathy of those who deplored the lawless excess of the prohibition era. Campaigning with Calvin Coolidge in 1924, vice-presidential candidate Charles G. Dawes, while ostensibly attacking the Klan, condemned those who had provoked its growth.

> Consider what happened in Williamson County, Ill., where the town of Herrin is situated. A reign of lawlessness existed. It was marked by the terrible Herrin massacre. It was marked by a general breakdown in respect for law, which indicated that the officers of the county, including the Sheriff, had been intimidated by lawbreakers into inaction. A thousand members of the Ku Klux Klan, without disguise—they were brave men—marched to the office of the Sheriff of Williamson County to protest against the lawlessness in that section. If a secret organization to uphold law and order is justifiable anywhere in our country, it was justifiable there.[30]

Dawes's ambivalent remarks about the Klan reflected both its avowal of traditional ideals and its political power. In Chicago and its suburbs (where Dawes lived), Klan members numbered between forty and eighty thousand.[31] Although the Klan briefly flourished statewide, scattering threats of violence and provoking retaliation, murder followed only in Williamson County, where twenty deaths furnished the entire state total.[32] Quite clearly the county deserved both its bloody reputation and Angle's scrutiny.

Other Americans, however, had no excuse for smugness. Following Angle's pioneering exposure of the unsavory Williamson County Klan of the 1920s, numerous state and local studies have tracked the flaming crosses from Rhode Island to Oregon.[33] In southern Illinois traditionally lax law enforcement contributed to the gangster power of the Shelton brothers and Charlie Birger. Yet, driven from Williamson County, the Sheltons eventually established a secure and lucrative base in Peoria. And Al Capone dominated Chicago rackets with impunity.

What makes *Bloody Williamson* a classic is not merely the outrageous events but the rare skill with which Angle brought them to life. He led in perceiving that crime and violence deserved careful historical analysis. Changes in the national temperament in the past forty years will have altered the perspective readers bring to *Bloody Williamson*. No longer will this chronicle merely inspire revulsion for disorder in a unique and isolated county; it will more likely promote insight into a dark thread running throughout the American experience.

JOHN Y. SIMON
Southern Illinois University
at Carbondale

Notes

1. Ralph A. Stone, "Prosperity, Depression, and War, 1920–45," in *A Guide to the History of Illinois*, ed. John Hoffmann (Westport, Conn.: Greenwood Press, 1991), 97.

2. Paul M. Angle, *On a Variety of Subjects* (Chicago: Chicago Historical Society, 1974), ix–x; *Current Biography Yearbook, 1955*, ed. Marjorie Dent Candee (New York: H. W. Wilson, 1955), 20–21; *Chicago Tribune*, May 12, 1975; *New York Times*, May 13, 1975.

3. Pamphlets published 1926–30, each covering a single year, were revised, consolidated, and indexed in Angle, *Lincoln, 1854–1861* (Springfield, Ill.: Abraham Lincoln Association, 1933); Angle, *New Letters and Papers of Lincoln* (Boston: Houghton Mifflin, 1930); Angle, "The Minor Lincoln Collection: A Criticism," *Atlantic Monthly* 143 (April 1929): 516–25; Carl Sandburg and Angle, *Mary Lincoln: Wife and Widow* (New York: Harcourt, Brace, 1932).

4. Angle, *On a Variety of Subjects*, 73.

5. Ibid., 76–78. See Thomas B. Littlewood, *Horner of Illinois* (Evanston, Ill: Northwestern University Press, 1969), 126–27.

6. Angle, *A Shelf of Lincoln Books: A Critical, Selective Bibliography of Lincolniana* (New Brunswick, N.J.: Rutgers University Press, 1946); Angle, *The Lincoln Reader* (New Brunswick, N.J.: Rutgers University Press, 1947).

7. "Under Which Lyre" (1946), in *W. H. Auden: Collected Poems*, ed. Edward Mendelson (New York: Random House, 1976), 262.

8. Angle, *On a Variety of Subjects*, xvii–xviii.

9. See Irving Dilliard in *American Historical Review* 59 (January 1954): 397–98; David V. Felts in *Journal of the Illinois State Historical Society* 45 (Autumn 1952): 270–71; William E. Wilson in *Saturday Review*, October 18, 1952, 15; Theodore C. Link in *New York Times Book Review*, November 30, 1952, 16; Tarleton Collier in *New York Herald Tribune Book Review*, October 19, 1952, 17; Walter Yust in *Chicago Tribune Magazine of Books*, September 28, 1952, 3, 9.

10. Angle, *Philip K. Wrigley: A Memoir of a Modest Man* (Chicago: Rand, McNally, 1975), [7].

11. Angle, *On a Variety of Subjects*, 75–76.

12. Ibid., [165], xxi.

13. Barbara Burr Hubbs, *Pioneer Folks and Places: An Historic Gazetteer of Williamson County, Illinois* (Herrin, Ill.: Herrin Daily Journal, 1939), 37–38.

14. James P. Jones, *"Black Jack": John A. Logan and Southern Illinois*

in the Civil War Era (Tallahassee: Florida State University, 1967), 76–87; Milo Erwin, *The History of Williamson County, Illinois* (1876; Marion, Ill.: Williamson County Historical Society, 1976), 262–64.

15. J. N. Reece, *Report of the Adjutant General of the State of Illinois*, 8 vols. (Springfield, Ill.: Phillips Brothers, 1900), 6:532; *History of Gallatin, Saline, Hamilton, Franklin, and Williamson Counties, Illinois* (Chicago: Goodspeed, 1887), 499.

16. James D. Fox, *A True History of the Reign of Terror in Southern Illinois . . .* (Aurora, Ill.: J. D. Fox, 1884), 13.

17. Jasper William Cross, Jr., "Divided Loyalties in Southern Illinois during the Civil War" (Ph.D. diss., University of Illinois, 1942), 134.

18. Ibid., 138; *The War of the Rebellion: A Compilation of the Official Records of the Union and Confederate Armies*, 128 vols. (Washington, D.C.: Government Printing Office, 1880–1901), Series 3, 3:500–501, 508–9; ibid., 5:836; *Chicago Tribune*, July 30, 1863; [Springfield] *Illinois State Journal*, August 6, 1863; Robert E. Sterling, "Civil War Draft Resistance in Illinois," *Journal of the Illinois State Historical Society* 64 (Autumn 1971): 259.

19. *Chicago Tribune*, August 2, 1863; Cross, "Divided Loyalties," 140; Wood Gray, *The Hidden Civil War: The Story of the Copperheads* (New York: Viking Press, 1942), 155.

20. Erwin, *Williamson County*, 103, 281–82. See [Springfield] *Illinois State Register*, August 8, 23, 1863.

21. J. F. Wilcox, *Historical Souvenir of Williamson County, Illinois* (1905; Evansville, Ind.: Unigraphic, 1976), 26–27.

22. Erwin, *Williamson County*, 119.

23. Edgar F. Raines, Jr., "The Ku Klux Klan in Illinois, 1867–1875," *Illinois Historical Journal* 78 (Spring 1985): 17–44.

24. Angle, *Bloody Williamson*, ix.

25. Ibid., x.

26. *New York Times*, August 6, 1920; Dennis O'Connor, "Violence in Franklin County" (Seminar paper, 1973, Morris Library, Southern Illinois University), 24–33.

27. Daniel J. Prosser, "Coal Towns in Egypt: Portrait of an Illinois Mining Region, 1890–1930" (Ph.D. diss., Northwestern University, 1973), 123–26.

28. Harry Caudill, *Night Comes to the Cumberlands: A Biography of a Depressed Area* (Boston: Little, Brown, 1963), x. See also John W. Hevener, *Which Side Are You On? The Harlan County Coal Miners, 1931–39* (Urbana: University of Illinois Press, 1978); Paul F. Taylor,

Bloody Harlan: The United Mine Workers of America in Harlan County, Kentucky, 1931–1941 (Lanham, Md.: University Press of America, 1990).

29. Margaret N. O'Shea, *Oldham Paisley: A Community Editor and His Newspapers* . . . (Marion, Ill.: Marion Daily Republican, 1974), 54–55. See Edmund C. Hahesy, "The Newspaper Editor and Community Conflict: Williamson County, Illinois, 1922–1928" (M.A. thesis, Southern Illinois University, 1956).

30. Charles G. Dawes, quoted in the *New York Times*, August 24, 1924. See Michael R. McCormick, "A Political Study of Williamson County, Illinois, in the Early Twentieth Century" (M.A. thesis, Southern Illinois University, 1972).

31. Kenneth T. Jackson, *The Ku Klux Klan in the City, 1915–1930* (New York: Oxford University Press, 1967), 125.

32. Illinois Legislative Investigating Commission, *Ku Klux Klan: A Report to the Illinois General Assembly* (Chicago: Legislative Investigating Commission, 1976), 41.

33. See William H. Fisher, *The Invisible Empire: A Bibliography of the Ku Klux Klan* (Metuchen, N.J.: Scarecrow Press, 1980); Lenwood G. Davis and Janet L. Sims-Wood, *The Ku Klux Klan: A Bibliography* (Westport, Conn.: Greenwood Press, 1984).

FOREWORD

MY INTEREST in the subject of this book started with the Herrin Massacre. At that time I was a college graduate of two weeks' standing, and certain that there were at least two sides to every question, even when mass murder was involved. In the Herrin Massacre my father, a Republican of the McKinley school, could see only one side. We had some sharp arguments, and I think he must have questioned the wisdom of permitting his eldest son to be exposed to the "education" he himself had been denied.

Three years later I took a position in Springfield, Illinois, where I lived until 1945. There Herrin and Williamson County were frequent subjects of conversation. From former residents of southern Illinois, from state officials, from militia officers, from lawyers who had prosecuted or defended gangsters, from judges who had presided at their trials, I heard stories that were always fantastic and often incredible.

Then I came to know Williamson County at first hand, and to feel at home on the quiet, tree-shaded streets of Herrin and Marion, so different from the bare black camps of other coal-fields. I came to take it as a matter of course that I should spend an hour, one evening, talking with a Marion businessman about the works of Plato and Aristotle, and the relative merits of the various editions of the Encyclopædia Britannica—subjects about which his information far exceeded mine. "I keep goin' back to the ninth edition time after time," he said in the edgeless drawl that reminds one of Egypt's proximity to the South, "because of the high authority of the articles." He mentioned Huxley and

Darwin, and in philosophy Leibnitz and Schopenhauer. "And who was that monism fellow?" he asked. "I can't think of his name." I took two wild shots: "Kant? Fichte?" He shook his head, and we talked of other matters. "I've got it," he said as we parted. "Hegel!"

On another evening, in Herrin, the talk ran to fine printing, to an obscure pamphlet of Sir Thomas Browne's that my host had not been able to find, to London antiquarian booksellers, to the maps in William Camden's *Britannia,* which lay open before us.

I do not mean to imply that such interests are the rule in Williamson County. Neither are they the rule in Chicago or New York or Boston. I do contend that in friendliness and hospitality the people of this region are unsurpassed. Walk along the street in any town in Egypt—the proud name of the southernmost quarter of Illinois—and most of the pedestrians you pass will smile and wish you good morning. Walk a block or two farther, and a car will pull to the curb and stop. The driver, who has never seen you before, will ask whether he can't take you where you are going. One afternoon, as I was walking toward the square in Marion, a car stopped and the driver rolled down the window. "Ask that old fellow over there," he said, pointing to an elderly man, poorly dressed, who was leaning against a building, "if he's going anywhere. I'm going to Carterville, and I'll be glad to take him along." No, the old man replied, he wasn't going anywhere—and then he asked me, with grave courtesy, to thank the gentleman in the car. As I passed him after I had conveyed the message he nodded in gratitude.

This contrast between the people of Williamson County as I know them and their record of violence and lawlessness is one of the reasons why I decided to write this book. Another is the experience I had when I undertook, some years ago, to write a short paragraph on the Herrin Massacre for the *Dictionary of American History.* I could find no accounts of that event on which I could rely, so I spent many hours quarrying what I took to be the essential facts. (I now know that that article, of only 150 words, contains at least two inaccuracies.) My third reason is the superficiality, not to say shoddiness, of almost everything that I have seen in print on this subject. I decided that if there was enough interest in "Bloody Williamson" to justify magazine articles and feature stories every few months, there should be a place for one book based on careful research and written with as much objectivity as a fallible human could achieve.

My fourth and most compelling reason is my conviction that the story of "Bloody Williamson" is much more than a record of lawlessness in one small Illinois county. That county, as I have pointed out, is strongly "American" in population and background; I fear that it is no less "American" in those phases of its history which are my concern.

We Americans—and now I apply the term to the people who have occupied the present United States since the first English settlements in North America—have never been slow to resort to violence, sometimes in passion, sometimes in the conviction that legal processes were either inadequate or too slow in their operations; sometimes simply because the law interfered with what we wanted to do. The resort to violence may take the form of a Boston Tea Party or a Whiskey Rebellion and become a matter of national pride; it may assume the shape of a Civil War draft riot or a reprisal crusade of the Molly Maguires and go down in obloquy; it may manifest itself in Frank and Jesse James or the Hatfields and McCoys and become a legend; it may materialize at Cripple Creek or the Haymarket, and appear as a blaze of tragic glory to some and a dark stain to others. It may erupt in the latest lynching or the Cicero race riot of 1951. Its forms are as diverse as the emotions of our people, and its power to break through conventional barriers, and to thrive on itself, has been demonstrated in every part of the country at every period in our history.

Williamson County, Illinois, I believe, offers an almost unrivaled setting for a study of this phenomenon. There one can identify a wide variety of its causes—family hatreds, labor strife, religious bigotry, nativistic narrowness, a desire for money and to hell with the rules; one can observe its recurrences over more than half a century; and, because of the setting's limited geographical extent, one can see what went on with a degree of clarity impossible on a larger stage. With the possible exception of Harlan County, Kentucky, I know of no other American locality possessed of these attributes.

Some of my Williamson County friends will criticize me for writing this book. They are sensitive about their county's history, and doubtless the more so because they know their own innate decency and friendliness, and realize that odium was brought upon them either by a small minority, or by a majority acting abnormally for short periods. They contend that what Williamson County is known for is misrepresentative, and they resent, understandably, the books and articles that treat of its past, as this book does, in terms of crime and violence.

Others of my southern Illinois friends—a majority, I believe —will agree with my contention that no segment of the American past is immune to investigation, and that the story of "Bloody Williamson," so long the province of the sensationalist, needs a thoroughgoing recital more than most.

I have put the free time of five years into this book. As it stands, after repeated revisions, it is as good a book as I am capable of writing. (That is not to say, of course, that it is as good a book as could be written.) Its weaknesses stem from my deficiencies as historian and writer; it owes its merits to many besides myself. I wish I could name all who have been helpful, but if I were to do so, the list would exceed any reader's patience. Nothing, however, could excuse me for not thanking publicly those who have read my entire manuscript, and improved it greatly, in style and accuracy, by their criticisms: Willard L. King, Chicago lawyer, author, and grammarian; Margaret Scriven, librarian of the Chicago Historical Society; Virginia Marmaduke of the editorial staff of the *Chicago Sun-Times;*

Earl Schenck Miers, author and publisher; and E. W. Puttkammer of the University of Chicago Law School. To others—Elizabeth P. Brush of Rockford, Illinois; R. H. Sherwood of Indianapolis; Dr. Chauncey C. Maher of Chicago; and Dean Robert B. Browne of the University of Illinois—I am equally grateful for help with certain phases of the story. As a research assistant, Julian S. Rammelkamp placed me permanently in his debt. One tends to take the services of librarians for granted, but Winifred Ver Noy of the University of Chicago Library, David C. Mearns of the Library of Congress, and Louis M. Nourse of the St. Louis Public Library took more trouble in my behalf than I had a right to expect.

I hope all those whom I have not named will accept my assurance that I am well aware of my obligation.

PAUL M. ANGLE

Chicago

CONTENTS

BLOODY WILLIAMSON

1

MASSACRE

June 21–2, 1922

■■

The most brutal and horrifying crime that
has ever stained the garments of organized
labor. *St. Louis Globe-Democrat, June 24,
1922.*

ALL THROUGH the night the mine guards and workmen hud-
dled beneath empty coal-cars. Soon after sundown they were
jolted by a series of explosions, and no one needed to tell them
that their water plant had been blown to bits. Behind piles of
railroad ties they were safe enough, even though now and then
bullets spattered against the steel sides of the cars or thudded
into the tough wood. But they were trapped, and they knew it.

At dawn John E. Shoemaker, assistant superintendent, and
Robert Officer, timekeeper, ran from the barricade to the office
to telephone for help. The line was dead. While the two men
worked with the phone, shots crashed through the flimsy siding.
Looking out, they saw armed men lying behind the crests of the
high piles of dirt that surrounded the strip mine in which they
were besieged. The men underneath the cars, now near panic,
begged C. K. McDowell, the superintendent, to surrender. He
agreed, reluctantly.

Bernard Jones, a mine guard, tied a cook's apron to a broom-
stick and came out from the barricade.

"I want to talk to your leader," he called to the men lying behind the hills of raw earth.

3

One of the attackers rose to his feet. "What do you want?" he asked.

Jones replied that the men inside would surrender if they could come out of the mine unmolested.

"Come on out and we'll get you out of the county," was the answer.

Behind the barricade the guards and workmen threw down their arms. As they emerged they put up their hands and formed a line. Then they walked along the railroad track and through the cut in the piles of overburden through which the spur entered the mine.

The besiegers—some five hundred miners on strike and their sympathizers—surged forward, a rifle or revolver in almost every hand. They searched the prisoners and lined them up two abreast. One of the captives near the end of the line went back to the bunk car and returned with his grip. A striker took it from him.

"You won't need that where you are going," he said.

The procession started along the railroad toward Herrin, five miles to the northwest. After a short distance the prisoners were ordered to lower their hands and take off their hats. The mob grew ugly. Some of its members fired their guns into the air, some swore at the captives, and some called out to newcomers: "We got the scabs! We got the scabs!" A Negro armed with a long rifle ran up and down the line in a frenzy. Several white men urged him to use his fists on the prisoners. One of them called out:

"See these white sons-of-bitches that we don't think as much of as we do of you, colored boy!"

At Crenshaw Crossing, a hamlet half a mile from the mine, a number of men waited for the procession. The column halted. A dark, burly man with a revolver—not the leader who had promised safe conduct—waved his hat for quiet and started to talk. As the noise subsided his words carried to the frightened captives:

4

"The only way to free the county of strikebreakers is to kill them all off and stop the breed."

Someone in the crowd demurred. "Listen, buddy, don't rush things," he warned. "Don't go too fast. We have them out of the mine now. Let it go at that."

"Hell! You don't know nothing," the first speaker answered with a burst of temper. "You've only been here a day or so. I've been here for years. I've lost my sleep four or five nights watching those scab sons-of-bitches and I'm going to see them taken care of."

The mob, moving again, became uglier. Some of its members struck the prisoners with pistol butts, and blood began to streak sweaty faces caked with the dust raised by shuffling feet. As the crowd approached Moake Crossing, a half mile beyond Crenshaw, McDowell was bleeding from several head wounds. A cork leg made it impossible for him to keep the pace the captors had set.

"We ought to hang that old peglegged son-of-a-bitch," someone muttered.

Several times the superintendent faltered and almost fell; each time his captors jabbed him with rifle barrels and jerked him to his feet.

At Moake Crossing he stopped. "I can't walk any farther," he groaned.

The burly man who had talked about stopping the breed stepped up. "You bastard," he snarled, "I'm going to kill you and use you for bait to catch the other scabs."

He took one of McDowell's arms and motioned to another man in the mob to take the other. When the crowd moved on the three men started down a crossroad. Before the prisoners had covered a hundred yards they heard shots from the direction in which McDowell had been taken.

"There goes your God-damned superintendent," one of the mob members boasted. "That's what we're going to do to you fellows, too."

A farmer living near by also heard the shots. After a safe interval he walked down the crossroad. There lay McDowell, two bullet holes in his chest. He was dead.

At the powerhouse,* a mile farther on, the procession came to a halt.

"We'll take four scabs down the road, kill them, and come back and get four more and kill them," the leader of the column announced.

At that moment an automobile came up, and a man with an air of authority stepped out. Several of the prisoners heard him referred to as "Hugh Willis," and "the president."

"Listen, don't you go killing these fellows on a public highway," the frightened captives heard him say. "There are too many women and children around to do that. Take them over in the woods and give it to them. Kill all you can."

With that, he drove away.

Across the tracks and to the north of the powerhouse was a strip of woodland, green with the fresh foliage of early summer, lush with the undergrowth of many years. Into it the mob herded its captives. In less than three hundred feet they came to a stout fence strung with four strands of barbed wire. A big, bearded man in overalls and a slouch hat called out:

"Here's where you run the gantlet. Now, damn you, let's see how fast you can run between here and Chicago, you damned gutter-bums!"

He fired. An instant later the woods rang with rifle and pistol shots. Several of the terrified strikebreakers fell. Those who escaped the first volley leaped for the fence, vaulting it or tearing their way through the barbs.

Sherman Holman, a mine guard, went down in the first fusillade. As he dropped, he fell across the arm of the assistant superintendent, Shoemaker, who was wounded and unconscious. One of the mob came up and kicked Shoemaker's body.

---

* *Where current was generated for the Coal Belt Electic Railroad, which then connected Herrin, Marion, and Carterville.*

6

"The son-of-a-bitch is still breathing," he said. "Anybody got a shell?"

A man with a revolver stooped over and sent a bullet into the assistant superintendent's brain.

William Cairns, another guard, was part way through the fence before his clothing caught. While he struggled to free himself he was shot twice. He fell, but he could still see and hear what went on around him. Not far away a strikebreaker, spattered with blood, leaned against a tree, screaming. With every scream someone hit him. One of the mob lost patience.

"You big son-of-a-bitch, we can kill you," he said. Then he drew his pistol, and fired.

The strikebreaker crumpled to the ground.

Edward Rose, also a guard, wriggled through the fence, but not far beyond it tripped and fell. With the attackers close behind his only chance was to lie still and hope that he would be taken for dead. The bearded man who had fired the first shot noticed him.

"By God! Some of 'em are breathing," he announced. "They're hell to kill, ain't they?"

He fired, hitting Rose in the back. The wounded man remained conscious. From the ground he could see boots swing as their wearers kicked men who had been shot, and he could hear pistols crack when bodies gave signs of life. The shooting moved into the distance, but now and then a faint scream gave notice that some terrified fugitive had been trapped. Finally the noise died away.

Miraculously, some of the strikebreakers emerged from the barbed-wire fence with only cuts and scratches. Most of them simply deferred their fate.

Between the powerhouse woods and Herrin lay a strip of timber known, from its owner, as the Harrison woods. About 8.30 in the morning Harrison and his son, working in the barn lot, heard shooting to the southeast. As they turned in that direction they saw a man running toward them, with fifteen or twenty

7

others in pursuit. Several of the pursuers stopped and fired. The fugitive fell. The Harrisons watched three or four men drag the body into the timber. A few minutes later another group came up with two prisoners at gunpoint. They too disappeared in the trees. Shots followed. After a safe interval father and son walked to the spot where the men had entered the woods. There they found a body hanging from a small tree. Three other bodies lay beneath the dead man's feet.

One of those who vaulted the fence at the powerhouse was Patrick O'Rourke, a mine guard from Chicago. In the woods he was hit twice, but since he was still conscious and able to move, he hid in the underbrush and his pursuers missed him. When they had gone he started up a road toward Herrin. On a bend a car caught him by surprise. He ran to a near-by farmhouse and hid in the cellar, but the occupants of the automobile had seen him. All were armed, and he had no choice but to surrender when they ordered him out of his hiding-place. As he emerged, one of the men hit him over the head with a pistol butt, and then they dragged him to their car.

By this time other cars had stopped and a small crowd had gathered. Some wanted to shoot the captive, others to hang him. During the argument a newcomer reported that five more prisoners were being held at the schoolhouse in Herrin. O'Rourke's captors decided to take him there.

In the schoolyard the prisoners—now, with O'Rourke, six in number—were forced to take off their shoes. Someone in the mob made one of the captives, a World War veteran, remove his army shirt. Then all were ordered to crawl on their hands and knees. After fifty or sixty feet they were allowed to walk again, though still without their shoes.

The crowd, some two hundred in number, headed for the Herrin cemetery, a mile distant. They were in a vicious mood, kicking and beating the bleeding prisoners as they stumbled along the road. Even the children—and there were many in the mob—yelled "scab" and other epithets at the captives.

8

At the cemetery, the procession halted. As the prisoners stood on the highway bordering the burial ground, several members of the mob came up with a rope and yoked the six men together. Once more they were ordered to move on, but they had covered only a short distance when word spread that the sheriff was coming. Taunts came from the crowd:

"God damn you, if you've never prayed before you'd better do it now!" and in derision: "Nearer my God to Thee!"

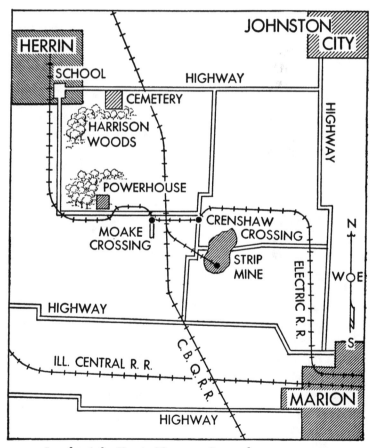

Locale of the Herrin Massacre, September 21–2, 1922

Two or three shots were fired. O'Rourke, hit again, fell to the ground, pulling the other five with him. More pistols cracked, and the stricken men writhed in agony. After their bodies were quiet one member of the mob filled the magazine of his revolver and methodically fired into each inert form.

In a few minutes three of the men on the ground showed signs of life. Thereupon one of the bystanders drew a heavy pocket-knife, knelt, and slashed the throats of those who still lived.

About 9.30 Don Ewing, a Chicago newspaperman, arrived at the cemetery. O'Rourke and a man named Hoffman, both partly conscious, were calling for water. Ewing found a small pail, filled it at a near-by house, and started to give Hoffman a drink.

"Keep away, God damn you!" a bystander warned, and backed the threat with a cocked rifle.

A young woman holding a baby taunted the dying man: "I'll see you in hell before you get any water." As she spoke, she casually put her foot, and part of her weight, on the man's body. Blood bubbled from his wounds.

Without protest from the crowd, one of the mob urinated in the faces of the victims.

About midmorning, when it was perfectly safe to do so, Sheriff Melvin Thaxton of Williamson County, and one deputy, took up the trail of the mob. Wherever they found dead and wounded men they called for ambulances and undertakers. Those still alive were taken to the Herrin Hospital; the dead were sent to a vacant storeroom in the same city. There they were stripped, washed, laid on pine boxes, and covered with sheets. Then the doors were opened, and for hours men and women (often with babies in their arms) filed past. Some spat on the corpses; some said to the children whose hands they held: "Look at the dirty bums who tried to take the bread out of your mouths!"

Late June in southern Illinois is hot, and the door of the improvised morgue had no screen. Long before nightfall flies blackened the wounds that still seeped in the eighteen bodies.*

* *Another body was found the following day.*

2

APPROACH TO MASSACRE

September 1921–June 1922

▄▄

> God damn them, they ought to have known
> better than to come down here; but now
> that they're here, let them take what's com-
> ing to them. *Hugh Willis, United Mine
> Workers official, June 21, 1922.*

IN THE immediate sense, the succession of events that led to
the bloody morning of June 22, 1922, began in the preceding
September. Early in that month the Southern Illinois Coal Company opened a strip mine * midway between Herrin and Marion
in Williamson County, Illinois. About the first of November the
mine shipped its first coal. From then until April 1, 1922, when
the soft-coal miners of the country went on strike, it operated
regularly. About fifty men, all United Mine Workers, were employed.

The Southern Illinois Coal Company was owned by William J.
Lester, then living in Cleveland, Ohio. Lester, Cornell graduate and civil engineer by profession, had had some eight years'
experience in strip mines, but this was his first independent venture. A promoter at heart, a man of energy and determination,

---

* *In strip mining, or surface mining as operators now prefer to call it, the
vein of coal nearest the surface (if no more than fifty feet underground) is
uncovered by a giant shovel, after which a smaller shovel is used to break
up the coal and load it on trucks or cars. The process is much more eco-
nomical than shaft mining. In 1922 it was relatively new.*

11

he did not intend to see it fail at the outset. Moreover, he was heavily in debt for his equipment, and could not afford a long period of idleness. In his predicament he turned to the local union officials. In order to keep men at work, and perhaps for less laudable reasons—rumors of a "fix" have persisted to this day—they gave him permission to repair the two steamshovels used for stripping the overlying earth from the coal. This finished, they made a further concession: he could uncover as much coal as he chose on condition that he refrained from loading and shipping.

This in itself was an important privilege, for the operator who could fill orders the minute the strike ended would have an advantage over his competitors. But Lester was not satisfied. By early June he had sixty thousand tons of coal uncovered, and with the price pushed sky-high by the strike, sixty thousand tons of coal meant a profit of a quarter million dollars. He could not resist the temptation. In spite of the remonstrances of friends and other operators, who warned him of certain bloodshed, he decided to load and ship. "It's legal," he insisted, "and I need the money. Why shouldn't I?"

On June 13 the Southern Illinois Coal Company dismissed its union miners. Two days later a contingent of some fifty men arrived at the mine and were put up in bunk cars. About half of them were private mine-guards, hated by union men as professional strikebreakers. The others were steam shovel operators, locomotive engineers and firemen, and commissary workers. All came from Chicago agencies.

On June 16 Lester notified the Burlington Railroad, which had a spur to the mine, that sixteen cars of coal were ready for shipment. The first train crew refused to take them out, but a second crew came in and hauled them away.

Word that Lester was mining and shipping coal on an open-shop basis flashed through Williamson County and near-by mining camps. The striking miners could hardly believe that any operator would be so foolhardy. Throughout Illinois, the miners

were so thoroughly organized that no serious attempt had been
made to operate non-union for fifteen years. Moreover, the locals
in Williamson and the adjoining county of Franklin were the
union's citadel. There lived half of the state's sixty thousand
miners; to a man they held union cards. Unionism had permeated every craft and industry, so that the miners had the active
sympathy of the entire laboring population. Even the merchants
and bankers depended so much upon the good will of organized
labor that they were hardly less ardent in their sympathies than
they would have been as union members.

The loyalty of members of the United Mine Workers of America to their organization had a deep and durable quality impossible to overestimate. Investigators for the United States Coal
Commission, probing the causes of the Herrin Massacre a year
after it happened, contrasted conditions in Williamson County
before and after unionization.

> When mining began [their report read] . . . it was upon
> a ruinously competitive basis. Profit was the sole object; the
> life and health of the employees was of no moment. Men
> worked in water half-way up to their knees, in gas-filled
> rooms, in unventilated mines where the air was so foul that
> no man could work long without seriously impairing his
> health. There was no workmen's compensation law; ac-
> cidents were frequent. . . . The average daily wage of the
> miner was from $1.25 to $2.00.

> Then, in 1898 and 1899, came the union.

> The Workmen's Compensation Law was enacted. Earn-
> ings advanced to $7.00 and even $15.00 a day; improvement
> in the working conditions was reflected in the appearance
> of the workmen, their families, their manner of life and
> their growing cities and public improvements.

Small wonder, the Coal Commission men implied, that Williamson County miners "believe in the union, for they think it
brought them out of the land of bondage into the promised land

when their government had been careless or indifferent to their needs."

When Lester started to ship coal, the striking miners saw his action as a threat to all they had gained in a quarter of a century. If he succeeded in operating with nonunion labor, other coal companies would follow his example. The union would be broken, and before long there would be a reversion to the conditions that prevailed before the days of organization.

The man had already accumulated a burden of dislike. Farmers in the vicinity of the mine resented the fact that he had closed a road they had used for thirty years, even though he had built a detour to replace it. And when guards took up posts along the detour, which skirted the edge of his property, irritation turned into hostility. For several days after June 16, when they first went on duty, the guards behaved with the utmost arrogance. One old resident, picking berries by the roadside, suddenly found the barrel of a revolver against his ribs.

"What the God-damned hell are you doing here?" the guard snarled. "Beat it, and that God-damned quick!"

A farmer who lived in the vicinity was stopped several times. When he threatened to go to the State's Attorney and swear out a warrant, the guard snorted: "You and the State's Attorney can go to hell."

A deputy sheriff stopped near the mine, his car stalled by a blowout. He flashed his badge, only to have a guard snap at him: "We don't give a damn if you're the President of the United States; you move on."

As another local resident drove along the detour, two guards signaled him to stop and ordered him out of his car.

"He's a God-damned son-of-a-bitchin' spy," one remarked. "Yes, that's just what he is," the other replied.

They slapped the man in the face, punched him with gun barrels, took his small change, and told him to move on.

"If you ever cheep this I'll bump you off," one of them warned him.

Lester's superintendent, C. K. McDowell, was almost as arrogant as the guards. When a local man went to the mine to collect a bill, McDowell told him:

"We came down here to work this mine, union or no union. We will work it with blood if necessary, and you tell all the Goddamned union men to stay away if they don't want trouble."

A powder salesman who visited the mine a day or two after the strikebreakers moved in heard the same kind of swaggering talk. When he reminded Lester of earlier attempts to operate nonunion that had ended in violence and failure, the latter replied:

"Our operation is different. We use less men and can pay a certain amount for protection, and if the shovel is blown up we will get $800 a day insurance."

At that moment McDowell came into the office.

"If McDowell doesn't make me $7,500 a day," Lester commented, "I'll run him over the hill. Isn't that right, Mac?" he added. The superintendent nodded.

A few minutes later Lester told the salesman: "I've broken strikes before and I'll break this one." *

Talk such as this, with the insolent actions of the guards, was intended to frighten the striking miners and their sympathizers —which meant nearly the entire population—into docility. Actually, it only intensified existing fears and hatreds.

That disorder was likely to be the result of Lester's venture was apparent to experienced observers from the beginning. One of these was Colonel Samuel N. Hunter, personnel officer in the office of the Adjutant General at Springfield. Prior to his appointment in 1920, Hunter had been active in politics in Perry County, which almost touches Williamson on the northwest; hence he

---

* *If Lester made this statement—and the powder salesman testified under oath that he did—he made it for effect, and without regard for truth. His only experience in strip mining had been as a superintendent in companies controlled by R. H. Sherwood, now of Indianapolis. Mr. Sherwood tells me that no company of his has ever attempted to operate during an authorized strike.*

had had experience in gauging public opinion, and he knew the temper of southern Illinois. When he picked up the *Chicago Tribune* shortly after noon on Saturday, June 17, and read that the Southern Illinois Coal Company had started to ship coal, whatever hope he had had for a pleasant weekend vanished.

At the moment Adjutant General Carlos E. Black was at Camp Logan in the northern part of the state; the Assistant Adjutant General was on vacation. In their absence Hunter was the ranking officer. Disturbed by the *Tribune* story, he tried to reach Black by long-distance but failed. Then he called State's Attorney Delos Duty of Williamson County. From what Duty told him he concluded that the situation there was serious. Len Small, the governor, was at Waukegan, also in the northern part of the state, defending a suit for misappropriation of funds. After a talk with the governor's secretary, Hunter decided to go at once to Marion, the Williamson County seat. He wired the State's Attorney that he would arrive at noon the next day, and asked him to arrange a conference to be attended by himself, Sheriff Thaxton, and representatives of the Southern Illinois Coal Company and the striking miners. Then he telegraphed Major Robert W. Davis, a capable National Guard officer who lived in Carbondale, to join him on the train to Marion.

Hunter and Davis arrived at the county seat shortly after noon on Sunday, June 18. They called on the sheriff, who outlined the situation for them, and spent the rest of the afternoon on the streets forming their own estimate of public sentiment. That evening, with a Marion police officer, they went out to the mine. Guards stopped their car but recognized their uniforms and took them to McDowell. The superintendent told Hunter that no one had threatened him in the operation of the mine, but he asked the Guard officer for a company of troops. Then he could discharge his private guards and save money. If Hunter would agree, he would make him an "interesting proposition." Hunter advised him to close down the mine: he was courting serious danger by using strikebreakers in a union stronghold. McDowell

16

replied that he knew his rights and intended to mine coal.

On Monday morning, June 19, Hunter and Davis met with Duty and the men he had called together—Lester, A. B. McLaren, a local mine-operator, and the sheriff. No one represented the striking miners. Both Duty and Hunter pleaded with Lester to shut down the mine, Duty warning him that he would lose his investment and perhaps his life if he persisted. Lester was obdurate. In the course of the conference he asked the sheriff to deputize the guards at the mine. Thaxton refused, but promised ample protection. After the meeting Hunter took Lester aside, told him that he did not believe the sheriff would make any effort to prevent trouble, and again urged him to close the mine.

"I'll be damned if I will," Lester answered.

As soon as the conference ended, Hunter reported by telephone to Adjutant General Black, now in Springfield. He informed his superior that the feeling among the miners in Marion and near-by towns was intense, and that the local officials sympathized with the union men. The fact that Sheriff Thaxton was a candidate for the office of county treasurer did not help the situation. With the labor vote amounting to seventy-five or eighty per cent of the total, Hunter doubted that the sheriff would exert himself to protect the property of a mine being worked by strikebreakers. In Hunter's opinion, troops would be needed, and he recommended that two companies be held in readiness.

This estimate of conditions was decidedly at variance with the public statement that Hunter gave to Oldham Paisley, editor of the *Marion Republican,* immediately after his report to Black. He was certain, he said, that in the morning's conference the officials of the coal company and local authorities had reached an understanding that would preclude trouble.

"It is not General Black's policy," he asserted, "to use troops until such time as the emergency gets beyond the control of the civil law officers, and we feel confident that the civil authorities of Williamson County are entirely competent to handle any emergency. We have every confidence in their performing every official duty."

Paisley also interviewed Lester. The operator assured him that he did not expect trouble from the striking mine-workers. His steamshovel men, he said, all belonged to the Steam Shovelers Union. He admitted that this union had withdrawn from the American Federation of Labor some years previously, but he claimed that it had recently been invited to reaffiliate. His railroad men, he said, were union members in good standing. He was required to have guards to comply with insurance regulations, but he promised to keep them off the public highway. As soon as practical he would reopen the closed road by bridging the shovel cuts that had been made across it.

That afternoon Hunter, Thaxton, State Senator William J. Sneed (president of the United Mine Workers' subdistrict that embraced Williamson County), and several newspapermen made another inspection of the mine. McDowell took Hunter aside and renewed his plea for troops. This time he made his "interesting proposition": fifty dollars a day to the officer if he would send troops to guard the property. Hunter told the superintendent to keep his money, and urged him again to close the mine. Again McDowell refused. If there should be trouble, he argued, the state would have to send in troops sooner or later, and he was prepared to hold out until they came.

In the evening Hunter telephoned the Adjutant General—his second report of the day—to say that the sheriff had not sworn in additional deputies, as he had urged him to do, and to reiterate his own belief that the local officer could not be depended upon to get the nonunion men out of the county.

On the following day, Tuesday, June 20, Hunter spoke before the Herrin Lions Club. After the meeting he walked about town, talking with the idle men who loitered on the streets. From them he learned that that very morning hundreds of union miners had held a mass meeting at the Sunnyside Mine near

Herrin. Apprehensive, he asked Senator Sneed what the meeting was about. Sneed dodged the question, but assured him that he need not be alarmed. The sheriff, informed of the gathering, promised to investigate.

That same day the telegraph wires injected another explosive element into the situation. On Monday, after his visit to the Lester mine, Sneed had wired to John L. Lewis, president of the United Mine Workers of America, to ask whether the American Federation of Labor had given the Steam Shovelmen's Union permission to strip and load coal. In his reply Lewis stated that no such agreement existed, that "this outlaw organization" was furnishing strikebreakers at strip mines in Ohio, and that its officers had paid no attention to remonstrances made by the United Mine Workers. "Representatives of our organization," he concluded, "are justified in treating this crowd as an outlaw organization and in viewing its members in the same light as they do any other common strikebreakers."

Sneed's telegram and Lewis's answer were published in the local newspapers on the afternoon of the 20th.

On the morning of the 21st, Hunter decided that something must be done. Once more he called at the office of the sheriff to urge that impassive official to swear in additional deputies. Thaxton was out, but a deputy said that all was quiet at the mine, and that no new men had been deputized. Hunter, aware that tensions were perilously close to the breaking-point, appealed to the State's Attorney. Duty sent for the sheriff and added his appeal to Hunter's. Thaxton remained noncommittal.

As a last resort Hunter, with the sheriff, called on C. R. Edrington, secretary of the Greater Marion Association, as the local chamber of commerce was known. Edrington proposed that a local citizens' committee be formed to avert violence at the mine, and named the men who should be its members. Thaxton assented.

At noon they assembled in Edrington's office: R. B. Mitchell, a mine manager; William H. Warder, attorney; William Rix, president of the Marion Trades Council; Oldham Paisley of the *Marion Republican;* A. B. McLaren, the coal operator who had been present at the first conference Hunter had held; Hunter; and Edrington. But Thaxton, who by virtue of his position held the key to the whole situation, failed to appear. His office was closed, and no one could locate him.

The conferees agreed that there would be violence if Lester persisted in operating with nonunion labor and mine guards. But before a plan to stop him could be devised, an ominous report came in. That morning a truck carrying a new contingent of strikebreakers had been ambushed between Carbondale and Herrin. Three of the men were in the hospital at Carbondale; the others were said to have escaped.

Hunter went to the sheriff's office immediately. There he learned why Thaxton had not attended the meeting at the Greater Marion Association. As soon as the attack on the truck had been reported to him, he had left for the scene of the shooting. Since he was uncertain whether it had taken place in his own county or in the one to the west, he had persuaded State's Attorney Duty to accompany him. The office deputy had no idea when he would return or how he could be reached by telephone. Hunter went back to the conference.

Within a few minutes even more ominous news reached the committee: miners, several hundred strong, were holding an indignation meeting in the Herrin cemetery. The telegram from Lewis to Sneed had just been read, and feeling was running high.* Almost at once other calls came from Herrin: mobs were looting the hardware stores and helping themselves to guns and ammunition.

---

* *Since John L. Lewis has been accused repeatedly of precipitating the Herrin Massacre, the findings of Theodore Cronyn, representing the* New York Herald, *are pertinent. Cronyn wrote from Herrin on July 11, 1922:*

"Officers of the union deny that Lewis's telegram had any provocative effect whatever or that it was intended to have. Lewis has denied it; his whole organization has denied it. And men who are as free from prejudice as can be found in the county tell the writer that however the telegram may have been construed by those who read it the mine would have been

The men in the office of the Greater Marion Association worked feverishly. Hunter called Black in Springfield to report on developments, and warned McDowell at the mine that a mob was forming and arming itself. Paisley urged the Marion hardware dealers to hide their guns and ammunition. One store had already been looted. He remembered several rifles that the American Legion used on ceremonial occasions and saw to it that they were concealed in the police station. Every few minutes someone called the sheriff's office, only to be told that the county's chief law-enforcement officer could not be located.

About 3.30 came the call that all feared—McDowell announcing that the mine was surrounded and that so far five hundred shots had been exchanged. None of his men had been hit, although several bullets had ripped through the makeshift office where he was telephoning. He thought two and perhaps three of the attackers had been wounded. Where was Thaxton? He hadn't been able to locate him. He must have troops!

As soon as McDowell hung up, Hunter called the sheriff's office deputy and urged him to take all available deputies to the mine, stop the fighting, and disperse the mob. He also urged the deputy to telephone the Adjutant General for troops. Once again he received the stock reply: Thaxton could handle the situation. For the remainder of the afternoon the sheriff's door was locked and no one answered the telephone.

Calls continued to come in from the mine: the mob was in-

---

attacked anyway—*that the attack was being planned several days before Lewis sent his message."*

One "veteran of Williamson County" told Cronyn:

"Well, you can never make me believe John Lewis intended to have anybody go out and do some killing. I should say he was merely settling a disputed point in the routine of his business. But I will say that John Lewis was unfortunate in his choice of language. Everybody down here knows how the union miners feel about these things. . . . When Lewis officially told them that those fellows out at Lester's mine were to be treated like any other strikebreakers I should say it was about the same as saying, 'Hike out there to the mine and clean 'em out.' I don't believe that John Lewis gave the matter enough thought, or may be he didn't know how bad conditions were down here."

21

creasing in number, the firing becoming heavier. Hunter called Black again to report that the mine was now under attack, that the sheriff could not be located, that his office deputy would take no responsibility, and that McDowell wanted troops. He himself thought they would be needed.

By this time the men at the Greater Marion Association knew there would be no reprieve: if heavy bloodshed were to be avoided, a settlement had to be worked out that very afternoon. Lester had left the mine a day or two previously. If he could be found, perhaps he could now be persuaded to stop operations. Charles F. Hamilton, who had known him a long time, was the man to approach him. McLaren found Hamilton on the street and brought him into the conference. Hamilton succeeded in reaching Lester at the Great Northern Hotel in Chicago. The mine owner, who had already learned of the attack through a call from McDowell, had lost his nerve. He agreed to shut down for the duration of the strike. Hamilton immediately relayed word to the superintendent.

From that time—about 4.30—until 6.00 the little group of men worked on the terms of a truce.

First of all, the shooting must be stopped. That would follow if each side would raise a white flag. Then, in return for Lester's promise to quit, the strikebreakers should be given safe conduct from the county. If attackers and attacked could be brought to parley, the safe conduct could be arranged.

Hunter called McDowell, who agreed to put up a white flag if the besiegers would also raise one, and promised to confer with the union officials. Then, in the belief that the sheriff should head any group of mediators, another effort was made to find the missing official. As usual, he could not be located. Someone suggested a citizens' mediating committee, but the men in the office could not agree upon its composition. They decided, therefore, to put the truce into effect, and work out the details later.

Edrington called the office of the subdistrict of the United Mine Workers in Herrin. Neither Sneed, the president, nor Hugh

Willis, state board member, was present. In their absence he talked with Fox Hughes, subdistrict vice-president, explained what the committee planned to do, and turned the phone over to Hunter. Hunter asked Hughes to take several men to the mine, put up a white flag, and see that the attackers stopped shooting. The Lester men would have their own flag up before he arrived. As soon as the firing ceased, he and his party could arrange for the withdrawal of the strikebreakers. Hughes agreed. Hunter called the mine, told the officials there that Hughes had agreed to the truce and would be out soon, and directed them to place their white flag where it could be seen. Hunter also asked that they telephone him as soon as the truce was effected.

Time passed, and the men in the office of the Greater Marion Association became apprehensive. A call to the mine brought word that the strikebreakers' flag, a sheet thrown over a telegraph wire above a pile of overburden, had been up for some time, but that nobody on the outside had appeared with a flag of any kind. And the firing persisted, though with diminishing intensity. The peacemakers called the subdistrict office again, and learned to their consternation that Hughes had not yet started to the mine. He promised to go at once, and did leave a few minutes later. By phone Hunter told McDowell that Hughes was coming at last, and cautioned him to make certain that his own men held their fire when the union official approached. Soon afterward the mine phone went dead.

Believing that they had achieved their purpose, all the members of the citizens' committee except Edrington and Hunter left for their homes. The two men sent out for sandwiches. Hunter took advantage of the lull to make his third report of the day to General Black. By this time he had confirmed McDowell's report that there had been casualties among the attacking miners. One man had been killed and two others seriously wounded. The miners, nevertheless, had agreed to the truce he proposed, and it was now being put into effect. There was no longer cause for apprehension.

23

To the Adjutant General, Hunter's call brought great relief. That afternoon, after he had learned from Hunter that the mine was under attack, he had received two telephone calls that had convinced him the situation in Williamson County was about to blow up. One came from Lester, who demanded in great excitement that troops be sent to protect his men and property. The other call was from Governor Small at Waukegan. The governor said that Lester had appealed to him, too, for troops, and asked Black what steps he had taken. Black replied that immediately after talking with Lester he had ordered the commanders of three National Guard companies in southern Illinois to have their men ready for an imminent call to active duty. The three units could be mobilized and on their way to the scene of trouble within two hours. Before calling them out, however, he wanted to hear from Colonel Hunter on the ground. What he did would depend upon that officer's next report. Small approved Black's course.

Then came the call from Hunter reporting that a truce was in the making. Black immediately telephoned the news to the governor. Both men agreed that the three companies of guardsmen should be held in readiness, but that they should not be called out that night.

If Hunter, Black, and Small had been aware of what was happening while they exchanged congratulations on the passing of the crisis, they would have been less complacent. For Fox Hughes bungled the mission he had agreed to undertake. He did go to the mine, but with the piece of white bunting he took along stuffed inside his shirt, and he kept it there. Instead of taking several responsible men with him, he went alone except for the driver of his car. From Crenshaw Crossing he proceeded on foot. By his own story, there was still desultory shooting, and he could see no flag on any part of the mine dump. (The next morning, when the Lester men surrendered, their sheet hung forlornly from the telephone wire on which they had placed it.) Concluding that the strikebreakers had not kept their promise, Hughes returned to Herrin. When he learned there that after his own departure Hunter had been in touch with Hugh Willis, his superior in the union organization, he concluded that the truce was no longer his concern, and made no further effort to do anything about it.

Thus, as darkness fell, the best chance of peace slipped away. And on the streets of Marion and Herrin there was plain evidence that the chance had gone for good. In both towns mobs formed; once again they tried to obtain arms and ammunition from stores and even from individuals. Men and boys, many of them armed, packed the streets. Policemen had great difficulty in keeping traffic moving. Cars loaded with armed men made their way at high speed in the direction of the Lester mine. The officers on duty asked no questions. What might happen several miles away was no concern of theirs.

Early in the evening Circuit Judge D. T. Hartwell, who had been holding court at Metropolis, reached Marion. During supper his wife told him what had happened, and what threatened. He drove uptown. There he heard all kinds of rumors, but learned nothing except that serious trouble was impending.

Shortly after nine p.m. he found the sheriff in the State's Attorney's office. Thaxton and Duty had just come in from investigating the morning's shooting. In a short time Hugh Willis appeared. He had heard in Herrin, he said, that a group at the Greater Marion Association had induced Lester to shut down the strip mine; he had come to find out about it. Duty located Hunter and asked him to come to his office. After some delay the colonel and Major Davis, who had come over from Carbondale that evening, joined the meeting.

Once again the group faced the problem of putting into effect the truce that had been agreed upon late that afternoon. There was no argument over the terms: the mine was to be shut down, and Lester's men were to be given safe conduct from the county. The sheriff, they decided, should see that the truce was carried out. Hunter and Hartwell urged him to take his deputies and go to the mine immediately, and Hunter, Davis, and Hugh Willis offered to accompany him. Thaxton refused: he must have sleep. He would go to the mine, but not until morning. With that the others had to be satisfied. Before the conference ended, Hunter, Davis, and the sheriff agreed to meet at Thaxton's office at six o'clock the following morning.

Hunter put through a final call to General Black. The truce, he reported, would still go into effect. Troops would not be needed.

After the meeting broke up, Hunter and Davis returned to the office of the Greater Marion Association. There they found Edrington, his wife, and his secretary. For two hours the five people talked about what had been the most eventful day of their lives. As they talked, the sheriff slept. Hugh Willis, back in Herrin, made a little speech to a group in front of the union office. Thaxton, he told them, was a mighty good fellow: they shouldn't forget him at the election in the fall. At the mine, he said, there was nothing more to do until morning; then the scabs would come out.

"God damn them," Willis concluded, "they ought to have known better than to come down here; but now that they're here, let them take what's coming to them."

Under their coal cars and behind their barricades of ties lay Lester's hungry, frightened men. Shortly before dawn two of them slipped out from their place of refuge and brought back pitchers of lukewarm coffee. They remembered later that it was as "bitter as gall."

At six o'clock on the morning of June 22, Hunter and Davis knocked on the sheriff's door. No one responded. They waited, walking around in the vicinity to kill time. On the street they heard that the men had come out of the mine, and that some of them had been roughly treated. More than two hours passed before Thaxton made his appearance; he had understood, he said, that he was to meet the officers at eight. Davis told him of the rumors they had heard, and urged that they try to head off the

Lester men and their escort of striking miners before some of the former were killed. The sheriff made light of the possibility, and insisted on proceeding directly to the mine.

It was nine a.m. when the three men, with one of Thaxton's deputies, reached the mine. All the cars and buildings were on fire. From the crowd they learned that the strikebreakers had surrendered and had been marched off toward Herrin three hours earlier.

After deciding that the mob was beyond control, the party separated. The sheriff and his deputy started for Herrin, Hunter and Davis returned to Marion. There, at 11.15, Hunter telephoned the Adjutant General and reported that the men had surrendered that morning and were on their way to Herrin in accordance with the terms of the truce. When Black informed him that he was certain, from newspaper dispatches, that the terms of the truce had been violated, and that many men had already been killed, Hunter was incredulous.

The two officers picked up Judge Hartwell, drove back to the mine, and started over the route the prisoners had taken. They found the spot where McDowell had been killed, and at the powerhouse woods saw bloodsoaked ground and fragments of flesh and clothing on the barbs of the fence. By that time there was nothing to do but collect the dead bodies, and make sure that those who still lived suffered no more from the mob.

3

MASSACRE: THE AFTERMATH

June 1922–October 1922

■■

> Where whole communities openly sympa-
> thize with ruthless murder of inoffensive
> people in the exercise of the right to earn
> a livelihood, and where wholesale murder
> goes unpunished, it is imperative that pub-
> lic opinion should demand that the strong
> arm of the law, under fearless officials, take
> positive action. *General John J. Pershing,*
> *July 4, 1922.*

NO EPISODE in the history of American industrial warfare has
ever shocked public opinion more violently than the Herrin Massacre. In country weeklies as well as metropolitan dailies, in papers all the way from Maine to California, editors flayed Herrin,
Williamson County, and union labor. The events of June 22,
1922, constituted "the most brutal and horrifying crime that has
ever stained the garments of organized labor"; the massacre was
"hideous," an "archdeed of savagery," a succession of "bestial
horrors"; those who took part in it were "unspeakable moral
Turks." "In justice Herrin, Illinois, should be ostracized," wrote
the editor of the *Journal* of Augusta, Maine, in a denunciation
representative of hundreds, "shut off from all communication
with the outside world and [the people] left to soak in the blood
they have spilled . . . until they learn that this affair is everybody's business."

In the Senate of the United States, on June 24, Henry Lee

Myers, Democrat, of Montana, read several newspaper accounts of the Williamson County killings and then declared: "German atrocities of the World War horrified this country from one end to the other; but I doubt if any German atrocities were perpetrated . . . that were more horrible, more shocking, more inexcusable, than the atrocities of which I have just read. . . ."

Two days later, in the House of Representatives, Wells Goodykoontz of West Virginia, a Republican, took the floor to say of the massacre: "There were no palliating facts, no mitigating circumstances. No crime ever committed could have been more inhuman or revolting in its nature. . . ."

If the people of Williamson County had any hope that such reprobation as this might soon lose its virulence, that hope was shattered by the coroner's jury. After deliberating for a few hours the six jurors, three of whom were union miners, found that all the men killed on June 21 and June 22 except one—Jordie Henderson, a union miner whose death was attributed to Lester's superintendent—were killed by unknown parties. They also found "that the deaths of the decedents were due to the acts direct and indirect of the officials of the Southern Illinois Coal Company," and recommended that an investigation be undertaken to fix the blame upon those officers.

The verdict started a new wave of denunciation. Again Senator Myers took the floor, this time to refer to the Herrin killings as "anarchy pure and simple, ruthless defiance of the Federal government and State government . . . defiance of all constituted law and authority. . . .

"What is worse," he concluded, "than the commission of the crime itself is the fact that the united populace of the county where it occurred appears to approve of it. The populace of Williamson County, Illinois, appears to be unitedly and one hundred per cent disloyal to the United States and its Constitution."

Newspapers, equally bitter, saw similar significance in the finding of the coroner's jury. The people of Williamson County, the *Chicago Tribune* asserted, have recognized the conventions by holding an inquest and returning a verdict. Apparently that will be satisfactory to them. The fact that there has not been an arrest for the murders, that there has not been an indictment by the grand jury, that there has not been a charge of murder placed against any living man, means nothing but justification in such a community.

But it means more than that outside the community. It means that here in the heart of the state a community has set itself above the law, and that those within it, who are not party to the massacre, are so intimidated that they ignore the crime and attribute the guilt only to those outside the circle.

"Shall unionism be set above the laws of God and of man?" the *St. Louis Times* asked. "Can any red-handed murderer defend himself by saying: 'If this had not been done, I would not have slit this helpless captive's throat'?" Others saw in the coroner's inquest "a travesty of justice . . . as appalling and as menacing as the crime itself," "a piece of callous shamelessness and a deliberate taunt flung at the United States," which "would be regarded as a joke if any humor could attach to the butchery at Herrin."

In Williamson County many deplored the killings, but outsiders saw only sympathy for the rioters and scorn for the victims. At the funeral of Jordie Henderson a twenty-piece band, two thousand men on foot, and a row of automobiles more than a mile long followed the hearse. Four thousand mourners awaited the casket at the Herrin cemetery. A similar throng attended the last rites for Joe Pitkewicius,* also killed by strikebreakers' bullets on the afternoon of June 21.

(While the funerals of Henderson and Pitkewicius were being held, sixteen bodies were buried in the potter's field of the Herrin cemetery. As the rough boxes were lowered into graves dug

---

* *This name, Lithuanian in origin, appeared in all kinds of variant spellings in the press of the time. I follow the form recommended by a Lithuanian friend of mine, although he suggests that it might have been shortened to Pitkewicis, or even Pitkewics.*

by union miners, three of Herrin's four Protestant ministers sang
a hymn, and then each said a prayer. A few spectators looked on
impassively. After the yellow clay had been piled on top of the
caskets, the sexton marked each mound with a plain board bearing the simple inscription: "Died, June 22, 1922.") *

More striking evidence of local approbation came from certain
southern Illinois newspapers, which incautiously printed stories
of the massacre before the nationwide revulsion had become evident. The following eyewitness account, by Editor Robert Dro-
beck of the *Williamson County Miner,* shocked millions when
they read it in a pamphlet circulated by the National Coal Association:

> At daybreak the 3,000 armed citizens [surrounding the
> mine] realizing that the future peace of their county was at
> stake, formed what has been termed by many, one of the
> neatest columns of troops ever seen in the vicinity, worked
> their way into the stronghold of the outlaws and captured
> those that remained alive. Several of those that were taken
> from the pit alive were taken to the woods near Herrin,
> where later they were found dead and dying. There were
> no riots, merely the citizens of the county acting in the only
> way left them for the safety of their homes. The faces of the
> men who were killed in the disturbance are horrible sights.
> Uncouth, as all crooks must be at the beginning, they were
> doubly unattractive as seen after justice had triumphed and
> the county had again resumed its normal peace-time be-
> havior.

Visiting the region in mid-August, George E. Lyndon, Jr., representing the *Brooklyn Daily Eagle,* found Herrin and Marion
"sullenly ashamed, but not repentant." By local standards, as he
interpreted them, the victims were outcasts. "They committed
the cardinal crime, the unforgiveable treachery of selling their
labor without the sanction of unionism. Theirs was a treason in
the eyes of organized labor above and beyond the treason to

---

* *When I visited the site in the summer of 1951 no sign of the graves
could be seen.*

country, even as the terrible vengeance of organized labor was above and beyond the majesty of the law."

From the beginning, editorials condemning the Herrin killings had been salted with demands that the authorities—county, state, or national—bring the participants to justice. Day after day the *Chicago Journal of Commerce* ran a box on its front page headed: "Ten Days Since Herrin," or: "Fourteen Days Since Herrin," calling for the indictment of those who had taken part in the rioting. On June 29 that same paper reprinted several columns of editorials under the heading: "Press of Nation Demands Justice for Murders That Disgrace State," and added its own assertion that "forty-seven states of the Union are looking to Illinois to administer justice to all responsible for the murder of workingmen, the torture of wounded, the desecration of the dead and the defiance to law and order on the part of the Miners' Union at Herrin."

As time passed without any apparent action, one organization after another demanded that something be done. The Chicago Association of Commerce passed resolutions urging that the offenders be brought to justice and that the officials whose negligence contributed to the disorders be disciplined. The Board of Directors of the National Association of Manufacturers chided the American Federation of Labor, in session when the massacre took place, for its failure to rebuke the mine workers, and called on every loyal American "to join in demanding the protection, by state and nation, of these fundamental rights of the citizen, that no man shall live his life by the consent of others, and no official shall refuse or neglect to guard these living truths of the day's work." In a letter to Governor Small the president of the National Coal Association charged that Williamson County officials had done little or nothing to punish the rioters, urged that the state use its law-enforcement agencies, and offered the Association's resources to the prosecution. The Illinois Manufacturers Association sent its members a communication headed, "The Home of Lincoln Threatened with Disgrace," in which it asked that they write or wire the governor requesting him to place Williamson County under martial law so that residents having knowledge of the events of June 22 could offer their evidence without fear.

In early August the National Coal Association distributed hundreds of thousands of copies of a thirty-eight page pamphlet entitled *The Herrin Conspiracy.* On the outside front cover were several excerpts from newspaper editorials, concluding with this from the *New York Sun* of July 6: "Until this coal mine butchery is legally avenged Americans can no longer boast that in the United States the Constitution is supreme." The body of the publication was a reasonably objective account of the massacre and the events leading up to it—there was no need to color the facts—but its final paragraphs drove home its real point:

> More than a month after the massacre scarcely a visible effort has been made to discover or punish perpetrators of the crime. . . .
> Shall the assassins of innocent American citizens go unpunished?
> It cannot be possible that Illinois will not take further official cognizance of these infamous acts, as the first and last tribunal of the country, our American citizenship, will demand that lawlessness, murder and massacre are not and never shall be permitted to undermine the security not only of the nation's industries, but the very lives and homes of our people.

Prominent Americans made the same demands. At Marion, Ohio, on July 4, 1922, General John J. Pershing alluded to the Herrin massacre without naming it, called it wholesale murder that was as yet unpunished, and asserted: ". . . it is imperative that public opinion should demand that the strong arm of the law, under fearless officials, take positive action." On July 13 Colonel Theodore Roosevelt, Assistant Secretary of the Navy, told delegates to the Elks' National Convention that Herrin was "as atrocious a massacre   .   as is contained in our annals" and reminded his audience that poor man and rich man were equal before the law. Reversing the usual emphasis, he declared: "The offender of great wealth must be brought to task for his iniquities, and the offender of small wealth must be brought to task also." But the sharpest reproof of all came from President Harding. In the course of an address to Congress the President referred to Herrin as "a shocking crime" that shamed and horrified the country," as "butchery . . . wrought in madness," and asked for legislation extending the jurisdiction of the federal courts so that such "barbarity" could be punished.

The President's address was read before Congress on August 18. On the following day he received a telegram from John H. Camlin, president of the Illinois Chamber of Commerce, informing him that despite appearances the people of Illinois were determined that the mine rioters should be apprehended and punished, and that his own organization had taken steps to see that there would be an effective prosecution. "There is, of course, a conscience in Illinois which will not tolerate such a disgraceful thing," Harding replied. "It will be very pleasing to me and reassuring to the whole country to know that this conscience is finding expression."

In his telegram Camlin referred to a letter that his office had sent to each of the state's 102 chambers of commerce two days earlier. In this communication the Illinois Chamber declared that neither State's Attorney Duty of Williamson County nor Attorney General Edward J. Brundage had adequate funds for prosecuting the murderers, yet they were the only officials in the state who could take action. Contributions totaling at least twenty-five thousand dollars were requested, and a quota was assigned to each local chamber.

> In this emergency the State of Illinois is on trial [the appeal concluded]. Our citizens visiting elsewhere have been compelled to hang their heads in shame. The world is asking us, "What are you going to do about it?" We believe the only possible answer is that the business men of this state will

*Williamson County in Relation to the
Principal Cities of Illinois*

contribute of their funds to the utmost in order to prove to the world that justice still reigns and human life shall be safe in Illinois.

On the day this letter was released Judge Hartwell summoned a special grand jury to convene at Marion on Monday, August 28, to investigate the Herrin killings.

All over the country editors commended the Illinois Chamber for its action, though many wondered why Illinois, one of the wealthiest states in the Union, had to depend on a private organization for the money with which to prosecute murder. (The reason was to be found in a political feud between Brundage and Governor Small. In 1921 Small had vetoed a large part of Brundage's appropriation, leaving him barely enough money for the routine functions of his office.) Only a few Illinois papers spoke out in opposition, taking the position that it was the duty of the state in its official capacity to enforce the law, and not the concern of a chamber of commerce.

In some places, however, the action of the state chamber aroused more than theoretical dissent. Months earlier the Illinois Chamber had planned to make a tour of southern Illinois in late September. The schedule called for a half day in Marion, with a barbecue and a visit to a mine. After the massacre, the half day was cut to forty-five minutes. When the state chamber issued its appeal for funds, an officer of the Greater Marion Association asked that the city be omitted altogether. "I do not believe the average business man in Marion," he informed the state secretary, "is in a proper frame of mind to make a genial host for your party." The trip was abandoned.

Much more important was the reaction of the United Mine Workers of Illinois. Two weeks after the state chamber asked for contributions, Frank Farrington, the miners' district president, and other officers conferred with the union's lawyer. After the conference Farrington pledged all the resources of the district for the defense of any union miner who might be indicted for participation in the Herrin riots. "We have a proper appreciation of the magnitude of the forces that have combined to convict our members," he said, "and we shall leave nothing undone that will enable us to combat these forces." What that meant became clear when the union miners of the state met in convention at Peoria early in September. There, in executive session, they voted a one-per-cent assessment on the earnings of all their members after September 1, 1922, and directed that the money be used for the defense of those whose indictments were expected.

Equally significant was the opportunity the action of the Illinois Chamber gave to the labor press.

The smoke of gunpowder at the powerhouse woods had hardly cleared before the Associated Employers of Indianapolis, an organization dedicated to the open shop, addressed a letter to its clientele calling upon "red-blooded citizenship" to urge Governor Small "to afford the fullest possible protection to life and property in the legitimate mining of coal, notwithstanding the miners' union." When President Harding, on the Fourth of July, proclaimed that "a free American has the right to labor without any other's leave," no labor editor, with public opinion as inflamed as it was, had the temerity to contradict him. When associations of employers—and particularly the National Coal Association—began to blanket the country with pamphlets, labor's friends saw, or professed that they saw, an anti-union conspiracy. But not until the Illinois Chamber of Commerce made its financial appeal did they have what could be presented as convincing evidence.

They were quick to use it. Announcing that henceforth he would devote his entire time to defending any miners who might be indicted, A. C. Lewis, a lawyer of Harrisburg, Illinois, charged the "organized wealth of the nation" with "poisoning the minds of the public" and with trying to create "a public sentiment which will prevent these men from receiving a fair trial. . . . It is apparent," he continued, "they have raised and are spending fabulous sums of money, not for the purpose of bringing the guilty to justice, but with the intention of seeking victims in the hope that . . . they can in some measure discredit organized labor."

Behind the prosecution [asserted the *Illinois Miner,* official organ of the Illinois district], crowding it, whispering to it, pointing a dark finger now at one point of labor's defense front and now at another point, is the allied employing class. . . . They advocate more things than conviction. They talk solemnly of the "inalienable right of every man to work, wherever he will, at whatever wage he will."

Such pronouncements as these led Philip Kinsley, level-headed representative of the *Chicago Tribune,* to write from Marion on September 1: "The murder charge will be lost sight of in the trials of the rioters and the cause of the open shop versus labor will be the central issue."

Appearances to the contrary, Illinois officials had not turned their backs on the Herrin killings. Two days after the massacre, representatives of the Attorney General were in Williamson County interviewing county officers and leading citizens. Three weeks later Brundage offered a reward of one thousand dollars for information leading to the arrest and conviction of the murderers. Moreover, Judge Hartwell had summoned a special grand jury for July 9 in the expectation that it would investigate the mine riot, only to be told by the prosecution that it was not yet ready. Consequently, only routine cases were presented to the jurors, and the county officials suffered charges of neglect and nonfeasance in silence.

By the end of August the prosecution had gathered its evidence. The judge, having called one grand jury prematurely, wanted to defer the investigation until the September term of court, when a jury called in due course would be available, but the State's Attorney insisted that a special grand jury be called at the earliest possible moment. Judge Hartwell yielded, and issued his summons for a venire to be present at the courthouse in Marion on August 28.

At the roll call that morning twenty-six men came forward. Four were excused for personal reasons, so one more was selected from the panel to make the necessary twenty-three. Philip Kinsley classified twenty-one of the group as farmers, one as a furniture and lumber dealer, and one as a part-time farmer and coal miner. "All," he wrote, were Americans "of the normal back-country type of Anglo-Saxon-Celtic descent through the southern mountains . . . a little harder of eye, perhaps, than the average farmer of the corn belt."

The judge delivered his charge with the utmost informality, standing with one foot on the railing of the witness box, leaning forward, and speaking as if in conversation. His words, however, contradicted his nonchalance. He reminded the jurors that they had not been summoned to settle a labor dispute, and that they represented neither operators nor miners. They owed allegiance only to the people of Illinois; their guide should be their oath to inquire "fully, fairly, and impartially" into the facts.

"I do not mean to lecture you," Hartwell said. "A good many of you are older than I am. I am not going to indulge in any moral sermon. You and I live in this county. You and I have enjoyed the protection of its laws and of the laws of the state and government. . . ."

He concluded with quiet impressiveness: "There comes a time in the life of all of us when a man will have to take a stand. If a man stands for the things he believes to be right, who can complain? With full confidence in you, I now ask you to go to your jury room to commence the performance of your duty as grand jurors."

Within two days, the grand jury returned its first indictment, charging Otis Clark, farmer and miner, with murder. Hearing of his indictment, Clark came to Marion and surrendered before the sheriff could serve the warrant for his arrest. Frank Farrington, president of the Illinois District of the U.M.W.A.; Harry Fishwick, vice-president; Walter Nesbit, secretary-treasurer; Hugh Willis, subdistrict board member; A. W. Kerr, chief counsel for the defense, and associate counsel George R. Stone and A. C. Lewis ostentatiously escorted him from the courthouse to the county jail.

At intervals throughout the next three weeks the grand jury returned additional indictments. By September 23, when it recessed for thirty days, it had brought in a total of 214—forty-four for murder, fifty-eight for conspiracy, fifty-eight for rioting, and fifty-four for assault to murder.

Before recessing, the grand jury filed a report. After reviewing what had happened on June 22 and the preceding days, the jurors made some pointed observations. The sheriff—"holder of a card in the Miners' Union and a candidate for county treasurer"—had refused to ask for troops and had taken no adequate measures to preserve the peace, although he could not have been unaware of the strikers' plans to attack and close the mine. The Adjutant General's office had tried to shift responsibility to the sheriff, and had not taken decisive action to prevent disorder. The laxity of the police in the towns where stores were looted for firearms was deplorable. John L. Lewis's telegram advising that members of the steamshovelmen's union be treated as common strikebreakers was quoted in full, and although no comment was offered, the jury pointed out that preparations for the attack on the mine followed its publication. The Southern Illinois Coal Company had been within its legal rights in resuming operations, but "was either woefully ignorant of the danger of its operations or blindly determined to risk strife and conflict if profits could be made."

In view of the fact that the labor press was to make much of the grand jury's failure to indict anyone for the killings on the day before the massacre, one paragraph of the report deserves quotation in full:

> On the first day of the attack upon the mine two union miners were killed by the answering fire from the men in the strip mine and another so seriously injured as to die subsequently from his wounds. It has been difficult for this

grand jury to determine who fired the shots from the strip mine which caused the deaths of the Union miners. When asked to present evidence to the grand jury which would tend to fix responsibility, counsel for the Miners' Union announced they would lend no aid to the Grand Jury.*

To the press of the country the action of the grand jury and its outspoken report came as a surprise. Editors who had condemned Williamson County and the state of Illinois for inaction reversed themselves overnight. Delos Duty ("splendid name"), Attorney General Brundage, and the members of the grand jury deserved the thanks of the entire country for their "noble vindication of the law." What was more, the law could be expected to operate effectively in the trial of those against whom indictments had been brought. "America is still America," the *New Haven Journal-Courier* proclaimed ". . . and the flag lifts its drooping folds."

Labor and the labor press, on the other hand, were bitter. The grand jury had played into the hands of the Illinois Chamber of Commerce and other organizations whose purpose was not to bring murderers to justice but to smash union labor. A. W. Kerr, chief counsel for the defense, struck the keynote in a statement that he issued two days after the grand jury filed its report. That document, he charged, bore "all the ear-marks" of having been prepared by the Attorney General in collaboration with the officials of the Illinois Chamber of Commerce. The Attorney General had taken "so-called massacres" in different parts of the state with complacency: not until violence took on a capital-labor aspect did he become aroused. And the Illinois Chamber of Commerce, Kerr charged, was an organization "whose only record is that of an effort to destroy organized labor; to break

---

* *A lawyer who has read this chapter comments as follows: "I wonder if you couldn't be accused of bias in quoting this without explanation. It was not the duty of the union to present the evidence. It would have been better if the grand jury had also indicted Lester for these homicides. He might not have been guilty but there was certainly some evidence to indicate his guilt. The entire story should have been brought out."*

the morale of those organizations; to take little children out of school before their time; to give less food to the wives and chil-dren of Illinois."

Labor papers repeated Kerr's theme. "American capital is get-ting ready to stage a bloodier orgy than ever was staged on the industrial arena of this country," one editor announced. Another sneered: "It's a Roman holiday for the union haters and all tal-ented folk who can get their feet in the slush fund." Still others pounced on the failure of the grand jury to return indictments f∩r the killings on the day before the massacre. The Illinois Chamber of Commerce had obtained 214 indictments against workers, commented *The Worker,* of New York, without "one indictment being returned against a mine owner or any of his retinue," while the *Minneapolis Labor Review* pointed out caus-tically that "this grand jury that indicted the union miners re-fused to indict those, who on the day previous to the engagement at Herrin, had shot down and murdered unarmed unionists, who were attempting to reach the mine officials for a conference"—ignoring the grand jury's statement that the miners' attorneys had refused to offer any evidence on which indictments might be based.

Herrin made its attitude toward the indicted men plain by ac-tions rather than words. When the defendants were arraigned on September 25, Judge Hartwell announced that eight would be held without bail, while the others would be released on bonds ranging from five to twenty thousand dollars each. Eighty-six citizens of Herrin promptly stepped forward and signed bonds aggregating $410,000. Writing down their names, the judge re-marked that it was like taking the census.

One week after the arraignment Ignatz Kubens, a Lester em-ployee from Chicago who had been shot at the powerhouse fence, died in the Herrin hospital, bringing the total number of massacre victims to twenty-three—three union miners and twenty guards and strikebreakers. His death led to forty-eight additional indictments when the grand jury convened in late

October for its final meeting at the end of its month's recess.

In the Williamson County jail the eight defendants who were held there escaped the worst rigors of confinement. The Illinois miners' union furnished fans to keep them comfortable; a Herrin local donated a Victrola and a supply of records. From time to time friends brought delicacies to supplement the prison fare, and the wives of the married prisoners took turns at cooking chicken dinners with all the fixin's.

4

TWO TRIALS
AND AN INVESTIGATION

November 1922–June 1923

●●

> The murder charge will be lost sight of in
> the trials of the rioters and the cause of the
> open shop versus labor will be the central
> issue. *Philip Kingsley in the Chicago Trib-*
> *une, September 2, 1922.*

ON THE morning of November 8, 1922, crowds pushed into
the Williamson County courthouse as soon as the sheriff un-
locked the doors. Long before ten a.m., when the trial of eight
men charged with the murder of Howard Hoffman, Lester mine
guard, was to begin, spectators had filled the circuit courtroom
on the second floor. If they noticed their surroundings at all, they
saw nothing incongruous in features that visiting correspondents
were describing in dispatches sent out to the entire country—the
cracked plaster of the walls and ceiling, the flyspecked campaign poster of President Harding draped with a far-from-fresh
American flag, the signs admonishing against spitting hanging
over cuspidors that resounded with an almost continuous fusillade of tobacco juice. In this room justice had been measured
out, by local standards, for more than thirty years, and the people were used to it.

As the clock struck ten the bailiff called for order. Judge Hartwell, youthful, debonair, casually but immaculately dressed,

44

walked from his chambers to the bench and asked the regular panel of jurors to come forward. Before there could be a response the state requested an hour's recess for the purpose of preparing a motion. At eleven o'clock, when court reconvened, the motion was made and granted: indictments against all the defendants except Otis Clark, Bert Grace, Peter Hiller, Joseph Carnaghi, and Leva Mann were nol-prossed. Court adjourned until afternoon.

After lunch—"dinner" in the Marion of 1922—the first panel of veniremen stood before the bench, and the attorneys began to ask their interminable questions. This man was rejected because he had formed an opinion in the case, this one because he did not believe in the death penalty, this one because he was a relative of a defendant, this one was challenged peremptorily. The day dragged to its close without a juror in the box.

Many such days followed. The defendants, keenly alert in the beginning, read newspapers or dozed in their chairs, the clerk of the court lost himself in adventure magazines, the court reporter studied the *Ladies' Home Journal* until even the new styles lost their interest. But one by one, jurymen were accepted. On December 8, exactly one month after the trial began, and after 220 veniremen had been examined, the jury was completed. Judge Hartwell set December 13 as the date for opening statements.

On that morning the defendants were brought into the courtroom early. Otis Clark, forty or thereabouts, of medium height and weight, bearing himself with habitual soberness, looked as much the insurance salesman (which he had been) as the miner (which he was). Bert Grace was all animation, calling to his friends and exchanging jokes with them. Neatly dressed, his thinning hair prematurely gray, he could have passed for a traveling salesman as easily as for a coal miner. Peter Hiller, young, round-faced, stolid, bore himself like a garage mechanic on a Sunday outing, and with no more concern. Joe Carnaghi's black hair and olive skin confirmed his Italian parentage; his pleasant, good-humored expression explained his popularity in the community. By contrast, Leva Mann's grave face seemed almost mis-anthropic as he sat with one knee in his big muscular hands waiting for the proceedings to begin.

"There is little to tell about them [the defendants]," Philip Kinsley wrote, "because they are ordinary men and have led ordinary lives. They are Americans, proud of their country, proud of the power of their union. There is no tinge of 'red' about them. They are not of the bolshevik persuasion. They are not 'wild, ignorant foreigners.' They are conservative and commonplace, an indistinguishable part of the herd washed from the main current by accident."

Conservative and commonplace, too, were the jurymen whom State's Attorney Duty faced when he rose to make his opening statement. One of the twelve was a miner; the others were farmers, though two had worked in mines. The youngest was twenty-seven, the oldest fifty-six; their average age was forty-four. Such names as Swanner, Weaver, Riddle, and Cox testified to their "American" lineage.

Duty opened by reviewing the events of June 21 and June 22. Not until he outlined what the state expected to prove did his high-pitched voice become tense. The state would show, he asserted, that Otis Clark was one of the two men who led McDowell to his death, and that he was the leader who gave the order to fire, by the fence in the powerhouse woods. It would show that Bert Grace took part in the hangings and shootings in the Harrison woods, and that he was the man in the Herrin cemetery who threatened to shoot anyone who should attempt to give water to the wounded. It would show that Leva Mann, Joe Carnaghi, and Peter Hiller were participants in the killings at the cemetery, and that it was Hiller who cut the throats of the dying strikebreakers.

Kerr rose to reply to Duty. Heavyset, fatherly, he had endeared himself to union labor by his defense of the copper miners in the Calumet strike of 1913; the defendants and the miners' union looked to him with complete confidence. As he described the early days of coal mining in Illinois—the low wages, long hours, hazardous working-conditions, the uphill pull of the diggers to better themselves—the intensity of the zealot supplanted his customary graciousness.

"In that battle," he shouted, "at every step these determined workers were met with the powerful forces of organized capital. . . . Private armies of gunmen in the employ of the organized operators directed their guns against the breasts of the workers. The miners fought on against all the power of the organized employers of this state until finally they won for themselves an organization. . . . And now in this case they are assailed for wanting to protect and conserve this organization. . . ."

Kerr described Lester's operation, his violation of his agreement with the union, the provocative acts of the guards.

"We will show," he promised, "that their avowed purpose was to assault, abuse, intimidate and, as a last resort, to kill and murder in order to make tremendous profits and break up the Miners' Union. For remember, that other operators all through the country were watching the progress of the efforts in this county with the keenest interest. If Lester had been successful in his attempt to mine coal during the strike his tactics would have been adopted by other operators and the strike would have been broken."

Against these tactics the citizens of Williamson County rose in defense of their homes. In the sequel some of the "invaders" lost their lives. The killing of Howard Hoffman, for which the defendants were on trial, was "homicide and not murder." "Some day and in some courtroom," Kerr predicted, "a jury will say that the time has come to stop that importation into peaceful communities of this type of men. I believe that day will come in this trial. I believe that it is this jury that will immortalize itself by freeing all communities for all time from the sinister influence of the American gunman."

Kerr concluded with a vehement attack on the Illinois Chamber of Commerce:

"Why, then, you ask, are these five indicted? Because the prosecuting authorities of the State of Illinois yielded to private influences. Their place and their status is taken by a private organization composed of men of great wealth, the Illinois Chamber of Commerce. Actuated by a desire for vengeance, eager to do anything that will help to destroy organized labor, the Chamber of Commerce is the organization that prosecutes in this case. You and you alone stand between these defendants and this cry for revenge. Let the law be your guide, let the facts be your support, and let justice be your product. We want nothing more."

(Under the title, "The Other Side of Herrin," Kerr's speech was printed as a supplement to the December 16 issue of *The Illinois Miner,* and widely circulated in an effort to counteract the propaganda of the National Coal Association and similar organizations.)

The opening statements took up the morning of the 13th. In the afternoon the state put its first witness on the stand. The testimony was routine, but on the following day the prosecution edged toward the heart of its case. One witness identified Joe Carnaghi as a member of the crowd that marched the six prisoners to the Herrin cemetery; another placed Leva Mann in the same gathering. A third—George Harrison—testified that he saw two men, both armed, come out of the woods on his farm where he later found three dead strikebreakers, and admitted that he knew one of them.

"Look around the courtroom," he was told, "and see if you can point out such a man."

Harrison pointed to Bert Grace, in the act of shooting a stream of tobacco juice at a cuspidor. "There is one," he said.

Friday, December 15—the third day of the trial—offered drama. Harrison's son Fred, a student at the University of Illinois, corroborated his father by naming Bert Grace as the man who had come from the woods on the morning of June 22, pistol in hand, twenty minutes after shots were fired there. William Goodman, a farmer who had known Otis Clark for twenty-five years, told of watching the mob bring the prisoners along the road from the mine to Crenshaw Crossing.

> QUESTION (*by State's Attorney Duty*): "Did you see anyone in the crowd you recognized?"
> ANSWER: "Yes, I saw Otis Clark, who sits right over there." [Goodman pointed to Clark.]
> QUESTION: "What did he have?"
> ANSWER: "A big, heavy pistol."
> QUESTION: "Did you hear Clark say anything?"
> ANSWER: "Yes, he said, 'We ought to take these men out and kill them and stop the breed.'"

In the afternoon, Don Ewing held the stand for several hours. He was the Chicago newspaperman who had been prevented from giving water to the men who died at the Herrin cemetery. Because he was one of the two state's witnesses who connected any of the defendants with the death of Howard Hoffman, his testimony was of crucial importance. Under Duty's questioning he related how he had reached Marion on the morning of June 22, hired an automobile, and proceeded to the strip mine, which he left almost immediately for the Herrin cemetery. There he found the six prisoners lying on the road, roped together. One of them, bleeding from a gash in the neck and a bullet hole in the abdomen, begged for water. When Ewing tried to give him a drink a member of the mob, armed with a rifle or shotgun, held him off.

Could he identify the wounded man who had asked for water? He could: he had seen him that afternoon at the Herrin hospital, where he had learned that his name was Howard Hoffman.

Could he identify the man with the gun who threatened him? Pointing a steady finger, and speaking in a clear, firm voice, Ewing answered: "Bert Grace." No sound came from the crowded courtroom as Grace stared back at his accuser.

Cross-examination, detailed and severe, failed to shake Ewing's testimony in any material particular.

On Monday morning George Nelson, who lived at Moake

Crossing, identified Otis Clark as one of the two men who led McDowell down the road to his death; another witness pointed him out as the leader who had urged the mob to kill the prisoners and stop the breed. In the afternoon Dr. O. F. Shipman, an eye-ear-nose-and-throat specialist of Herrin, took the stand. Again there was drama, for Shipman was the second—and last—state's witness to establish a direct connection between the defendants and the death of Hoffman.

The physician said that on the morning of June 22 he had walked from his office toward the cemetery. Near the schoolhouse he met the mob with their prisoners, several of them bleeding and seriously injured. He described the march to the cemetery, the roping of the captives, the shooting when one of them fell.

QUESTION: "Did you see anyone you knew?"

ANSWER: "I saw faces of men whom I afterwards identified as Joe Carnaghi, Percy Hall, Leva Mann and Jim Galligan. I was within twenty or thirty feet of them. All had revolvers."

QUESTION: "How did you identify Howard Hoffman, around whose neck you say the rope was tied first?"

ANSWER: "I saw him in the Herrin hospital and learned his name there."

QUESTION: "Did you see who shot Hoffman?"

ANSWER: "I saw two."

QUESTION: "Who were they?"

ANSWER: "One man whose name I do not know, but who was about five feet eight inches high, weighed about 160 to 170 pounds and had a wart or mole on the right side of his nose, under the eye. He shot every man, borrowing a gun from the crowd to finish up. A boy gave him some cartridges and he reloaded his gun and shot some more. He shot Hoffman in the neck. Hoffman raised up his head and said, 'Men, men, what are you doing?' "

QUESTION: "Who else shot Hoffman?"

ANSWER: "Joe Carnaghi, whom I was close enough to, to touch, pulled an automatic revolver from his pocket and shot a round, then reloaded."

The next two days were devoted to the testimony of four survivors of the massacre—Robert Officer (Lester's timekeeper),
and William Cairns, Patrick O'Rourke, and Bernard Jones, all
guards. They told detailed and explicit stories of the morning of
June 22, but only Cairns and Jones could identify any of the defendants as participants in the killings. Cairns placed Otis Clark
and Peter Hiller among the mob who took the prisoners from
the mine, and accused Hiller of murder at the powerhouse
woods. He himself was wounded when he tried to get through
the fence. Then, he continued:

> "I fell down on my side. I saw one of our men standing by
> a tree bleeding and yelling. Every time he hollered some-
> one hit him again. Finally I saw a heavyset man walk up
> to him and say, 'You big son-of-a-bitch, we can kill you.' He
> then fired a shot into the man and the man fell down by the
> side of the tree."
>
> QUESTION: "Who was the man that fired that shot?"
> ANSWER: "There he is." [Cairns pointed to Peter Hiller.]

Jones testified that Clark was the man who, at Crenshaw
Crossing, urged that the scabs be killed, and that he was one of
the two men who led McDowell away at Moake Crossing.

At 2.10 p.m. on Thursday, December 21, after having called
thirty-nine witnesses, the state rested. Court was then dismissed
until the following morning. Chief counsel Kerr took advantage
of the recess to outline for the press the tactics of the defense.
He and his associates would prove that the guards and gunmen
were the aggressors, and that they brought the fatal attack upon
themselves. The defense would prove that Ewing's account of
the water incident at the cemetery was fictitious, and that several of the other state's witnesses testified falsely. And they
would prove, by many of the most reliable citizens of the
county, that the men now on trial could have had no connection
with the killings.

The defense followed Kerr's forecast without deviation. As
soon as court convened on the morning of December 22 two wit-

nesses were called to testify to the closing of the road, one of the original causes of community resentment. A third described the provocative acts of Lester's guards. That afternoon four members of the Conroy family—father, mother, son, and daughter—related what had happened on the afternoon before the massacre. According to John, the son, whose story was most explicit, the crowd gathered outside the mine between 1.30 and 2.00 p.m., were fired upon by the guards, and returned the fire. The witness saw a white flag raised on a pile of overburden between 5.30 and 6.00 p.m., but insisted that the guards continued their firing. He saw no one whom he knew with a gun. After the Conroys had finished, Ed Crenshaw, who also lived near the mine, described the killing of Jordie Henderson. According to his story, Henderson was lying on the ground about a hundred yards from the Crenshaw house, his head raised so that he could watch the shooting from the mine. Suddenly he slumped, rolled on his side, and lay still. He was unarmed, Crenshaw said, when he was shot.

The next morning the judge announced that court would recess until January 2, 1923.

For three days after the trial was resumed witnesses told of the provocations of the guards—their interference with berry pickers, their roughness, their abusive language. Others described the firearms and ammunition which they had seen in the mine before the attack. Still others swore that on the afternoon of June 21 the first shots were fired from the mine, and that the shooting continued after the strikebreakers had hoisted their white flag.

By January 5 the defense had completed the testimony by which it sought to show that the striking miners were justified in attacking the mine. Now it turned to alibis. On that day alone fifteen witnesses took the stand to swear that they had watched the "death march" on the morning of the 22nd, that they knew all the defendants, and that they saw none of them in the mob. Similar testimony took up the next several days. Then the defense became specific. Kerr and his associates started with Joe Carnaghi. A Herrin woman who ran a small dairy testified that she had sold him milk between 7.00 and 7.30 on the morning of June 22; three others corroborated her story. According to the next two witnesses, Carnaghi was working in his garden between 7.45 and 8.15. Two people saw him pulling a cake of ice along the street in a child's wagon before 9.00; five others placed him in downtown Herrin not later than 9.00. One of these, F. L. Baucher, picked up Carnaghi and a companion and drove them to the Herrin cemetery. By the time of their arrival the Lester men were lying in the road, dead. From there the three drove to the powerhouse where, of course, only dead bodies were to be found.

Carnaghi's alibi was the most elaborate, but an ample number of witnesses testified on behalf of the other defendants. Six people—three men and three women—had seen Leva Mann near the line of march, but all were certain that he had not been in the mob. Bert Grace was on the public square in Marion practically all morning on the 22nd. Peter Hiller and four friends had driven from Herrin to the powerhouse, had seen the column approaching, had turned around and driven back to Herrin. Otis Clark had been with the mob at Crenshaw Crossing, but instead of wanting to kill the scabs and stop the breed, he was the man who had said that if there was to be any killing, he was through. So said nine men under oath.

Its alibis offered, the defense spent four days in an effort to impugn the state's witnesses, particularly William Goodman and Dr. O. F. Shipman. According to defense evidence, their reputation for veracity was execrable, they were prejudiced, and Shipman at least was moved by desire for a reward.

The last defense witness stepped from the stand late in the afternoon on January 16. Kerr offered to send the case to the jury at once, without argument and without instructions. Otis Glenn, Assistant Attorney General, objected strenuously: the state wanted to review the evidence and proposed that each side take

53

six hours for argument. While the lawyers wrangled, the judge intervened to say that he would call the case at ten o'clock the next morning and send it to the jury when there were no more arguments to be made.

Shortly after ten, Duty began the argument for the prosecution. For two hours he reviewed the evidence, recalling particularly damaging testimony offered by the state's witnesses, ridiculing the alibis of the defendants, stressing the brutality of the mob's actions. "If these men," he said, pointing to the defendants, "had any part in the conspiracy, whether they fired a shot or not, they were guilty of murder. . . . There are no mitigating circumstances. There was no self-defense. . . ." He concluded by appealing to the jury to do its duty.

When court convened at two o'clock Kerr announced that the defense would make no argument, thus cutting off further argument on the part of the state. Judge Hartwell announced a recess until the following morning.

On Thursday, the 18th of January, well over two months since the trial had begun, spectators who crowded the dingy courtroom to capacity listened intently while the judge delivered his charge. At 11.15 the jurors, their faces solemn, filed into the jury room.

Hours passed. Friends and families of the prisoners sat in groups in the courtroom, now strangely silent, and talked in whispers. Late into the night, in spite of the winter weather, people stood on the walks around the public square, hoping to divine the meaning of the lights that burned in the jury room. Soon after dawn they were on the streets again, joined now by miners dressed in their working clothes, their faces streaked with the black dust of the pits. Still no word came from the courthouse.

At 1.30 p.m., twenty-six hours after the jury had received the case, word spread that a verdict had been reached. The groups on the streets raced to the courtroom. There the judge, already on the bench, warned that there must be no demonstration.

The jury filed in; the foreman handed Hartwell a slip of paper. Slowly, evenly, the judge read:

"Otis Clark, not guilty. Leva Mann, not guilty. Peter Hiller, not guilty. Joe Carnaghi, not guilty. Bert Grace, not guilty."

No sound came from the spectators—only the shuffling of feet as they filed out and down the steps. The jurymen, unable to realize that their long ordeal was over, wandered back to the jury room.

That afternoon came post mortems. "It was a fair and orderly trial," Judge Hartwell said. "The jury is the judge of the facts and they have passed upon them. I have nothing to say, except that I did the best I could to give and believe I did give a fair and impartial trial."

Defense counsel, in a written statement, emphasized the point that Kerr had made in his opening statement:

> The defense was directed against the vicious and unwarranted, brutal and murderous use of a private army of gunmen. If this trial has taught the lesson well that hereafter the weapons of the employers' private army shall not be directed against human breasts, then the trial with all its sacrifices has not been in vain. . . . It was the only righteous verdict which could have been rendered against an army of invaders.

C. W. Middlekauff, for the state, was disappointed but determined. The jury had been misled, he asserted, into considering the case as a controversy between Lester's strikebreakers and the miners' union, while the real issue was whether the law of the land should prevail in Williamson County. The prosecution would proceed with the next case. "The issues involved in this whole transaction are important," he concluded; "the people of the entire United States are interested in their solution. We are desirous of putting it square up to another jury in Williamson County whether they will be ruled by the laws of Illinois or whether the domination of the mob shall prevail. . . ."

Over the nation editors echoed Middlekauff's comments,

though without his restraint. "The acquittal . . . is denounced by the daily press from one end of the country to the other as a travesty upon justice," said the *Literary Digest,* "the editors rising almost as one man to point the finger of scorn at the town of Herrin and the County of Williamson, in the State of Illinois." Herrin was "an unconquered province of lawlessness," "a stench in the nostrils of humanity" that was "about to complete its secession from the United States of America." The people of the county had proved that they chose "to condone murder and shield assassins," and were content to leave "the stain of atrocious murder" on the annals of the state.

Labor papers might—and did—call the jury's verdict "a vindication of the traditional American right of self-defense" and "a crushing condemnation of the practice of 'protecting property' with privately employed gunmen who usurp the police power of the State"; they might assert that it proved that liberty still lived in the United States; they might ask why there was not some punishment that could be dealt out to an "outlaw operator" who invaded "a peaceable and law-abiding county" and goaded it to violence. Editorial opinions such as these converted few readers. The vast majority continued to hold with the Illinois Chamber of Commerce, dismayed but unbowed, when it demanded in its official publication:

> Every man still under indictment should be prosecuted as vigorously as those who have just been acquitted. . . . Let nothing stand in the way of the prosecution of every man suspected of having any part in that damnable outrage.

For its second case, the state chose to prosecute those who had been indicted for the murder of Antonio Molkovich, a cook who had lost his life at the powerhouse woods. Perhaps the fact that Molkovich, though of Russian birth, had served in the United States Army during the World War was counted on to nullify some of the prejudice against strikebreakers. The grand jury had returned eighteen indictments for his murder, but on the first day of the trial the state moved to nol-pros all but six. Otis Clark and Bert Grace again stood in jeopardy; with them, at the table for the defendants, sat Hugh Willis, Phillip Fontanetta, Oscar Howard, and James Brown, a Negro.

When the trial began on February 12, 1923, the appearance of the courtroom contrasted sharply with what it had looked like when the first trial opened three months earlier. The same cracked plaster threatened to fall at any moment; the same fly-specked picture of the President stared from the wall, the same battered cuspidors stood in corners, but instead of hundreds of spectators a mere handful lounged in boredom while a winter rain beat against the windows. Three reporters—two for local papers and one for the *Illinois Miner*—sat at the table that had been crowded with metropolitan correspondents.

Even the lawyers seemed to be affected by a feeling of futility. Their examination of prospective jurors followed the same lines as before, but was more rapid and more cursory. As a result, though more talesmen were examined than at the first trial, the jury was completed in slightly more than two weeks instead of a month. Again the jury consisted mainly of farmers, one or two of whom had worked in the mines. All were of the old American stock.

The state opened its case on the morning of March 2, 1923. This time C. W. Middlekauff, the middle-aged, experienced prosecutor whom Brundage had borrowed from the United States District Attorney's office, made the first statement. The state would show, he promised, that Hugh Willis, Otis Clark, and many others conspired to drive the Lester strikebreakers from the county. No man with "even horse sense," he admitted, would have attempted to operate on a nonunion basis in that locality, but that fact was of no pertinence in this trial. He and his associates did not represent scabs or Lester or the Southern Illinois Coal Company: they stood in the place of the people of the commonwealth.

After recounting, once more, the events of June 22, Middlekauff outlined what the state expected to prove. It would show that Otis Clark and Oscar Howard killed McDowell. James Brown was the colored man who maltreated the marching captives with frenzied cruelty. The union official who came up in a car and waved the prisoners to their death on the barbed-wire fence was the defendant Hugh Willis. Phillip Fontanetta had killed one of the men who had been wounded there; Bert Grace had taken part in the killings in the Harrison woods, and he was also the person who kept Don Ewing from giving a drink of water to the dying man at the Herrin cemetery.

In the afternoon Kerr took the floor for the defense. As at the first trial, he laid the blame for the riot on Lester and the strike-breakers. "We will show you, not by strangers, but by your own citizens," he promised, "that the real murderers were the men that were brought in to work in the Lester mine. . . . This trouble . . . started in the greed of Lester for money."

The defense would prove, Kerr continued, that Henderson had been dead for thirty minutes "before the community arose and started the aggression." It would also prove that the men charged with killing Molkovich were not at the scene of that murder when it was committed.

The defense had been criticized for paying its witnesses. "We do so," Kerr admitted, "and we do it proudly. These witnesses are laboring men and are now getting about one day's work a week. If you had a lawsuit and were to need a witness from the hayfield during harvest time, you would probably pay that witness for his time lost. We are only paying our witnesses for the time we take them away from their regular work."

"The miners' union is standing behind these men," he concluded, "because the Illinois Chamber of Commerce, two months before the miners' union got behind these miners, had raised a fund to prosecute the miners and to send them to the penitentiary."

The prosecution lost no time in producing its most important witnesses. After an undertaker and the coroner had given testimony regarding the body of Molkovich, thus establishing the corpus delicti, William Cairns was sworn in. He pointed out Otis Clark, as he had in the first trial, as one of the men who had led McDowell away. Under questioning he continued:

"We were halted again and a machine went by and I heard the crowd say, 'Willis is coming.' That auto went on ahead and I don't know what happened there."
"What else?"
"I saw a colored man with a rifle. [Cairns pointed to James Brown.] I remember him because part of his left ear is gone. He had on overalls and a piece of a war helmet."

Cairns described the ordeal at the powerhouse woods, repeating the testimony he had given at the first trial against Peter Hiller, and then added:

"John Shoemaker, mining engineer and assistant superindent, was lying within ten feet of me and two men walked up to him saying, 'Here's that machine gunner.' These two men kicked my head to one side. One of them [Cairns paused to identify Phillip Fontanetta] had on an army uniform. He put a gun up against the face of Shoemaker and fired a shot, blowing away a portion of his jaw."

Bernard Jones and Odis Lawrence, Lester's locomotive engineer, followed Cairns and confirmed what he had said about Clark, Brown, and Fontanetta. It was Robert Officer, however, who gave the most damaging testimony against Hugh Willis. At the first trial he had been unable to identify any of the defendants; now he pointed a steady finger at Willis and said:

"That man with glasses got out of the car. I was thirty feet from him when he got out of the car and I saw him walk around in front of the column and ask for the leader. . . . Willis said, . . . 'Don't kill any men here on the highway, there are too many women and children. Take them over into the woods and let them run under fire, killing all you can.'"

59

After Officer stepped from the stand the judge declared **a** recess because of serious illness in the family of one of the jurors, and eleven days passed without a session. When the trial was resumed familiar witnesses told familiar stories—of the looting of stores for guns, of the killing of McDowell, of Otis Clark and the "stop the breed" speech. Then came another recess—this time of four days—because of the illness of a juror's child. When court reconvened Don Ewing described again how the man whom he identified as Bert Grace kept him from giving water to the wounded prisoners. Again the defense attorneys could not shake his story.

The state finished its case on March 29, and the defense introduced its first witnesses the same day. As before, they testified to the provocative conduct of the mine guards and swore that on the afternoon of June 21 the first shots came from the strip mine. After two days, the parade of alibi witnesses began. Oscar Howard, according to four residents of Crenshaw Crossing, was there instead of at Moake when McDowell was killed. A Herrin miner who knew both Howard and Clark had stood within twenty feet of the crippled superintendent when he was led down the road, yet the witness recognized neither of the men who held McDowell's arms. Several others confirmed his statement. Five men declared that it was Clark who told the mob he was washing his hands of the affair if they were going to kill the strikebreakers; a sixth swore that he took Clark in his car from Crenshaw to Moake at 9.20 a.m., hours after the killing of McDowell.

The proceedings became monotonous. Some of the defendants dozed; Otis Clark spent more and more time with his books. Judge Hartwell, always nervous and high-strung, wandered about the courtroom looking from the windows, inspecting the picture of President Harding, sitting on the court reporter's bench, on the newspaper reporters' bench, on the defense attorneys' bench, on the State's Attorneys' bench, on the window-sills, yet ever alert even though he might sustain or overrule **an** objection in a voice that sounded, as one reporter put it, "like a bored stud-poker player dealing a 'last round' at three o'clock in the morning."

Alibis were offered for every defendant. Fontanetta was playing cards at the time the Lester men were being killed; Bert Grace was loitering on the Marion public square; James Brown was plowing with a borrowed horse; Hugh Willis was in Herrin. None, according to many witnesses, could have had a part in the murder of Antonio Molkovich.

On the morning of April 6 the defense rested, the state announced that there would be no rebuttal evidence, and Otis Glenn rose to make the opening argument. Early in his address he pointed to the logical weakness of the defense case.

"Someone was killed that day," he reminded the jury. "The defense has spent several days in trying to prove that the killing of these men at the powerhouse was justified. Then, on the other hand, they have produced scores of witnesses to try to prove that their men did not do the thing which they said was the right thing to do."

He made no effort to defend Lester. The man was a "fool" and "insane," and as far as his property was concerned, he "committed suicide." Yet no law forbade him to bring men, union or nonunion, into Williamson County to work a mine.

Irony gave a sting to Glenn's voice as he reviewed the testimony of the witnesses for the defense, pointing out flaws and implausibilities in their statements. But irony gave way to fervor when he came to his conclusion:

"You have an opportunity to strike at murder and lawlessness. If this crime is endorsed murder will grow upon the community and assassination will increase. Life, home and family will not be safe. You have the opportunity of stamping this out and I believe you will do it."

Glenn finished late in the morning. After the noon recess the defense waived its right of argument. Judge Hartwell called in the jurors and gave them his charge. At 4.20 p.m. they retired.

61

Shortly after eleven o'clock that night word came that a verdict had been reached. The judge appeared, took his place on
the bench; Middlekauff shuffled in in carpet slippers; twenty-
five or thirty friends and relatives of the defendants found seats
in the dimly lighted room.

"Gentlemen, have you reached a verdict?" Hartwell asked
when the jury stood before him.

"We have," the foreman answered, and handed over several
sheets of paper.

The judge adjusted his horn-rimmed glasses, then read
slowly:

"We, the jury, find the defendant, Hugh Willis, not guilty of
the crime as charged in the indictment."

He paused, then resumed:

"We, the jury, find the defendant, Phillip Fontanetta, not
guilty of the crime as charged in the indictment."

And so for the other four defendants.

There was no demonstration.

Middlekauff pulled himself to his feet.

"I ask your honor to poll the jury."

The judge asked the first juror to stand.

"Were these and are these your verdicts?" he asked, holding
up the papers.

"Yes, sir," came the answer in a firm voice.

"Are you satisfied with them?"

"Yes, sir."

Each juror, asked identical questions, responded in the af-
firmative.

The second trial was over. And the greater case into which
this trial and the one that preceded it had somehow been transformed—the case of organized labor against the strikebreaker,
the private guard, the organizations of employers who wanted
a return to the open shop, against the law itself—that too had
been decided.

On the following morning State's Attorney Duty announced

that there would be no more trials. "I intend to nolle every one of these cases," he said. "I have my personal opinion as to who did the crime and I tried to convince two juries. . . . I am not complaining, but it's a hopeless proposition." Middlekauff deferred to the State's Attorney's decision, although he reminded the court that the state legislature had recently appropriated $75,000 for the prosecution, and said he believed that body should have some voice in the matter. Brundage showed less restraint than his associate, issuing a statement in which he charged that many of the defense witnesses testified falsely, and that the court had permitted the selection of jurors who should have been disqualified. "The prosecution is reluctantly obliged to admit that justice cannot be obtained in Williamson County," he concluded. To which the seven lawyers for the defense replied by pointing out that when the second-trial jury was completed, there were left to the prosecution, unused, almost a hundred peremptory challenges. "It is strange," they commented with reference to Brundage's charges of false testimony, "that because witnesses happen to be laboring men rather than gunmen their motives must be questioned."

Amid these recriminations Judge Hartwell granted Duty's motion that all remaining indictments be dismissed.

Herrin faded from the front pages, even from the editorial columns, of all but the few papers that followed the investigation authorized by the Illinois House of Representatives during the course of the second trial.

The occasion for legislative intervention was offered in mid-March 1923, when a deficiency appropriation of $120,000 for the Adjutant General's office was under discussion. Representative Michael Igoe of Chicago declared that the responsibility for the Herrin riots ought to be fixed before this appropriation was voted. Adjutant General Black, he asserted, was trying to put the blame on Colonel Hunter, yet Hunter's report, which had been read before the Appropriations Committee, showed that on three separate occasions Hunter had asked Black to send troops to Williamson County, only to be told that the request could not be granted because the local authorities had not asked for troops. Igoe introduced a resolution providing for a committee to investigate and report its findings to the House. Representative McCarthy of Kane County pointed out that Igoe's resolution was so worded that it practically fixed responsibility in advance of the investigation, and proposed a milder, less prejudicial substitute, which was adopted immediately.

A few days later the Speaker picked the seven members of the committee: Frank A. McCarthy, chairman, and Norman G. Flagg, W. B. Phillips, Thomas Curran, Michael L. Igoe, and M. P. Rice. Igoe and Rice were Democrats, the others Republicans. Phillips and Flagg lived in southern Illinois; the other five members represented constituencies in the northern part of the state.

As soon as the second trial ended, Chairman McCarthy announced that the committee would hold its first meeting in Springfield on April 11. The members plunged at once into the main purpose of the investigation—to ascertain the delinquencies, if any, of the state officials concerned—by putting Adjutant General Black on the stand. That day and the next he and Colonel Hunter told their stories. Most of the pertinent facts were brought out during their first appearances, though later witnesses added some information of value.

Reduced to its essentials, the question between the two officers was one of veracity. Had Hunter—not once but several times—asked Black to send troops, or had he led his superior officer to believe that they would not be necessary? The issue came out nakedly in their conflicting accounts of what was said in the course of the several reports Hunter made to Black by telephone on June 21.

1.00 *p.m.* HUNTER: Reported the attack on the truckload of Lester men near Carbondale, the raids on the stores in Herrin and Marion, his inability to find the sheriff. Black ordered him to get after the sheriff again, and said: "Let them damn fools go to it. Some of them will get killed off. Maybe they will quit."

BLACK: Hunter reported only that a citizens' committee had been formed.

3.15 p.m. HUNTER: Reported the attack on the mine, the killing of two union men, the continued absence of the sheriff, and McDowell's request for troops. "General Black advised me to see to it that the sheriff got on the job, and told me to stay in the clear; that he could not send troops yet, as the civil authorities had not requested them."

BLACK: Hunter reported the attack on the mine, but said he believed the situation could be handled locally. (Black also stated that he alerted commanders of the National Guard companies at Mt. Vernon, Salem, and Cairo in response to the call he received from the panic-stricken Lester soon after Hunter reported.)

6.30 p.m. HUNTER: Reported the truce that was in the making, but asked Black to send troops. Black refused. "The Adjutant General maintained all the way through that he could not or would not send troops until requested by civil authorities."

BLACK: Hunter reported that a truce had been arranged and that there was no further reason for apprehension.

11.00 p.m. BLACK: Hunter verified his earlier report regarding the truce.

Hunter denied that he ever made this call. Later in the investigation, telephone-company records proved that he did make it. The toll slip was filed at Springfield instead of Marion or Murphysboro, as was the case with the records of the other calls, and did not come to light for several weeks.

Other evidence indicated that Hunter's repeated requests for troops were inventions after the damage had been done. Three days prior to the massacre, he had told Oldham Paisley of the *Marion Republican* that troops would not be used because the local authorities had the situation in hand. Two days after the massacre he had talked freely to the Board of Officers, headed by Major General Milton J. Foreman of the 33rd Division, Illinois National Guard, who had made an investigation on the scene, and said nothing to any of its members to indicate that he had asked the Adjutant General or anyone else to send troops to the danger spot.

The fact was that at the time of the massacre Hunter believed that under the law state troops could not be sent into a county unless local authorities asked for them. On June 24, 1922, he had made that clear to a representative of the *Marion Post.* "Let me say right here," he was quoted, "that I did not have the power to call out troops at any time. The law compels me to wait until the local authorities announce the situation is beyond their control and ask for troops." Abundant testimony given during the investigation showed that this was his understanding at the time; hence his frantic efforts to induce the sheriff to make the appeal that he believed to be essential. When he learned, sometime after the riots, that the governor, acting through the Adjutant General, could send troops into any community on his own initiative, he altered his story to fit the newly discovered provisions of the state's military code.

Having grilled the military in Springfield, the committee decided to move to the scene of the trouble. On April 26 it met in Marion. There, after a visit to the site of the Lester mine, it took up the question of local responsibility for the riot.

Melvin Thaxton, now county treasurer by virtue of the largest majority in the county's history, was one of the first witnesses. Under questioning by Chairman McCarthy he was less than cooperative, but when Representative Igoe took over the examination his memory failed him almost completely.

> IGOE: "What do you do down here in the case of murder?"
> THAXTON: "Try to make arrests."
> IGOE: "Why didn't you make arrests before June 22?"
> THAXTON: "I couldn't find anybody to arrest."
> IGOE: "Name a single act which you did in connection with the murder of the two union men."

THAXTON: "Well, I talked around. Nobody seemed to know."

IGOE: "Why didn't you go to the strip mine that night [June 21]?"

THAXTON: "Well, we didn't go."

IGOE: "Did you bring anybody before the grand jury concerning the murder of these union men?"

THAXTON: "No."

IGOE: "Isn't it true that you told Earl Miller, a newspaper reporter, and Colonel Hunter that on June 21 you heard of the murders while you were at Carterville and said that you thought you ought to go and that Duty told you not to go?"

THAXTON: "No."

IGOE: "You didn't find out who killed the union or non-union men?"

THAXTON: "No, sir."

IGOE: "Did you ever get a letter from Lester?"

THAXTON: "I probably might."

IGOE: "Don't you know that you got a letter dated June 18 in which Lester said: 'We expect trouble and therefore we expect you to provide protection for our men and our property'?"

THAXTON: "I don't know."

Representative Pierce had no more success with the form sheriff than Representative Igoe.

PIERCE: "Did you hear Colonel Hunter report to the Adjutant General [on the night of June 21]?"

THAXTON: "He said that everything was quiet and that no further trouble was expected."

PIERCE: "You knew that that report was false, didn't you?"

THAXTON: "No."

PIERCE: "If seven men had been shot why didn't you expect trouble?"

THAXTON: I don't know."

PIERCE: "You don't think that you did your duty, do you?"

THAXTON: "I felt like I did."

PIERCE: "You have told us all you did and you call that the fulfilling of the answer you gave the people of Williamson County in response to your oath of office?"

THAXTON: "Yes, sir."

Thaxton's deputies, and the police officers of Herrin and Marion, were uncommunicative, even defiant, on the stand. Jake Jones, a Herrin policeman, admitted that while he was on duty on the night of June 21 he learned that several hardware stores had been raided for guns.

QUESTION: "What did you do then?"
JONES: "Nothing. I didn't have any right to do anything. It was too far gone and I didn't know what had been done."
QUESTION: "Don't you think that a crime?"
JONES: "It wasn't a crime. They just went in and got them. I didn't think it was any of my business. I don't know whether they charged them or not. I never asked."

Police officers on duty on the night of June 21 saw nothing unusual in the crowds that almost blocked the streets in Marion or Herrin; or if they did, they were content to regulate traffic, and asked no questions. They showed no more concern on the morning of June 22. Al Richardson, one of Thaxton's deputies, arrived in Herrin about nine a.m. He noticed crowds in the downtown section, but never asked the reason for them. Jake Jones knew well enough what was taking place, but simply ignored it.

QUESTION: "How did you hear of the mob coming?"
JONES: "A woman telephoned that the mob was coming up 13th Street."
QUESTION: "Did you tell the chief? Did you make a record of the call?"
JONES: "No."
QUESTION: "Why didn't you go to 13th Street?"
JONES: "One man himself couldn't have done anything."
QUESTION: "Why didn't you tell the chief?"
JONES: "It was already rumored that the mob was coming down 13th Street."
QUESTION: "And you and the chief of police stood there and did nothing?"
JONES: "Yes."
IGOE: "You ought to be indicted for complicity in this murder."

By the end of a week in Marion most of the members of the investigating committee had lost their patience completely. Chairman McCarthy put into the record the statement that he had been practicing law for eighteen years and had never seen more reluctant witnesses; Igoe simply refused to ask questions; Pierce commented that he would feel safer in Springfield than in the hostile atmosphere of Williamson County. So the committee voted to resume its hearings in the state capital.

Altogether, some sixty witnesses appeared before it. W. J. Lester refused to testify,* Hugh Willis left the state and could not be called, and one deputy sheriff and two Herrin policemen departed after the Marion sessions. But the testimony was sufficient to fill in whatever gaps in the story remained after the two trials.

On the basis of its hearing the committee drew up a report which ranks with that of the grand jury as an authoritative account of the events of June 22 and the preceding days. Its assigning of responsibility, however, was much more comprehensive. Few escaped censure. Adjutant General Black was blamed for not taking personal charge before the massacre and ordering out troops on his own responsibility, but that was a mild reproof in comparison with the castigation Colonel Hunter received. "We believe that he was absolutely incompetent, unreliable and unworthy to perform the duties assigned to him," the committee stated. Sheriff Thaxton and his deputies were

---

* *A year after the massacre the Illinois District, United Mine Workers of America, bought the Lester mine in order to forestall heavy damage-suits. The purchase price was $726,000, considered fabulous by all who knew the value of the property. There are reasons for believing that Lester "kicked back" substantial sums to several union officials: even so, he made a handsome profit.*

After his Illinois venture Lester attempted to develop a strip mine in Kentucky and lost heavily in the undertaking. When it failed, he promoted a bauxite mine in Arkansas. In that, too, he was unsuccessful. The depression found him penniless, but he succeeded in establishing a modest practice as a consulting engineer in and about Indianapolis. There, in the spring of 1934, he was stricken with paralysis. He died at the family home of his wife, Emily Hill Lester, at Augusta, Georgia, on January 5, 1935.

"criminally negligent"; all the local police-officers were "absolutely derelict in their duty." Hugh Willis could be convicted of murder in any county in the state but Williamson. If he, Fox Hughes, and other union officials "had been prompted by high and lofty motives," the disaster could easily have been prevented. Lester, on the other hand, should not be absolved from blame: his greed and foolhardiness were sharply condemned. Of all those of whose activities the committee took cognizance, only Delos Duty drew words of praise. "His untiring efforts in trying to convict those whom he believed responsible for the murders lead us to the conclusion that he did his full duty, even to the sacrifice of his health. He deserves the commendation of this committee, the people of his county and the State of Illinois."

Five members of the committee signed the report. The other two, Representatives Pierce and Curran, filed a minority report.

In the main, the two minority members accepted the majority's statement of facts, though they omitted some of the most harrowing incidents, and challenged several passages reflecting on Hugh Willis and Colonel Hunter. Of the majority conclusions, however, only the condemnation of Lester was retained. All other participants were exonerated in the concluding paragraph:

> It is the opinion that the evidence heard by the committee is of such controversial nature, that we are unable to definitely fix the responsibility, because of the mob spirit prevalent at the time, nor that there was any real or intended neglect of duty on the part of the public officials; furthermore . . . the committee believes that this massacre could not have been anticipated and that everything that could be done had been done by the State to forestall this trouble, because . . . these mobs were composed of people from other towns and localities.

Both reports were presented on June 30, 1923, in the last hours of the biennial session. As many members of the House were not in their seats, Representative Curran tried to force the Speaker to recognize the absence of a quorum, and thus prevent either report from becoming a matter of official record. In this he failed, but he succeeded in blocking the adoption of the majority report and in keeping it from being printed as a separate document.

That same night, in the Illinois State Senate, other union sympathizers gave the Herrin investigation the *coup de grâce*. Because Hugh Willis and other witnesses were not accessible, the House investigating committee had introduced a bill setting up another commission to prolong the investigation. The House passed the bill by a vote of 84 to 11. But a few opponents in the Senate prevented a vote before adjournment, bringing this bitter comment from the five signers of the majority report: "The committee hopes that these Senators will be replaced by men of high moral stamina and courage, who will think more of the protection of the fair name of the State of Illinois than their own selfish political ambitions."

Thus the last echoes of the guns of Herrin died away in the popping of firecrackers and the noise of the horseplay that Illinois lawmakers consider appropriate to the final hours of a legislative session.

5

THE BLOODY VENDETTA

July 1868–January 1876

●●

The feud is a disgrace to the whole State
of Illinois—a disgrace to the courts of the
State, to the government of the State, to the
Governor of the State, and to the people of
the State. *Chicago Tribune, August 9, 1875.*

In newspaper accounts of the Herrin Massacre the phrase,
"Bloody Williamson," occurred repeatedly. Most readers assumed that it originated in the killings that took place on June
22, 1922, but to residents of southern Illinois the words reached
far into the past. They brought to mind, first of all, the days of
the "Bloody Vendetta" half a century earlier, and after that,
mine wars and riots that kept alive the county's reputation for
lawlessness and bloodshed. In such a background many a
thoughtful observer found an explanation, if not a cause, of the
savagery that had shocked the entire nation.

Like most of southern Illinois, Williamson County was settled
by immigrants from Kentucky, Tennessee, the Carolinas, and
Virginia. Many of them came from the hill regions, and they
were slow to lose the peculiar characteristics of mountain folk.
They were generous, hospitable, hardy, independent, brave, and
intelligent, but undisciplined by education. Their superstitions
were many and strong, their prejudices deep and unyielding. In
religion they were Protestant—usually Methodist, Missionary

Baptist, or Campbellite—and inclined to find emotional release in the excesses of the camp meeting.

Almost without exception they were hot-blooded, proud, obstinate, jealous of family honor, and quick to resent an insult. Given what they considered sufficient provocation, they could kill with little compunction. Milo Erwin, the first historian of

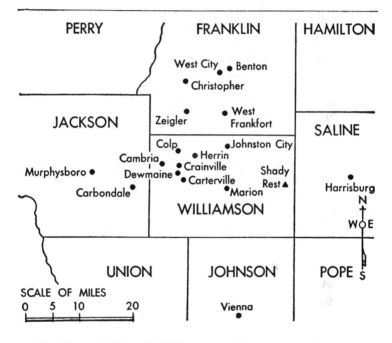

The Heart of "Egypt": Williamson and Contiguous Counties

the county, counted 495 assaults with a deadly weapon and 285 murderous assaults between 1839, when the county was organized, and 1876, the year in which he wrote. He also listed almost fifty murders that had been committed in those same years. Of the murderers, he could find only six who had been convicted and given prison sentences, although two were under indictment or awaiting trial at the time he made his compilation. All the others had either escaped detection, fled the country, or been acquitted on pleas of self-defense.

Murder, then, was no novelty. Yet in the "Bloody Vendetta" the taking of life became so commonplace that hundreds of people lived in mute fear, while to the rest of the state the mere fact of residence in Williamson County was a reproach.

By all accounts, the Vendetta began with an ordinary tavern brawl. On the Fourth of July, 1868, several members of a family named Bulliner were playing cards in a dramshop near Carbondale. Felix Henderson, commonly known as "Field" Henderson, took a hand in the game. Before long an argument developed, and Henderson made the mistake of calling one of the Bulliners "a damn lying son-of-a-bitch." In the fight that followed, Henderson was badly beaten.

Thus the Bulliner and Henderson families became bitter enemies. Both clans were relative newcomers. The Bulliners—two families headed by brothers—had lived in southwestern Tennessee until the last year of the Civil War, when they settled south of Crainville, a hamlet in the west-central part of Williamson County. There they bought good farms, established several business enterprises, and quickly came to be known as honest, industrious, and enterprising.

They also acquired the reputation of having "sand in their craws" and of not liking to be "put upon." The men were big-boned, broad-shouldered, muscular, good-looking, and pleasant in manner, yet they could be most disagreeable to anyone who crossed them. This propensity, with the influence that their standing in the community gave them, made them formidable enemies.

The Hendersons—three brothers and their families—were Kentuckians. Like the Bulliners, they settled in Williamson County, north of Crainville, during the last year of the war. All were large, strong, and fearless. Though not wealthy, they too owned good farms, and soon became as influential in their neighborhood as the Bulliners were in theirs.

74

While the enmity between the two families smoldered, another Bulliner quarrel gave the Hendersons an ally. On the farm adjoining that of "Old George" Bulliner lived George W. Sisney, one of the leading citizens of the county. He had served as captain in an Illinois regiment during the Civil War and had been elected sheriff in 1866. A contemporary characterized him as "a man of more than ordinary ability," of "medium size and compactly built, dark complexion, a very passionate and fearless man, but high-toned, generous and open-hearted." He had three grown sons, all "full of grit and fight."

A year after the first Bulliner-Henderson fracas Sisney and one of the Bulliner boys had a lawsuit over a crop of oats. In court, Sisney won. Some months later the two men met to settle several business transactions. Their accounts differed. In the argument that followed Bulliner accused Sisney of swearing to a lie in the lawsuit of the previous year, whereupon Sisney knocked him down. Young Bulliner rounded up his father and two brothers and the four men, all armed, set out to redress the wrong. As they approached the Sisney house on the run, with "Old George" shouting: "Here we come, God damn you, to kill you!" Sisney, armed with a repeating rifle, left by the back door. When the Bulliners saw him running across an adjoining field they opened fire. Every few yards Sisney stopped and fired back. Although hit four times, he managed to reach the shelter of a big tree. His assailants, afraid to close in on him, called off the fight.

Later, all the participants were fined one hundred dollars each. Then Sisney brought a suit for damages against the Bulliners which they settled out of court. Henceforward, however, the Sisney family was in the Vendetta.

For almost two years the animosities these incidents aroused lay dormant. A series of brawls brought them to life, and led the large and pugnacious Crain family, whose members had lived in the county for two generations, into the feud on the side of the Bulliners. The first trouble came on Christmas Day,

75

1872, when several Crains and Sisneys met by chance in the general store at Carterville, two miles west of Crainville. Bantering talk led to a full-scale fight, which bystanders finally quelled. Several of the participants were arrested, and ordered to appear for trial before a justice of the peace.

At the trial the Crains turned out in force. So did the Sisneys and Hendersons, now their enemies, and the Bulliners, allies of the Crains by virtue of their feud with the other two families. What had been scheduled as a judicial proceeding turned into a small-sized riot, with several of the participants seriously injured. The State's Attorney filed informations but failed to press the charges. Thus all went free.

By this time two trivial incidents—a game of cards and a lawsuit over a few bushels of oats—had separated four large and prominent families, each supported by many friends and relatives, into two groups of sworn enemies, with any Bulliner or Crain eager to assault a Sisney or Henderson simply because he was a Sisney or Henderson.

Throughout 1873 one brawl after another took place. Several times the rioters were arrested, but in every case either the accused was acquitted or the prosecution was dropped.

Then, on the morning of December 12, 1873, "Old George" Bulliner saddled his horse and set out for Carbondale. Later in the day neighbors found him lying by the side of the road, his back torn by a charge of buckshot fired at close range. The murder was never solved.

Three months afterward, two of Bulliner's sons were fired on from ambush, and one was mortally wounded. Friends carried the injured man home. He lingered until morning, when, as Milo Erwin put it, "the twilight shadow of death, cold and gray, came stealing on him. A supernatural lustre lighted up his eye, and illuminated the gathering darkness. At length his eyes closed, and an expression of ineffable placidity settled on his pallid lips, and he was no more."

Before he died, young Bulliner named Tom Russell as the

man who shot him. Russell had no family connection with the Vendetta, but everyone knew that two years earlier he had been jilted by a lady of somewhat easy virtue in favor of one of the Bulliner boys, and that since then he had hated them. He was arrested at once, and held for trial before a justice of the peace. He retained counsel, and the Bulliners, bent on vengeance, employed three lawyers to assist in the prosecution. A strong case was built up against him, but Monroe Bulliner, brother of the murdered man, failed to identify him as one of the assassins, while another witness provided an alibi. The result was a verdict of acquittal.

By this time the original causes of the feud were forgotten and it was feeding on itself. Two Bulliners had been killed, and no one doubted that there would soon be an attempt at retaliation.

There was. In mid-May 1874, James Henderson, acknowledged leader of the family and uncle of the "Field" Henderson who had been a party to the barroom quarrel with which the Vendetta began, was at work on his farm. For months he had lived in fear of his life, surrounding his house with watchdogs and posting his daughter and foster son as guards. This spring afternoon, while the girl helped her mother in the house, he and the boy lay down to rest. Assassins fired from a woodpile a few feet away, hitting Henderson in the back. One of them came into the open, and seeing that the victim was still alive, shot him with a pistol.

He lived for eight days. Before he died he named one of the Bulliner boys, and James Norris, who worked for them, as his attackers. Warrants for their arrest were issued, but three months passed before Bulliner was taken, while Norris was not apprehended until much later. Bulliner was indicted, tried, and acquitted when four witnesses from Tennessee swore that he was visiting there when Henderson was shot.

The day after the shooting of Henderson, a man plowing a field a mile distant was shot, though not fatally. He had no connection with the Vendetta; the supposition was that he had stumbled on evidence incriminating someone. Shortly afterward another innocent resident was shot from ambush, again for no apparent reason. In August 1874, an attempt was made on the life of George W. Sisney, but the charges of the assailants' guns, dampened by dew, failed to fire and he escaped. Although he watched his attackers run from the scene he would not reveal their names.

This wave of assaults and murders terrified the people of the western part of Williamson County. Fearing for their lives, they kept their suspicions, even their knowledge, to themselves, hoping thus to escape the bullets of the feudists. The murder of Dr. Vincent Hinchcliff proved that the hope was futile.

Hinchcliff was a substantial citizen. His family had lived in the county for many years, and all its members bore good reputations. He himself had been active enough in politics to be rewarded with the postmastership at Carterville, and as a country doctor he had a large number of stanch friends.

Hinchcliff's connection with the Vendetta came about through circumstances rather than family connections. He had testified against Tom Russell when Russell was charged with the murder of David Bulliner, and that had aligned him, in the minds of the community, with the Bulliners and Crains against the Hendersons and Sisneys.

On Sunday morning, October 4, 1874, Hinchcliff made a call on a sick man. Returning home, he was shot from ambush and died instantly. During the ensuing investigation, witnesses testified that they were close enough to hear not only the shots but also the exultant yells of the assassins, yet they could not identify the murderers. Two of the Hendersons were arrested and indicted, but were never brought to trial.

After the death of Hinchcliff [Milo Erwin wrote], consternation seized every mind; mutual distrust and a want of confidence was felt. The solemn pallor of cholera times hung over our people. Silence pervaded the air. The responsible men were seen standing around in groups, whispering questions that no man dare answer. . . .

One of those to whom the all-pervading suspicion and fear became intolerable was George W. Sisney. He knew that he might be chosen to pay with his life for the murder of Hinchcliff; he also knew that he had been lucky, a few months earlier, to escape death. In the fall of 1874 he ran for a second term as sheriff of Williamson County, but was defeated. Soon after the election he moved to Carbondale. There, though only a few miles from the scene of the feud, he thought he would be safe.

His peace of mind lasted only until the 12th of December, hardly a month after his removal. Early that evening, while he played dominoes with his wife and a young visitor, someone fired both barrels of a shotgun through a near-by window. Sisney was badly wounded; so was his young friend.

Both victims of the attack recovered. However, because of Sisney's prominence, and because, by leaving the scene of the Vendetta, he had obviously tried to sever any connection with it, the attempted murder attracted far more notice than earlier assaults. Newspapers made biting comments. "Where this will end," one editor moaned, "God only knows. Parties have visited Carbondale and ordered . . . double-barreled shot-guns, swearing vengeance, and boldly declaring that the fun has only begun." Another, in the county seat, admitted that the name of Williamson County had become "a hiss and a by-word." Strangers were shunning the region, property was dropping in value, and there was no prospect of exploiting the veins of coal that were known to underlie the topsoil. "To . . . bring these fiendish outlaws to justice seems to be the universal desire of the people," the writer concluded, "but to accomplish this seems to be the point that puts to silence the entire county."

One reason for this state of affairs—perhaps the only reason —was the ineffectiveness of the county authorities. The leading participants in the feud had influence, and weak-kneed officials were afraid to proceed against them. When Tom Russell was cleared, on preliminary examination, of the murder of Dave Bulliner, a deputy sheriff with a warrant for Russell's arrest on another murder charge in his pocket allowed him to walk out of the courtroom unmolested. The sheriff himself refused for months to arrest his cousin, Jim Norris, who was charged with the murder of James Henderson. But the worst delinquent was the State's Attorney, J. D. F. Jennings. According to Erwin, who doubtless wrote with prejudice, this worthy was "a professional doctor, lawyer, preacher, fiddler, horn-blower and libertine" and thoroughgoing hypocrite. "He was a rowdy among the rowdies, pious among the pious, Godless among the Godless, and a spooney among the women." But he could preach a sermon so persuasively that his hearers would still be shaking with remorse while he himself was gleefully drunk. His performance as a law-enforcement officer was on a par with his activities in the pulpit.

No wonder that a reporter for the *St. Louis Democrat*, writing a long account of the Vendetta a few weeks after the assault on Sisney, concluded: "As far as the officers of the law are concerned as to making arrests and prosecuting criminals, Williamson County might as well be without them."

The people of Illinois were coming to the same conclusion. If the local authorities could not be depended upon, then the time had come for the state government to act. In January 1875, soon after the General Assembly convened for its biennial session, a member introduced a bill directing the governor to take such action as he might find necessary to secure the arrest and conviction of the Williamson County outlaws, and authorizing him to spend ten thousand dollars for that purpose. Stubborn opposition developed. "The feeling seems strong," a correspondent wrote from Springfield ". . . that the proper thing is to leave the Williamson County murderers to go on killing each other till they are all exterminated." A sharp communication from the governor, and a petition from the sheriff, treasurer, county clerk, and leading citizens of Williamson County kept the bill alive, but its opponents succeeded in reducing the appropriation from ten thousand to three thousand dollars. Thus amended, it passed the House, but too late for the Senate to act upon it. The movement to obtain state aid served only to publicize the county's shame.

While the legislators wrangled over the relief bill, Jennings, the State's Attorney, disappeared, taking with him nine hundred dollars of public money. Soon afterward the office was declared vacant. At a special election in June, J. W. Hartwell, an able young lawyer and a man of courage, was elected to it.

During the first half of 1875 a few minor disorders were the only evidence that the Vendetta persisted. Then the feud blazed again. Once more the victim was George W. Sisney, and this time luck favored the assassin.

The circumstances were almost identical with those which had prevailed a few months earlier. On the night of July 28 Sisney retired early. About nine o'clock a friend knocked on his door. The man needed money and wanted Sisney to endorse his note. The ex-sheriff came downstairs, lighted a lamp, signed the note, and then sat and talked with his visitor before an open window until the blast of a shotgun ended the conversation. "As soon as we heard the shot," a neighbor said, "we knew that George Sisney was killed; everybody knew it would be Sisney's turn next." A crowd gathered. Inside the darkened house the hysterical sobs of women could be heard. Someone battered in the front door. Sisney, still erect in his chair, had a gaping hole in his chest. He was dead.

They took his body to Crainville for burial. On the day after the funeral service, several of his friends gathered in the store of William Spence, the principal merchant of the village. As they talked, Spence lost his Scotch taciturnity long enough to remark that if he told what he knew, someone would suffer for Sisney's murder. And, he added, they should.

The next morning Spence was found dead in his store, a shotgun wound in his body and pistol holes in his head and chest. Neighbors admitted that they had heard shots during the night, but none had been bold enough to investigate.

Two murders in quick succession shocked the people of the state as no previous killings in the Vendetta had done. Four days after the murder of Spence Governor Beveridge wrote a stern letter to the sheriff of Williamson County: "The State's Attorney must prosecute; grand juries must indict; witnesses must testify; courts and juries must try; and the Sheriff must execute the orders of the court." He had no funds with which to ferret out local criminals, he added, nor could he act unless called upon by the county authorities. He could, however, authorize the enrolling and equipping of local militia. But the law, he explained to a newspaper reporter, only allowed him to offer a reward of two hundred dollars, which would be a farce under the circumstances. The county officials, through whom he had to act, had not yet notified him of their inability to enforce the laws.

To many people over the state, the governor's attitude was inexcusably pusillanimous. From Cairo and St. Louis to Chicago, editors attacked the chief executive's supineness. What Williamson County needed was a hangman, with a governor in Springfield courageous enough to give him something to do. . . . The entire state was being disgraced by the lawlessness of a single county, and it was the governor's responsibility to find a way to restore order. . . . "This Williamson County business marks a black page on the annals of Illinois, and by the honor and power of the State there should be no more of it. . . ." "Let the Governor take a hand: the people will sustain him in driving out the ruffians. . . ." "Why does he not offer rewards for the apprehension of the Williamson assassins? What reward does he expect for his neglect of duty in this matter? Who can explain his conduct?"

This deluge of criticism had its effect. The Williamson County Commissioners offered rewards of one thousand dollars each for the arrest of the murderers of David Bulliner, James Henderson,

Vincent Hinchcliff, and William Spence. And Governor Beveridge, suddenly discovering that he had more money at his disposal than he had at first supposed, offered additional rewards of four hundred dollars each for the arrest and conviction of the murderers of these men, and a like amount for the arrest and conviction of the killers of George W. Sisney and George Bulliner. Shortly afterward the Jackson County Court offered rewards of four hundred dollars for the murderers of Sisney and George Bulliner, both of whom had been killed within its jurisdiction.

Nothing more was needed. A woman, to whom one of the killers had talked too freely, told her brother that she knew who had murdered William Spence. The brother decided that Benjamin F. Lowe of Marion—a former town marshal who had turned professional gambler—was the man to turn justice into a profit. Lowe agreed, and undertook to bring about the arrest of the murderers.

In less than a month he arrested a ne'er-do-well named Samuel Music at the post office in Cairo. The suspect had lived in the western part of Williamson County for seven or eight years, making a meager living as a teamster. He was illiterate and a drunkard. And he was the man who had gabbled about the killing of William Spence.

All the way from Cairo to Marion, Music drank steadily. When he reached his destination he was ready to talk. On the basis of his revelations the sheriff arrested John Bulliner, Samuel R. Crain, and three other members of the Crain family who went by the names of "Big Jep," "Black Bill," and "Yaller Bill." Lowe found Allen Baker, another Bulliner ally, at Du Quoin, arrested him, and brought him back to Marion. Marshall Crain, more directly implicated by Music than were any of the others, could not be located. Lowe heard that he was in Missouri. Soon afterward he ran him down in northeastern Arkansas. In a short time Crain was behind the bars of the Jackson County jail at Murphysboro, charged with the murder of George W. Sisney.

While Lowe was tracking his man, John Bulliner, Samuel R. Crain, and Allen Baker were arraigned before a justice of the peace. Music, the principal witness for the prosecution, testified that Marshall Crain had killed Sisney, and that the three men in court were his accomplices. Samuel R. Crain was released for want of evidence, but Bulliner and Baker were committed to jail. Soon afterward, they were indicted for murder.

Their trial opened at Murphysboro on October 8, 1875. Music, the star witness, told a lurid story. Early in July, he related, he had been present when John Bulliner offered Marshall Crain three hundred dollars if he would kill Sisney. Crain agreed. On the 28th of the month, Music continued, he had been in Carbondale where, by chance, he met Crain, who admitted readily enough that he was there for the purpose of killing Sisney. Music, unconcerned, went about his business.

The next day he met Crain and Allen Baker in Carterville. Crain related that about nine o'clock on the previous evening he had started for Sisney's home. Aided by rain, he reached there without being seen. The house was dark; evidently its occupants had gone to bed. He was about to give up hope when Sisney's visitor arrived, thus giving the killer his opportunity.

After firing one fatal shot, Crain ran. The rain, now a violent thunderstorm, aided him to escape. He made his way out of town, and then stumbled through swamps and mudholes until his reached his mother-in-law's home, nine miles from the scene of the killing, just before dawn.

From Carterville, Crain and Music went to Crainville, where they met John Bulliner. Again Crain described what he had done on the preceding evening. Bulliner gave him fifteen dollars and promised to pay the balance of the blood money when he sold his wheat. He had wanted Sisney killed, he added, because he believed that the ex-sheriff had been connected with the deaths of his own people.

The next day Music, Marshall Crain, and Big Jep Crain were passing the time in a card game. After several drinks Big Jep announced: "The next man to kill is Spence." The others agreed. Twenty-four hours later the three, with Black Bill, met in a field near Crainville. After the little town was dark and quiet Marshall Crain knocked on the door of Spence's store and called out the owner's name. From an upstairs window Spence asked who was there. "John Sisney," Crain answered. "I want to get shrouding for a child." When Spence appeared Crain fired both barrels of his shotgun into the storekeeper's abdomen, then put pistol shots into his victim's heart and brain.

From this story Music could not be shaken; no amount of cross-questioning could confuse him.

After Music had testified, Marshall Crain took the stand in his own defense. He knew nothing, he swore, about the murder for which he and the other two defendants were on trial. At this development, counsel for Bulliner and Baker produced a letter that Crain had written to their clients before the trial. In that communication he had asked his codefendants to have several people swear that he was at a surprise party on the night Sisney was killed, and at the home of a friend when Spence was murdered. In return he would testify that Music had admitted killing Spence. All three—Bulliner, Baker, and Crain himself—would then go free.

When Crain heard this letter read he knew that he was trapped. He also realized that Bulliner and Baker intended to help themselves as much as they could by establishing his own guilt. Enraged, he told the truth, corroborating Music's testimony on every material point. Thus he made his own fate certain, but he also assured the conviction of his accomplices. The jury brought in a verdict of guilty, and Bulliner and Baker were sentenced to twenty-five years in the state penitentiary.

A few days later Marshall Crain was brought before the Williamson Circuit Court at Marion to stand trial for the murder of William Spence. When arraigned he pleaded not guilty, but on the following day he changed his plea to guilty and threw himself on the mercy of the court. The case was continued until

85

witnesses could be called and examined. Their testimony established the guilt of the defendant beyond question.

After the last witness stepped from the stand Crain was called before the bar and asked why sentence of death should not be pronounced. The prisoner replied that he had been dominated by wills stronger than his own. "I was dragged into this work by other parties," he said. "I had a higher power and influence over me. I could not resist. I don't think I have done enough to be hung for. Spence was harboring parties that were trying to kill me. . . . I was influenced by John Bulliner, a man of good mind and education, but I am not a man of good mind, and no education."

Uninfluenced, the judge pronounced sentence: that Marshall Crain "be hanged by the neck until he is dead" on the 21st day of January, 1876. "And," he concluded, "may God have mercy upon you."

When the condemned man left the courtroom he was taciturn and apparently emotionless. Within two days, however, he lost his assurance and asked for permission to tell all that he knew about the Vendetta. Before the grand jury he confessed to killing both Sisney and Spence. Then he broke into loud lamentations, and continued his wailing for several days. At the same time, he sought peace in religion. A month after sentence was passed upon him, a heavy guard escorted him to a near-by millpond, and there, dressed in a long white robe, he was baptized and taken into the church.

At dawn on January 21, 1876, the town of Marion began to fill with people. In the jail Crain, who had slept well, ate a hearty breakfast. Throughout the morning he talked with his wife, relatives, and friends. Just before noon he dressed in a white suit, over which he put his baptismal robe. After saying farewell to his wife he walked to the window of his cell and called out to the crowd that now filled the jail yard:

"I must make a statement in regard to this matter. I feel it my duty to God and man to do so. I am guilty of killing the two men. My soul is stained with blood, and my punishment is just. I hope all will forgive me. I pray God to guide and prosper this country."

He then read a crude poem he had composed for the occasion. At its conclusion he walked to the trapdoor with a steady step. There he stood while a minister spoke of the solemnity of the occasion, read several passages from the Book of John, and led the crowd in the hymn, "There Is a Fountain Filled with Blood." When prayer was offered, Crain dropped to his knees.

The ceremony over, the hangman pulled the cap over the murderer's head and slipped the noose around his neck. When asked whether he had anything to say he answered: "I am the murderer of William Spence," paused, and concluded: "and George W. Sisney." At 12.56 the rope that held the trapdoor was severed. Twenty-six minutes later Crain was pronounced dead.

Attendants cut down the body and put it in an open coffin, which was placed in the street before the jail. For an hour and a half the crowd filed past. Then the coffin was closed and turned over to a brother. Burial took place on the following day.

"The wild winds of heaven," Milo Erwin wrote, "will sing their hoarse lullaby over his grave until the mighty Angel Gabriel writes the solemn legend, 'Finis,' on the hoary page of time."

The hanging of Marshall Crain, and the conviction of Bulliner and Baker for complicity in the murder of Sisney, signified the end of the Vendetta. Others, however, were still to be punished. During the early months of 1876 two other Crains were tried, found guilty, and sent to prison; a third member of the family, indicted as an accessory in the Spence murder, died of tuberculosis before he could be brought to trial. James Norris, implicated in the murder of James Henderson, drew a prison term. The last of the feudists to come into court was Samuel Music who, because of his testimony in behalf of the state, was let off with a fourteen-year prison sentence. After this the county authorities concluded that the requirements of justice had been satisfied, and made no serious effort to bring any members of the Sisney-Henderson faction to trial.

In bringing his narrative of the Vendetta to an end Milo Erwin wrote:

> With this, I seal the volume, and turn my eyes away from the bloody acts of depraved men, hoping with all the fervor of which my soul is capable, that God will add no other plague to our county. Enough has been done, to teach the world that sorrow is the first result of ambition, malice, or revenge. . . . We are beginning to have bright hopes of the future. . . . If those editors who labored so hard to traduce our character and disgrace our county, will do as much to restore it, soon peace and prosperity will be printed on the mangled tape of our county, and soon that odium that hangs around our name, like clouds around a mountain, will disappear, and Williamson county will stand forth resplendent in the light of a new civilization, conspicuous and honorable, and take the rank her sons and resources entitle her to.

6

DOCTRINAIRE VS. UNION

1890–1906

●●

> In the face of opposition from union
> miners throughout the State of Illinois and
> almost ostracism of the mine operators in
> the state, he has fought alone for what he
> deems is right. *Jewell H. Aubere in the*
> *St. Louis Globe-Democrat, December 11,*
> *1899.*

FOR MORE than twenty years Williamson County enjoyed
peace and prosperity—greater prosperity, in fact, than Milo
Erwin could have expected. Coal was the basis of the new
wealth.

The existence of coal in Illinois had been known ever since
1673, when Marquette and Jolliet made the voyage of discovery
with which the state's history begins. Many a later traveler noted
its presence in outcrops and creek banks, but the nineteenth
century was half gone before the commercial exploitation of this
great natural resource began in earnest. "The State has but recently commenced to make use of the coal with which nature
has so bountifully provided her," the statistician of the industry
wrote in 1855. "Except in the vicinity of the larger towns and
rivers, the business of mining coal here had made but small progress."

What little progress had been made in the first years of settlement—Illinois came into the Union in 1818—is shown by the

U.S. Census of 1840. There the state is credited with having produced 17,000 tons of coal in that year, with only 152 workmen engaged in coal mining. But annual production jumped to 300,-000 tons in 1850, and to 728,400 tons ten years later. The reason for the increase is to be found in three facts: between 1850 and 1860 the state's railroad mileage grew from slightly more than 100 miles to approximately 3,000; railroads haul coal cheaply; and they burn it. (Or did, until the advent of the diesel engine.) When, in 1854, the Galena and Chicago Union, parent line of the North-Western, purchased five locomotives that were guaranteed to burn Illinois coal instead of wood, the future of the state's mining industry was assured.

Railroad building, interrupted by the Civil War, was resumed after Appomattox. With almost miraculous rapidity Illinois transformed herself from an agricultural to an industrial state. The standard of living rose, and coal fed home furnaces as well as the boilers of great factories. Production shot upward—to 2,625,000 tons in 1870; 6,115,000 tons in 1880; 15,275,000 tons in 1890. (In 1918, its peak year, Illinois produced 90,000,000 tons of coal.)

In exploiting the wealth that lay beneath her thin and failing soil, Williamson County lagged behind other sections of the state. Her first mine was opened in 1869—by Laban Carter, who gave his name to the town of Carterville, which grew up around his workings—but for several years the output was insignificant. By 1880, however, with two mines in addition to Carter's in operation, 73,500 tons were brought to the surface, giving Williamson nineteenth place among the forty-eight coal-mining counties of the state. In 1890 production exceeded 200,000 tons, although the county stood one place lower in relative rank.

In that year Samuel T. Brush of Carbondale organized the company that was to put Williamson County in the front rank as a coal producer. His St. Louis and Big Muddy Coal Company, financed largely by St. Louis and Cincinnati capital, sank its shaft a mile north of Carterville. In 1893, after only two years of operation, it brought up more than 200,000 tons, and took rank as the sixth largest mine in Illinois. In that same year the district mine-inspector referred to its coal-washing plant, which represented an investment of thirty thousand dollars, as "the most extensive improvement of this kind in the State." The Panic of 1893 and the subsequent depression threw the company into receivership, but Brush stayed on as general manager, and the mine's output continued to rise. In the year 1897 it produced 319,697 tons, more than any other mine in the state.

But this was the peak. In 1898, with 300,600 tons, it slipped back to sixth place. The following year its production was only 172,335 tons; its rank an ignominious thirty-ninth. Brush had collided with the United Mine Workers of America, and doctrinaire and union were engaged in a fight to the finish.

Ever since the Civil War the coal miners of the country had been trying to form a permanent union on a national basis. Two organizations—the American Miners' Association and the Miners' National Association—won initial successes and then fell apart under the strain of internal dissension and countrywide depression. A third—the National Federation of Miners and Mine Laborers—was about to go the same way when a convention of all organized miners was called late in 1889. Somehow, differences were harmonized, and early in 1890 the United Mine Workers of America was formed.

That this union succeeded where its predecessors had failed was partly the result of farsighted leadership, and partly the effect of conditions in the industry, which rapidly became intolerable.

Beginning in the early 1880's, the selling-price of coal shrank steadily. Overproduction and fierce competition forced the operators to reduce costs. Wages, being vulnerable, dropped even faster than the price of the product. In 1890 the United Mine Workers, through joint conference with the operators, secured a substantial increase in pay rates, but the union was unable to hold its gains in the face of the Panic of 1893. By 1895 the operators in the bituminous field were paying only sixty per cent of the scale for 1894. Even so, men almost fought for the privilege of working. "The prevailing hard times," commented the Secretary of the Illinois Bureau of Labor Statistics in 1896, "has forced large numbers of men into the ranks of the army of the unemployed. Among these the struggle for a mere existence is constant and intense. The opportunity to earn the bare necessities of life, even at the hardest and most hazardous employment, is a prize to be fought for."

In 1895, in the seventh Illinois inspection district, which included Williamson County, the average daily wage of miners paid by the ton was $1.58, their average yearly income $235.01. Day men (as opposed to tonnage workers) fared a little better, averaging $1.63 and $273.61, respectively. Actually, the rates were even lower than these figures indicate.

> There are many days during the year [wrote the author of the *Illinois Coal Report* for 1896] in which work is nominally suspended and the mine is shut down, but the miners are in their rooms, getting their coal in readiness, and in other ways preparing for the time when the mine shall again be in active operation. . . . Then, too, the miner is entirely dependent upon that one industry for his livelihood. In most cases he is isolated from all opportunity of employment at any other calling, and in addition to this, even in times of idleness, he must hold himself in constant readiness to go down into the pit when the work starts up.

Most miners—and Brush's miners in particular—lived in company houses that rented at from four dollars a month, or thereabouts, for three rooms, or six dollars for four. Usually the dwellings were constructed of vertical planks, without weatherboarding on the outside, and devoid of either plaster or wallpaper on the inside. There was no central heating, no running water, and one privy served three or four houses. The surroundings, described with realism in the *Illinois Coal Report* for 1893, were depressing:

Everything is suggestive of coal; standing out promi-
nently is the black, grim-looking upper or outer equipment;
close by a large pile of slack or refuse, often towering high
above the house tops, the roads and spaces surrounding the
houses are usually covered with cinders or coal dust, there
being a total absence of flowers, grass or other vegetation.
The houses are small, the architecture the same throughout,
giving the entire place a very monotonous appearance.*

The miner worked under a contract of employment heavily
loaded in the operator's favor. If he took part in a strike he could
not only be discharged but also made to forfeit all pay that was
due him, and he could be, and often was, ejected instantly from
his company house. He had, of course, no assurance of employment, and no compensation in periods of unemployment.

Small wonder that miners should give their loyalty to any
organization that held out hope of better wages and working
conditions.

The new union did not wait long to test its strength. Before
the delegates to its annual convention, held in Columbus in early
April 1894, President John McBride proclaimed: "There is a
limit to human endurance and you have reached that limit. The
price paid for mining must go no lower, but it is absolutely necessary for both life and comfort, and you are entitled to both,
that the price should go higher, and that soon." The delegates

---

* *This is a general description, and may be too bleak for the St. Louis
and Big Muddy mine. Miss Elizabeth P. Brush, Samuel T. Brush's daughter,
comments on this passage:*
*"Occasionally my father took us to the mine to the Fourth of July picnic.
. . . I remember a grove of trees where the long tables were set, and I remember the rows of ugly little houses, but I do not believe there was 'a
total absence of vegetation'; the hideous mountain of slack which I recall so
well seeing from the train at Du Quoin must have had a rather incon-
spicuous counterpart at the Brush mine, for I do not recall it at all. . . .*
*"As for sanitary arrangements, running water was a rare luxury in rural
southern Illinois in the 1890's and for many years thereafter. Outdoor
privies were all but universal even in the towns. In our house, built on the
edge of town (Carbondale) in 1891, and considered 'modern' then, all the
water used for the bathroom, had to be pumped by hand into a tank in the
attic, and so the bathroom was used only in case of illness!"*

responded by passing a resolution calling for a strike to begin at noon on Saturday, April 21.

Although only a fraction of the soft-coal field was unionized, most of the miners obeyed the strike call. But they lacked both discipline and money. In a few weeks their ranks broke, and operator after operator made a local agreement with his men. Some won small increases, but in Illinois most of the diggers went back to work, after two months of idleness, at the rate which had prevailed before the strike.

Conditions speedily became worse. The hard times ushered in by the Panic of 1893 continued. In that year the average value of Illinois lump coal at the mine was $1.025 per ton; by 1897 it had dropped to $.852. The pay rate declined in even greater proportion.

On May 1, 1897, Illinois operators announced new reductions, amounting in some cases to as much as twenty per cent. The men accepted—at the moment they had no choice—but with the tacit reservation that at the earliest opportunity they would make a determined effort at least to restore the cut. In late June the executive board of the union met in secret session and ordered all miners to stop work on July 4. The board made no specific demands, and asked only for a living wage. Its hope of success lay in the fact that prevailing wages were below the subsistence level, and in the expectation that general business conditions would soon improve.

Although the United Mine Workers of America had a membership of fewer than 11,000 when the strike was called, 150,000 men walked out of the pits on July 4. In Illinois the union could count only 226 members, but a large majority of the state's 38,-000 miners stopped work. Soon the strike became a crusade, with groups of miners going from town to town with bands, banners, and speakers. Public opinion began to make its weight felt on the side of the strikers. Consumers, it became evident, were willing to pay more for their coal if thereby the miner could enjoy a living wage. After four months the operators yielded and the men obtained a substantial increase, their first in seven years.

By good fortune and astute management Brush escaped lightly in the strikes of 1894 and 1897. The former he rode out, in company with all other Illinois operators, and saw his men return to work, after being out fifty-six days, on the old terms. The second strike he circumvented by capitulating in advance. Believing that a prolonged suspension would raise the price of coal, he offered his employees an increase if they would stay on the job. They agreed, and kept their promise in spite of heavy pressure from striking miners in near-by counties.

To the local business community, Brush was an ideal industrialist. When the *Marion Leader,* in the fall of 1897, published a "Harvest and Industrial Edition," its editor wrote:

> The relations between the men and Mr. Brush are all that can be desired. He has displayed considerable tact in the management of the men, is approachable at all times and is ever ready to remedy any grievances that may exist, giving careful and impartial consideration both to the interests of the men and his company. The people of Williamson county are friends of the St. Louis & Big Muddy Coal Company which is the most important in Southern Illinois; it has done much to prove to the world the value of our coal bed and is deserving of the success and consideration which is due to an undertaking of this magnitude.

But Brush was also an individualist, bound sooner or later to clash with a militant union.

Victory in the strike of 1897 brought the United Mine Workers of America to real life. Membership rose from 11,000 in 1897 to 25,000 in 1898, to 54,000 in 1899, and to 91,000 in 1900. The greatest gain took place in Illinois, which John Mitchell, first as vice-president and, after September, 1898, as president of the union, made his special province. There membership jumped from a handful at the time of the strike to 30,000, almost eighty-five per cent of all the men employed in and about the mines of the state, by the end of 1898. Without Brush's knowledge, a local was organized at the St. Louis and Big Muddy mine in January of that year.

Conflict came soon. Early in 1898, union and operators agreed upon rates of pay for the states that made up the central competitive district. Subsequently, scales for the various districts within Illinois were worked out. For Williamson County the rate was set at thirty-six cents a ton, ten cents more than Brush was paying. Calling attention to the fact that he had not been represented at either conference, and claiming that the thirty-six-cent rate was disproportionately high, he refused to be bound by the agreement. Instead, when the miners' contracts expired on March 31, 1898, he offered new ones calling for a rate of thirty cents a ton. Immediately eighty per cent of his men struck.

For the next six weeks Brush operated his mine with the few men who had not walked out. Then he called the strike committee together and issued an ultimatum. Unless the men returned to work in five days he would bring in Negro miners whom he had already recruited in Tennessee. After that he would take back his former employees only as he needed additional men. On the other hand, if the strikers came back within the time limit, he would contribute one thousand dollars to the needy among them. The men rejected the proposal.

If—as Brush believed—the strikers thought he was bluffing, they were soon disillusioned. Before dawn on the morning of May 20 a solid train of Negro miners, some with their wives and children, unloaded at Carterville. Within a week he announced that he had 178 colored men, and several whites, at work, and that he was turning down nearly all his old hands who wanted their jobs back.

A few days later the other Carterville mines announced that in order to meet the competition of the Brush mine they would reduce their pay rate from thirty-six to thirty cents, effective May 30. The union took action at once. At 5.30 that morning some 250 miners from near-by towns arrived at Carterville and deployed along the roads leading to the various shafts. Miners going to work at all the mines except Brush's, where the men lived in company houses adjacent to the tipple, were turned back. Then the invaders pitched tents in the town park and prepared for a siege. "The strikers present," a reporter wrote, "say they are determined that Mr. Brush will pay the Springfield scale [thirty-six cents] or not run. Mr. Brush says he will run his own mine to suit himself."

While a committee of union men tried to persuade Brush's Negroes to walk out, the community lived in fear of serious trouble. Many of the strikers had brought their shotguns with them, and Brush had a large force of armed guards. If the men attempted to storm the mine, as they threatened to do, there would be bloodshed. The sheriff of Williamson County, however, swore in deputies and kept a mob from forming. And the Negroes were indifferent to the miners' persuasions. They were satisfied, they said, and intended to stay on the job. After a few days the union men admitted defeat and quietly returned to their homes.

For nearly a year the St. Louis and Big Muddy worked without trouble. During that time Brush made his position so clear that no one could mistake it. On March 29, 1899, he announced that he was instituting the eight-hour day (one of the union's chief objectives) and that henceforth he would pay thirty-seven and a half cents per ton, one and one-half cents more than the union scale. But he would not recognize the union.

By this time the St. Louis and Big Muddy was the only important mine in the state that remained unorganized. In it the union saw a challenge that could not be ignored. A new local was formed, drawing into its membership all Brush's white miners and a number of the Negroes who had originally come in as strikebreakers. On May 15, 1899, it called a strike, and all the members of the union walked out.

The issue was clear. Brush himself stated it in an interview with a reporter for the *Chicago Inter-Ocean*. About the first of May, he related, three of his men came to him to complain about their pay.

"I asked if they represented the Union, saying that I would not treat with anyone representing the Miners' Union, as that organization had utterly failed in the past to keep its promises to me."

The men denied any connection with the union and insisted that they came only to present their individual grievances. Brush listened and promised redress, only to learn from his mine manager that his callers constituted a committee from the local that had been organized without his knowledge. He discharged them immediately. "They had misrepresented the situation," he told the *Inter Ocean*, "and had induced me to make concessions that would have resulted in the claim being made that I had recognized the Miners' Union and would be bound to carry out such demands as my men might make."

The union demanded that the three committee members be reinstated by May 15. Brush ignored the ultimatum and the strike followed. Between 150 and 175 walked out; an equal number refused to quit.

The situation would have been dangerous enough with only strikers and strikebreakers involved. But it happened that every one of Brush's white miners, with no more than seven or eight Negroes, went on strike, while every one of those who remained at work was a black man. Carterville, moreover, had long imposed on the Negro a subhuman status. No colored person was permitted even to enter the town. (Even today, in several Williamson County towns, notably Herrin, no Negro is permitted to remain overnight.) ° Now black men threatened the existence

---

° *A woman who formerly lived in Williamson County comments: "Some Herrin families do keep hired Negro help in their homes overnight. I had a 'Clarissa' who lived with me for four years. The old feeling of 'being out of the city limits by dark' was still with her, however. She didn't like to answer my door after the evening meal and usually stayed right in her room. She never appeared on the streets after dark."*

of the union and endangered the livelihood that white men considered theirs.

Bitterness on both counts—union vs. nonunion and white vs. black—was the keener because of recent events in the central Illinois mining towns of Virden and Pana. At Virden, when a company that had locked out its men attempted in the fall of 1898 to bring in a trainload of Negro miners, a pitched battle between strikers and armed guards resulted. Nine white miners and ten guards were killed. The company had to abandon the attempt, and finally met the union's terms. At Pana the operators succeeded in bringing in Negro strikebreakers, but one riot followed another, several men lost their lives, and the state militia stood guard for months. The soldiers were still there, and Negroes were still working the Pana mines, when Brush's men walked out in May 1899.

Left by the strike with only half his normal labor force, Brush recruited some thirty-five or forty colored miners and put them into his company houses, from which the strikers had been evicted, without difficulty. Late in June he was about to import more when he learned that the Pana operators would soon settle with the union and let their Negroes go. With supreme foolhardiness, he decided to employ them.* On his behalf his son James approached the Pana operators, hired forty of their men, and arranged to bring them, with their families and belongings, to Carterville.

---

* *Miss Brush comments: "I recall that he thought the Pana operators craven to discard the Negroes after they had used them, and he liked the idea of befriending them (as he thought) as well as of breaking the strike against him. . . . What his admirers thought courage and optimism, a detached observer might well call rashness or I suppose, foolhardiness."*

That Brush had a deep interest in the welfare of the Negro—most unusual for a southern Illinoisan of fifty years ago—is beyond question. His daughter characterizes him as "a pillar of the Presbyterian Church of Carbondale, a friend of the Negroes of the town, and a stern enemy of the saloon." And Dean Robert B. Browne of the University of Illinois, who as a young man knew the Brush family well, tells me, in language gratifyingly unacademic: "Sam Brush always had the damnedest stream of colored folks coming to the back door and getting handouts. He took care of 'em."

The contingent, traveling in two special cars attached to an Illinois Central train, reached the little town of Lauder (now Cambria), three miles northwest of Carterville, on the morning of June 30, and made its usual station-stop. As soon as the train came to a halt an armed white man walked up to the conductor and ordered him not to proceed. The conductor signaled the engineer to start. Immediately a volley of rifle shots, fired by men lying in a wheatfield adjacent to the station, crashed into the two cars carrying the Negroes. Anna Karr, the wife of one of the Pana miners, died instantly; twenty others were wounded. Brush, who had boarded the train at Carbondale, his son, other mine officials, and as many of the Negroes as were armed returned the fire. The men in ambush let go another volley, but by this time the train had picked up speed and no one was hit.

At the Brush mine the Negroes disembarked without trouble. Later in the day, however, several hundred armed men surrounded the mine and the adjacent cluster of company houses. As night fell, desultory shooting began. The sheriff appeared but, having no arms for extra deputies, he was helpless.

Under the cover of darkness, Brush's men fought back. Near the mine stood a cluster of frame shacks, called Union City, which the union had built for the Negro members who had been evicted for joining the white strikers. Enraged by the killing of Anna Karr, the Brush Negroes surrounded the hamlet and opened fire. When the occupants ran, the attackers burned the houses. Then they scoured the woods where the union Negroes had taken refuge. Although shooting on both sides continued until daybreak, there were no fatalities.

As soon as the Brush men counterattacked, the sheriff asked for the militia. "I am powerless to control the factions or to enforce the law at Carterville," he telegraphed to Acting Governor Warder at Springfield. "Send me guns and ammunition and a force of 200 men to quell the riots and arrest offenders." A few minutes later Brush's superintendent made an independent appeal: "The situation . . . is such that ordering troops at once is necessary to prevent open violence and bloodshed." The following morning—Saturday, July 1—brought two more telegrams from the sheriff. "I am sure there will be a big fight soon," he announced in the first. "Ammunition and guns came to the strikers on 9 o'clock train. They are fixing to wipe out Brush mine tonight. Get us help as soon as possible." The second read: "Brush mine surrounded by 250 men. Men at train armed and got big lot of ammunition. Must have help at once." Brush himself joined the petitioners: "All our men, women, and children are so terrorized that they will not go to their homes, and have not eaten or slept since yesterday. The Sheriff seems powerless. We must have the militia immediately."

The acting governor refused to be stampeded. Before ordering out troops he telegraphed to W. W. Duncan of Marion, a leading citizen of the county, for an unbiased review of conditions. On the afternoon of July 1 Duncan reported:

> There are 500 or more union and non-union men at war in Carterville. Both sides are determined to fight it out. A Sheriff and posse can do nothing with the situation until the factions are disarmed by the state. The Sheriff's presence only increases the danger. My judgment is that many lives and the Brush mines will be destroyed without state aid to disarm both factions. Firing from ambush with Winchesters still continues. More union men are gathering, and while quiet now reigns the situation is ominous. I advise troops at once.

Warder acted on the advice, and ordered Company F of Mt. Vernon and Company C of Carbondale, both of which had seen service in the Spanish-American War, to Carterville. The troops arrived on the morning of Sunday, July 2, set up camp, and established guard posts around the mine and along the road connecting it with Carterville. Firing stopped immediately. Order prevailed even on the 3rd and 4th, when Brush brought in two more contingents of Negro miners. But this uneasy peace restrained only temporarily the deep bitterness that would surely erupt in violence as soon as the militia should be withdrawn.

A few weeks later Brush spent a day in Murphysboro on business, intending to take the evening train to Carterville. As he approached the station two men assaulted him. He was knocked down and beaten, though not seriously injured. Thereafter an armed guard accompanied him wherever he went.

As fall approached, and no disturbances occurred, Carterville became increasingly restive under the presence of the militia. The townspeople, wholly in sympathy with the union, had resented the sending of troops in the beginning; now they took steps to have them withdrawn. Leading citizens of the community assured the governor that the militia was no longer needed: there would be no further disorder. That official, well aware that the National Guard could not be kept on duty indefinitely, ordered the two companies home. On September 11, after having been on duty nearly two and a half months, they withdrew.

Six days passed before rioting broke out again.

Early on the morning of Sunday, September 17, two Carterville miners, Lem Shadowens and Elmer James, saw three of the Brush Negroes at a small Italian saloon within the town limits. James warned them to leave. The Negroes went away cursing, and one of them threatened:

"We'll go out of town and return, you damn son-of-a-bitch of a Spaniard, and I'll wash my hands in your blood and —— your wife before the sun goes down." *

About noon on the same day word spread through Carterville that fourteen or fifteen Negroes were on their way from the

---

* *Miss Brush writes: "Unless my father and my brother James lied repeatedly in their conversations with each other, the men who testified thus were most unsavory characters. The account is based on defense testimony, is it not? You quote my father's statement [see p. 104], but it seems to me you have not allowed it to influence your narrative of the killings. However blameworthy Sam T. Brush may have been for bringing the Negroes into Williamson County, his testimony as to what happened is surely deserving of enough weight to cast a shadow of doubt on what Shadowens and James said to save their skins. And is it likely that the Negroes, who cer-*

Brush mine to the Illinois Central station, and that they were armed. In a dozen homes white miners reached for their rifles and started for the station. Twenty-five or thirty men, all armed, arrived at the same time. Some of the Negroes stood on the platform, some inside the building. Those on the platform were ordered to get out of town and be quick about it, while Lem Shadowens opened the station door and called out:

"Come out, you damned black scab sons-of-bitches; we've got you—come out and take your medicine."

The Negroes hesitated, and then started up the railroad tracks. The white men followed at a distance. Suddenly one of the Negroes drew a pistol and fired at the group of pursuers. The miners answered with a volley. Several of the Negroes fell; the others ran for their lives. The whites followed, firing at the fugitives. In a few minutes not a black man could be seen. Five lay dead; the others, some of them wounded, escaped to the safety of the mining camp around the Brush shaft.

Immediately after the shooting the mayor of Carterville, fearing a reprisal, swore in a large number of deputy marshals and stationed them between the mine and the town limits. He had reason for his fears. Had it not been for the courage and foresight of Brush's son, there might have been a riot far bloodier than that which took place. As soon as the first fugitives reached the mine young Brush locked the storehouse in which the company arms were kept, and took his stand, gun in hand, before the door. Soon he faced two hundred Negroes, determined to arm themselves and avenge the murder of their comrades. He warned them that he would shoot the first man who took a forward step. The crowd wavered, then dispersed.

---

tainly went to Carterville with apprehension, made such threats? It would have been suicidal. As for their drinking, my father thought that story a lie."

In this comment Miss Brush, professor of history at Rockford College until her retirement in 1950, raises the problem that haunts everyone who tries to describe what happened in the past. In this instance my account is based on defense testimony. That testimony was not discredited at the time, and more than fifty years later it seems credible.

Before the day ended the two companies of militia that had left less than a week before were back in Carterville, to be joined by a third company the following week. Again, order prevailed.

News of the Carterville riot, coming less than three months after the attack on the Negroes at Lauder, shocked the entire state. Brush defended his men. The Negroes, he asserted, did not go to Carterville to make trouble. Some expected to meet friends or relatives arriving on the noon train, several intended to go to Marion for church services, one was starting to Tennessee to attend the funeral of his mother. Knowing the feeling against them, Brush continued, "the colored people got together at their school house on the mine property on Sunday morning, and selected a few of their best men to go to Carterville with their friends. They took men who did not drink and who were old enough to have good judgment. They did not go into the town until just in time to meet the train. They went to the depot quietly, and the agent of the Illinois Central Railroad states that they were not making any disturbance or provoking anyone, whatever."

On the other hand, the people of Carterville pointed out that the Negroes knew that the feeling against them was intense, that three of them (all killed) had been drinking at the Italian saloon that very morning, that many carried arms, and that one of their number fired the first shot. The townspeople resented deeply Governor Tanner's comment that the episode looked like an instance of premeditated murder, and contended that the conflict would not have occurred except for the taunts and threats of the Negroes themselves.

The local authorities had been unable to prevent two riots, but in both instances they moved quickly and courageously to apprehend the participants. On the very day of the Lauder riot the sheriff made six arrests, and others followed soon afterward. The sheriff was ill at the time of the killings at Carterville, but within twenty-four hours deputies arrested twenty-seven men charged with murder. Some were discharged for lack of evidence, but the Williamson County grand jury indicted nine men, seven of whom were colored, for the murder of Anna Karr at Lauder on June 30, and twelve men, all white, for the murder of the five Negroes killed at Carterville on September 17. On the petition of attorneys for the defense, who alleged that anti-union sentiment was so strong in most of Williamson County that a fair trial could not be had there, a change of venue to Johnson County, directly south of Williamson, was granted. Trial of the Lauder riot cases was set for Monday, December 4, at Vienna,* the county seat.

As the first week of December approached, Vienna became the focal point of life in southern Illinois. By early November every room in the town's two hotels was engaged for the duration of the trial. On Sunday, December 3, three hundred visitors appeared without warning from Carbondale, Carterville, and other communities; the townspeople had to throw open their homes to them. When the bailiff called out the familiar "oyez, oyez," on the morning of the 4th, Vienna's normal population of one thousand had been increased by five hundred strangers.

Their interest centered in the red brick courthouse, with white cornices and white belfry, that stood in the middle of a gently sloping square. Around the square, under the corrugated iron awnings that covered the sidewalks, groups of men who had not been able to crowd into the courtroom discussed the most exciting event in the county's history.

The soft drawl of their speech did not hide the tension that pervaded the atmosphere. Vienna, the seat of an agricultural county, cared little about the issues that were to be decided, but the strangers who thronged the town were violent partisans. Those from Carbondale backed Brush to a man; those from Carterville and the other mining towns hated him. Moreover, the prosecution had announced that it would produce a large number of Negro witnesses, and many predicted that they

---

* *Pronounced Vi-enna.*

would never testify. When the Negroes came in on the morning of the 4th, escorted by a heavy guard cf militiamen, and no attempt was made to molest them, Vienna relaxed and settled down to enjoy the proceedings.

Within the courthouse, the crowd showed as much interest in the legal luminaries whom the trial had attracted as in the defendants. On the bench sat Circuit Judge A. K. Vickers, middle-aged, bald, sedate, dignified, yet capable of laughter. Eight lawyers—some volunteers, some retained by the United Mine Workers—represented the defendants, but the spectators had eyes for one man only: "Governor" Charles P. Johnson of St. Louis. Sixty-three years of age and at the height of his reputation as a criminal lawyer, Johnson was known, feared, and respected in the courts of a dozen states for his ability to present the most intricate legal problem in terms that a plain juryman could understand, and to drive home his argument with an irresistible rush of oratory. He had earned his title by having served one year as lieutenant governor of Missouri. Heavyset, smooth-shaven, his strong round face capped with gray hair, he made an impressive figure in his black broadcloth and string bowtie. As he talked with his colleagues he radiated confidence.

Attorneys for the prosecution were State's Attorney George B. Gillespie of Johnson County; R. R. Fowler, State's Attorney of Williamson County—both young men of courage and ability —and five others retained by Brush. The prosecution, like the defense, had a star performer—"Judge" Francis M. Youngblood of Carbondale. At sixty-four Youngblood was old enough to wear the judicial title, although he had never presided over a court. He too had a reputation as a criminal lawyer, and was famed for his flow of speech.

But no one in the courtroom attracted as much attention as Samuel T. Brush. Those who expected to find in this dogged opponent of union labor a man of decisive manner and commanding presence were quickly disillusioned. Instead they saw a man of medium height, so thin that he hardly weighed 125 pounds. Brush was fifty-seven years of age, and many observers, noting his stooped form and rounded shoulders, would have guessed that he was older. Short, red-brown whiskers covered his chin, and his eyesight was so poor that he wore glasses constantly. The most noticeable feature of his face was a blue-black birthmark directly below his left eye. His appearance was not prepossessing, yet his gray eyes were kindly and often twinkled with humor. When he spoke he drew on a large vocabulary without affectation. His voice was well modulated, his manner pleasant and affable.

At nine o'clock on the morning of December 4 the nine men charged with the murder of Anna Karr were formally arraigned. The defense moved that the case be dismissed, alleging a defective indictment, but Judge Vickers overruled the motion. Court then recessed until the following morning.

On the 5th the process of selecting a jury began. That day and the next, sixty-three men were examined, and not one was acceptable to both sides. Hour after hour the lawyers questioned talesmen, trying to ascertain their attitudes toward union labor, capital punishment, and the Negro; probing for indications of intelligence and open-mindedness. Occasionally a solemn, nervous countryman broke the tedium with an answer that sent even the defendants into laughter. One old man tried hard to keep from answering the question:

"What was your wife's name before you married her?"

Finally, in desperation, the prospective juror appealed to the judge:

"Wall, now, Jedge, hain't thet pushin' a feller too fur? You see, it's thisaway: I've bin married so long I clean forgot what Sal's name was before I guv her mine."

Another shattered the decorum of the court when he defined his attitude toward capital punishment:

"No, sir: I don't believe in no capital punishment, and I'll tell you right here that any man who does ought to be hung!"

Many in the courtroom laughed at the answer a farmer gave

to the lawyer who tried to find out whether he was prejudiced against Negroes:

"Wall, sir, I don't believe in hangin' nobody for nothin', and I reckon I never could hang a white man for killin' a nigger, but if one nigger kills another, and it was right down awful murder, I reckon as how I could send him to the penitentiary."

Thirteen days passed before twelve men, selected from nearly five hundred talesmen, sat in the jury box. All were farmers, and most of them owned the land they worked. Only one had ever been a miner.

During the first days of the trial the state offered numerous witnesses to identify the defendants as members of the armed mob that had ambushed the Illinois Central train at Lauder station on the morning of June 30. None compared in effectiveness with Alfred Karr, the husband of the woman for whose murder the miners were on trial. As the tall, light-colored Negro with the reddish mustache and goatee took the stand, the spectators stiffened with expectancy, and a strained hush replaced the usual undercurrent of whispering and shuffling feet. In a calm voice Karr told how the bullets cut through the hair of the little child he held on his knee. Suddenly he stood, pointed to the dark face of George Durden, one of the defendants, and cried with passion:

"There is the man that killed my wife! I am sure of it. He shot her through the heart, and as she fell on the floor beside me and I called her by name, a stream of blood as big as this here cane [shaking the stick he held] burst from her bosom and soaked the floor where she fell."

From the defendants charged directly with murder the state turned to Thomas Jeremiah, one of the two white men on trial. The prosecution admitted that Jeremiah had not even been near the scene of the riot, but contended that he was its principal inciter, and procured the arms and ammunition the attackers had used.

To prove its case the state presented two private detectives whom Brush had hired several weeks before the outbreak. Both testified that Jeremiah, with John Paretti (indicted but never apprehended), had stored guns and ammunition in the boardinghouse in Carterville where all four men had lived, and that the weapons and cartridges had been removed on the early morning of June 30. The boardinghouse proprietor corroborated their testimony.

The state concluded its case dramatically. From the beginning Brush had taken an active part in the trial. He had filled several notebooks with abstracts of testimony, and had conferred repeatedly, in whispers, with the attorneys for the prosecution. Each night in his hotel rooms he had held a council of war, reviewing what had just happened and planning the next day's strategy. Now he was called as the state's last witness. Quietly and without perceptible emotion he told his story.

As the train stopped at Lauder, Brush related, he was sitting at an open window in a coach ahead of the one in which the Negroes were riding. Angry voices drew his attention. Looking out he saw Paretti, whom he knew, and heard him say to the conductor:

"I want to get to those Negroes."

The conductor asked Brush whether Paretti, and several others on the platform, were his men. Brush replied that they were not, and told the conductor to pull out. Looking Paretti in the eye, he warned him not to shoot. The conductor signaled the engineer, and the train jerked into motion.

"If you don't stop that train I'll shoot you!" Paretti yelled.

Instead of complying, the conductor jumped for the rear platform, and the train gained speed.

"Immediately," Brush said, "the Italian and the Negro behind him fired their guns. . . . Someone, whom I could not see, fired into the car, up toward the front end. Immediately after the two men fired at the conductor they fired at me. By this time there was a great deal of firing all around."

The quiet voice continued.

109

"I opened the valise which was on the seat in front of me, and, taking my revolver out, reached out of the window to return the fire. I was almost ready to shoot, and was looking for the men when I heard someone fall or jump on the ground near the depot platform, about the length of a car from the depot. I looked that way and saw a Negro firing wildly toward the train. . . . I fired at him that instant, and thought I hit him as he fell. I then turned and fired at the Italian and the Negro."

Brush concluded his testimony by describing the finding of the dead Negress and the removal of her body from the train at the mine.

The strategy of the defense was simple: to establish alibis for those defendants charged with participation in the riot, and to show that Thomas Jeremiah was not a conspirator.

To this end, witness after witness took the stand to testify that one or more of the defendants was somewhere else than at Lauder station when the train was fired on. Others, including the wife of the Carterville boardinghouse proprietor, swore that the ammunition Jeremiah was said to have stored up before the riot was inconsequential in amount. Still others testified to Jeremiah's good reputation and character, and impugned Brush's detectives.

With the testimony all in, Vienna prepared for an oratorical field day. Interest in the case had, if anything, been heightened by the testimony, and new spectators poured in to hear the closing arguments of the attorneys. These, it was evident, would take several days, for none of the fourteen lawyers had any intention of surrendering his right to make a speech.

On the afternoon of January 3, 1900, State's Attorney George B. Gillespie opened for the prosecution, taking three hours to expound the law and analyze the testimony of the witnesses for the defense. On the following day L. O. Whitnet, Gillespie's partner in private practice, consumed the entire morning on behalf of the defense. For the remainder of that day, and the two days that followed, the lawyers picked apart the stories of the

witnesses and attacked or defended the miners' union and Sam
T. Brush. One even read the Biblical accounts of the fall of man
and Cain's slaying of Abel, and from them drew precedents for
the application of the death penalty. The spectators, crowding
the courtroom from 8.30 in the morning until 9.00 each night,
sat enthralled.

The climax came on Saturday, January 6, when "Governor"
Johnson made the final argument for the defense and "Judge"
Youngblood closed for the prosecution. "This," wrote Jewell H.
Aubere, reporting the trial for the *St. Louis Globe-Democrat,*
"was the day for the battle royal. . . . Today the old court
house in Vienna was turned into an arena, and there before
breathless hundreds these venerable men struggled for the mas-
tery."

Johnson began quietly and disarmingly by reminiscing about
his boyhood in southern Illinois. He spoke of the jury as an in-
strument of justice, stressing the seriousness of each juror's responsibility, and emphasizing the fact that guilt must be proved
beyond a reasonable doubt. Turning to a defense of the miners'
union as an organization, he unleashed the eloquence that hundreds had come to hear. With a lump of coal in his hands he
described the hardships and dangers faced by the men who dug
the black mineral from the depths of the earth, and implored
the jurymen to deal simple justice to his clients.

Following Johnson's example, Youngblood traced the trials
of his own boyhood, and challenged any man to show that his
attitude toward the laboring classes had ever been anything but
friendly and sympathetic. But a crime had been committed, a
foul crime, and justice demanded that the penalty of the law be
applied. With a severity approaching passion he assailed Jeremiah and Durden as leaders of a conspiracy that had led to murder, and sarcasm gave a cutting edge to his voice as he reviewed
the arguments of the lawyers who had asked that these men go
unpunished. Then he dropped oratory, and closed with a cool
and logical discussion of the evidence.

After Youngblood finished, Judge Vickers read his instructions to the jury, and put the case in its hands.

As dawn broke on Sunday morning, the bailiff in charge of the jurors left the courthouse to summon the judge and the lawyers. The defendants were brought in from the jail. To the audience, which included half a dozen sleepy spectators, the judge read the verdict:

"We, the jurors sworn to inquire into this cause, find the defendants not guilty of the crime charged."

There was no demonstration.

That afternoon the lawyers, the defendants (except four who had been held for violating an injunction issued by the United States Court), and their friends and families started for their homes. At every station crowds prevented the train from proceeding until hundreds had shaken the hand of "Governor" Johnson, whom all credited with the acquittal. Nowhere did the celebration approach that at Carterville, where at least a thousand people, accompanied by a band, had assembled. There, from the platform of his car, Johnson made a short speech. On the 30th day of June, he said, Sam T. Brush looked from a car window at Carterville and saw his enemies. "On the 7th day of January," he continued, "we look out of a car window and see our friends. Brush and the attorneys for the prosecution tried to make the people of Vienna believe that the people of Carterville are all cut-throats and anarchists. But we convinced them that you are law-abiding and good citizens of this state."

After the Lauder case, the trial of the Carterville rioters was an anticlimax, in spite of the fact that the second riot far exceeded the first in seriousness. Everyone knew what the outcome would be. If a Johnson County jury would not convict Negroes for killing Negroes, could there be any real possibility that white men would be punished for the same offense?

The trial, which began at Vienna on January 23, 1900, followed the pattern of the earlier case. Once again strangers filled the county seat and crowded the courtroom from morning until

night. The same lawyers were on hand, with the defense banking heavily on Johnson. Once again weeks were consumed in examining almost six hundred talesmen before a jury was selected.
As before, the jury consisted mainly of farmers, all fairly young.

On February 13, Youngblood opened for the prosecution. In a
speech of an hour and a half he expounded the law and outlined
the state's case against the twelve prisoners, all charged with the
murder of the Negro, Sim Cummins. In reply, W. W. Duncan
indicated that the defense would be an alibi for some of the defendants, justifiable homicide for others.

The state took seven days to present its witnesses. Altogether,
fifty-two testified. Some had seen old man Shadowens, his two
sons, and Elmer James, all carrying guns, on their way to the
Carterville railroad station just before the riot. Some had seen
Willis Carney, or Robert Hatfield, or Mat Walker, fire at the Negroes as they ran down the tracks in terror. Others testified that
the colored men had been anything but provocative in their behavior, and that the riot was precipitated by the white miners
who had ordered them out of town. In all, nine of the defendants were positively identified as having taken part in the shooting. In order not to weaken its case, the state dismissed the indictments against the other three defendants, and yielded to the
defense.

The defense introduced a number of witnesses, some of them
colored, who swore that the Negroes had come to Carterville on
September 17 looking for trouble, and that their actions at the
Italian saloon early that morning, and at the railroad station later
in the day, had precipitated it. Three of the prisoners—Matthew
Walker, Willis Carney, and Lem Shadowens—admitted frankly
that they had taken part in the riot, but all swore that Sim Cummins had begun the shooting and that they had fired only in self-
defense.* Other defendants were located at points distant from

---

* *Miss Elizabeth P. Brush makes this comment: "Nothing in your account
would so distress my father as the implication that those poor black men
took the offensive in any way. Even if Sim Cummins had a gun, and I suppose he had, wasn't it natural that he should carry it? After the passage of*

the station at the time of the riot. A succession of witnesses, principally Carterville businessmen, testified to the good character of
the nine men standing trial.

On March 1, after six weeks had been spent in selecting a jury
and taking testimony, the lawyers began their closing arguments. For three days the old courtroom rang with sententious
oratory. The testimony of witnesses was emphasized or torn
apart, prejudice was charged and disavowed, the Bible, the Dec-
laration of Independence, and the Constitution were cited, and
the shades of Jefferson and Lincoln appealed to.

As in the Lauder case, Johnson closed for the defense. No one,
he asserted, was more keenly aware of the rights of Negroes than
he. As a young man he had fought for the abolition of slavery,
and as a resident of a one-time slave state he had been bitterly
condemned for championing the cause of freedom. But the right
of a Negro to equality before the law did not nullify the right of
self-defense. On that the defendants stood—that and the fact
that the state had not proved its case beyond a reasonable doubt,
as the law required.

The final summary of the state's case fell to George B. Gillespie who, though the youngest of the attorneys for the prosecution, had shown outstanding ability in this and the preceding
trial. Governor Johnson's address, Gillespie admitted, was "as
beautiful as a dream and smelled as sweet as new-mown hay,"
but facts, not flowery words, should influence juries. The defense
claimed self-defense, but against what? If an overt act had been
committed, it had been committed by the defendants. The Ne-

---

*so many years, the truth cannot be discovered. I am afraid that your readers
would not realize that.*

*"The development of our concepts of democracy and social justice makes
inevitable an adverse judgment of my father's attitude toward the union,
but I do not believe that that fact should influence our conclusion as to
what happened on that dreadful September day. It is, at the very least,
conceivable that Sam T. Brush, his son James, his nephew George Colton,
his trusted clerk John Maher, all men of unimpeachable integrity, were
right when they believed that the slain Negroes were good and sober men
innocent of any provocative conduct."*

groes, it was said, had formed an unlawful assembly, but they had as much right in Carterville as anyone, and if any assembly was unlawful on September 17, 1899, it was that of the armed whites. The men on trial brought about the death of Sim Cummins: they had the means, the opportunity, the motive, and malice in their hearts. "I make no passionate appeals," Gillespie concluded. "Decide this case according to the law and facts, and remember God's decree has gone forth 'that whosoever shall shed man's blood, by man shall his blood be shed.' "

Gillespie finished his argument late in the afternoon of March 3. That evening Judge Vickers gave the case to the jury. At four o'clock on the following morning the jurors reached a verdict of not guilty; three hours later the verdict was announced in open court. State's Attorney Fowler of Williamson County, recognizing the futility of further prosecutions, asked the court to dismiss the indictments, still pending, for the killing of the other four Negroes. The defendants walked out of the courtroom in full freedom.

As he discharged the prisoners Judge Vickers made a little speech. Let them forget the animosities that had been engendered during the trial, he asked, and cherish neither hatred nor desire for revenge because of it. Above all, he hoped that a spirit of mutual forbearance would prevail, and that peace, law, order, and tranquillity would be restored in Carterville.

The judge's hope was realized. Nonunion Negroes continued to work the St. Louis and Big Muddy mine without molestation. But for Brush it was a losing venture. Between 1900 and 1905 his production ranged from 213,000 tons to 245,000 tons, as opposed to 320,000 tons in 1897 and 300,000 tons in 1898. At the same time other mines in the state, and even in Williamson County, set new records. Moreover, his expenses ran high. At frequent intervals he had to replenish his labor force, which meant transportation not only for the miners but for their families as well, and at all times he had to keep his properties under heavy guard.

In 1906 he gave up—not by surrendering to the union, but by selling out to the Madison Coal Company. Thereafter the St. Louis and Big Muddy was known as Madison No. 8. And thereafter it was worked by the United Mine Workers of America.*

Fifty years afterward, one who had known Brush well, both directly and through close family associations, rendered a verdict sounder, perhaps, than those which were read in the courtroom at Vienna. "Sam Brush was no Lester," he said. "I am sure he fought the union because of principle, not because of money. He was the typical early American stubborn individualist who would not count the cost. He thought he was right."

---

* The Herrin News for June 15, 1906 carried this story of Brush's capitulation:

Brush and Colp mines, which for a long time have been non-union mines, will now be manned with union miners. This week they passed into the control of the Madison Coal Company, a New Jersey corporation. The price reported to have been paid for the property is $600,000.

Brush mine has employed negroes mostly and has been non-union. It is reported that when Brush told all of his "niggers" goodbye Monday that it was a pathetic scene.

"Well, Massah Brush, I'se guess we've got no job any more now?"

"No," replied Brush, "not unless you join the union."

Brush got up and addressed all of his men and was followed by the new manager who told the men that he was going to unionize the mine and that he would pay for the charter himself and that not a man could work at the mines that did not have a union card.

With his gatling gun hauled down from its mounting and his corps of office men Brush made his departure from a place that has in time witnessed a fierce clash between union and non-union labor, but finally witnessing the triumph of organized labor.

7

MILLIONAIRE VS. UNION

1901–1910

●●

> Labor unions at Zeigler or anywhere else
> can't put a collar around my neck and give
> me orders what kind of labor I shall buy
> with my money. *Joseph Leiter, December 5,*
> *1904.*

JOSEPH LEITER differed from Samuel T. Brush as much as Chicago differs from Carbondale. Where Brush had been orphaned in childhood, and had to depend upon an uncle for a home, Leiter had never known anything but the luxury with which one of Chicago's most opulent citizens surrounded his family. Where the one had spent short periods in subscription schools, had begun to work at the age of twelve, and had finally managed, years later, to study for one term at Illinois College, the other as a matter of course attended private schools in Chicago, then St. Paul's, then Harvard. Brush's first job was that of a newsboy on an Illinois Central train; Leiter started to work as the manager of the family real estate, with a million dollars, his father's gift, in his own name. While Brush, in the late nineties, was trying to bring his mine out of receivership, Leiter was attempting to corner the wheat market, losing, when he failed, something approaching ten million dollars—a loss that his father and others met.

The two men were as unlike in personality and character as in their circumstances. Brush was small, thin, and facially dis-

117

figured; Leiter, twenty-six years his junior, was tall, heavy, and robust. All his life the older man was a militant opponent of liquor and the saloon; the younger one a steady, and at times a heavy, drinker, and never one to shun other fleshly pleasures.

But Leiter, like Brush, had courage, stubbornness, and an adamant aversion to union labor.

The young Chicago millionaire became a southern Illinois mine operator by way of an experimental coking-plant in his home city. Experiments conducted there in 1900 and 1901 indicated that good coke could be made from Illinois coal, an achievement formerly believed to be impossible. The Leiters, father and son, decided to buy coal land in the southern part of the state, sink a shaft, erect coke ovens, and sell that product instead of the coal itself. Williamson County, zooming into big production, looked like the best prospect, but when young Leiter tried to buy acreage there in 1901 he found that he had come upon the scene too late. Proven coal land, in the amount that he and his father considered essential, was simply not available.

But in Franklin County, immediately north of Williamson, there was not a single mine. Local opinion held that in this region coal existed only in pockets, and that its presence in one place indicated that it would not be found near by. To Joe Leiter this was nonsense. He employed a geologist and put him to work in the southern part of the county. Borings showed that his amateur's hunch was sound: the Carterville vein extended northward and spread out in a field larger than any yet discovered. He began to buy land.

A severe attack of typhoid pneumonia incapacitated him for much of the year 1902, but upon his recovery he returned to the coalfield and bought land until a solid block of 7,500 acres stood in his father's name. Half of the tract was woodland, mostly in creek bottoms; the other half was farmland, so wastefully cropped for three quarters of a century as to be practically worthless for agriculture.

Leiter lost no time in developing the property. He chose a site for a shaft in the southwest corner of the county, about five miles north of the Williamson County line, began an extensive system of underground galleries, ordered the most up-to-date cutting and loading machines, and made arrangements with the railroads—none came nearer than six miles—to build into the field. A company town, called Zeigler after the elder Leiter's middle name, was laid out. The coking plant, with which the venture originated, was given up; the mine would be devoted to low-cost production of coal.

By early summer 1904, the Zeigler Coal Company, operating the Leiter mine, was ready to go into operation. In all respects, the establishment excelled anything of its kind in the country. Equipped with the latest machinery, the mine had a daily capacity of five thousand tons, the largest in the state. A bathroom, with hot and cold water and a locker for each man, was an unheard-of facility. Leiter took so much pride in the property that he caused the cornerstone of the powerhouse, the largest building, to be dated 2904, on the ground that the mine was a thousand years ahead of its time, and in his exuberance had the cement out of which the cornerstone was made mixed with champagne instead of water.

The town of Zeigler was even more remarkable than the mine. Wide streets, bordered by good walks, extended like spokes from a circular park in which the company office, with an apartment for Leiter's use, was located. No house—and they numbered 115—had fewer than three rooms, and all were weatherboarded, plastered, and calcimined. Rents ranged from six to nine dollars a month, including running water, and for an extra charge of twenty-five cents a month any occupant could have electricity. "Superior to the class of dwellings usually found in an exclusively mining village," the secretary of the Illinois State Mining Board commented, "and furnished at reasonable rates." In addition to good houses, the company provided a brick schoolhouse and a well-equipped hospital.

119

On June 9, 1904, just as the Zeigler Coal Company hoisted its first coal, Levi Z. Leiter died. His will devised his mining properties to his wife, his son, his two daughters, and one other as trustees, and vested the management in the son.

To a young man who often chafed under parental restraint, the future must have seemed bright. Yet he was soon to encounter, in union labor, an obstacle far more intractable than his father.

During the development of the Zeigler properties all work was done at day-wage rates. A local of the United Mine Workers of America had been organized at the mine, but its members, along with a large number of laborers and mechanics, were employed in sinking shafts, grading surfaces, laying tracks, and erecting buildings rather than in mining coal. Leiter had not dealt with the union, and did not pay the union scale, but no attempt had been made to interfere with his operations or to prevent union men from working for him on an open-shop basis.

As it turned out, the union was merely waiting until the mine started to hoist coal. When it did, the miners presented three demands: first, that he recognize the union; second, that he hire only union men; and third, that he pay the Jackson County scale of 56¢ a ton, recently agreed upon by the miners and operators of the district, without any differential for machine mining. Leiter replied, on July 7, with an announcement that thereafter the rate at the Zeigler mine would be 38¢ a ton. The union called a strike immediately, and on the next day 268 men walked out.

The principal grievance, ostensibly, was Leiter's introduction of mining machinery on a scale far beyond that which any other operator in the district had attempted. The Zeigler mine approached complete mechanization as closely as was then possible. By the use of machinery the company claimed that miners working at a rate of 38¢ a ton would earn at least as much as they would in the hand mines at 56¢. This contention the men denied, and alleged further that the loading and weighing machine that had been installed was inaccurate, and that they were not receiving credit for all their tonnage. The situation was made more difficult by the fact that the union had not adopted a pay scale for a fully mechanized mine, and would not admit that there should be a differential.

Company policy pushed the question of union recognition into the background. Leiter's attorney, Henry R. Platt of Chicago, interviewed after the strike had been in progress two weeks, expressed his client's position officially:

"The best of skilled labor is desired. Mr. Leiter believes, and will put into practice, the theory that a well-paid, intelligent employee is preferable to a non-union man. . . . He desires union men, believing that they are better laborers. He has no fight to make against unionism, but rather is its friend, and as such expects to continue."

But years later, testifying under oath, Leiter gave a different version.

"We knew," he said, "we would have trouble with the unions over the question of working mechanically, the unions being opposed to it because it decreased the number of men to be employed and it decreased the cost of production. . . . Knowing we would have to have the thing out with them we thought we would protect ourselves by buying all of the land, and owning the top so that we could chase them off of that."

From Carbondale, ten days after the strike had been called, a correspondent of the *St. Louis Globe-Democrat* summarized the situation. Ten thousand union miners, he wrote, were lined up against the great Leiter fortune. "Never before in all the history of coal mining in this section has such a tremendous struggle been on."

The struggle began on July 8, the first day of the strike. Leiter took the initiative and moved fast. Before nightfall forty-two Pinkerton guards patrolled the property. All striking employees were given eviction notices, although with unusual clemency they were allowed a week in which to move. (The company

leases contained a twenty-four-hour eviction clause.) Work
commenced immediately on an elaborate system of fortifica-
tions: a high fence surrounding an enclosure, 1,500 feet by 400
feet, in which the top works of the mine stood; two-story blockhouses, built of double thicknesses of oak logs with dirt between
them, at two corners of the rectangle; smaller blockhouses on
top of the office building and at the pumping-station on the Big
Muddy River, the source of water for both mine and town. Machine guns were mounted in the blockhouses and a large searchlight was placed on the mine tipple, 125 feet above the ground.
As a final protective measure Leiter, on July 16, incorporated the
Zeigler Coal Company under the laws of Delaware, thus en-
abling it to come into the United States District Court and file
a bill for an injunction against the striking miners.

In three weeks town and mine were ready to stand a seige. On
August 1 a Du Quoin newspaperman reported the delivery, at
Zeigler, of a carload of beer, five cases of cartridges, and two
safes full of money, adding: "The stockade is completed, the
rapid-firing guns being placed in position, and, with the addition of today's supply of ammunition, Zeigler can defy the
strikers." On the same day Judge Otis M. Humphrey, in the
United States District Court at Springfield, issued a temporary
injunction restraining the officers of the Seventh Illinois District,
U.M.W.A., and some three hundred striking miners from going on the property of the Zeigler Coal Company without permission, from picketing the town or mine, or from interfering in
any way with the operations of the company. United States
deputy marshals could now be added to the force of Pinkerton
men.

On the other side, the strikers made such dispositions as their
limited resources allowed. Most of them moved into a hastily
constructed tent city near the town of Christopher, five miles
north of Zeigler, where any imported strikebreakers would have
to be transferred from the Illinois Central to the railroad running to the mine. Then they sent men to every large city for

miles around to watch the trains and report the movements of gangs of workmen who might be headed for Zeigler.

The first test came on July 27, when a carload of nonunion men, mostly laborers hired to complete the Zeigler stockade, was attached to an Illinois Central train departing from East St. Louis. Twenty-five of Leiter's guards and a number of railroad special agents provided protection. Even so, at Belleville several United Mine Worker officials succeeded in boarding the train and tried to induce the men not to continue. None got off— the guards saw to that—but several promised to leave the stockade at the first chance. At Christopher shots were fired into the train, but no one was hit, and the contingent landed at Zeigler with whole skins.

Three days later Leiter guards attempted to bring in thirty-seven men, this time miners as well as laborers, in another chartered car. Somehow a number of strikers gained access, and between East St. Louis and Pinckneyville persuaded the strikebreakers to desert. The guards locked the car doors, but when the train stopped the men jumped out the windows. Zeigler, they had come to believe, would turn out to be a less desirable spot than they had at first supposed.

Nevertheless, Leiter succeeded in importing a labor force, though at great expense and danger. His efforts in August 1904 typified the first several months of nonunion operation. On the 10th Leiter himself brought in forty miners from West Virginia without disorder. Two days later a special car containing fifteen men from Pittsburgh was stoned and fired on, but without casualties except to the car windows. On the 15th, striking miners at Du Quoin tried to board cars in which seventy-five Italians were riding to Zeigler, but the guards kept them off and the miners could do nothing but shout abuse at the foreigners. On the 17th eighty-four Pennsylvania strikebreakers came through without trouble by using a different route, but on the next day a special train with more men aboard was fired on near Christopher and three of the guards were wounded.

Bringing nonunion miners into Zeigler was one thing; keeping them there was another. As early as August 10 the Carbondale correspondent of the *St. Louis Globe-Democrat* reported that sixty per cent of the men imported had already deserted, and that the union camp at Christopher was growing daily through recruits from Zeigler. On October 1 the same reporter asserted that ninety of Leiter's miners had quit during the preceding twenty-four hours. On November 19 all the men who had been brought in during the last week deserted. Despite the hundreds of men Leiter imported, he could keep no more than a hundred, on the average, at work during his first year of nonunion operation.

According to the newspapers, the men left because conditions at Zeigler had been misrepresented to them, or because they earned less money than they expected, but it is probable that bullets also had an influence. As the strike wore into late summer and fall the strikers became bolder, working their way into Zeigler after dark, firing into the stockade and the company houses. The guards returned the fire. "There was shooting in town practically every night," said Leiter's chief engineer, "or the blowing of dynamite here and there . . . half a mile to a mile from the town. . . . We would shoot at them [the strikers] at various times and when they fired into town we would fire into that particular locality."

Yet all the shooting caused only one fatality. That occurred in mid-November when an Austrian, one of a contingent on the way to Zeigler, was killed by a rifle bullet fired from ambush. His death, however, heightened apprehension to such a point that the sheriff applied to the Adjutant General for rifles and ammunition with which to arm fifty deputies. No sooner had the arms been received than an attempt was made to assassinate two of Leiter's principal officials, Henry R. Platt and William Browning. On the afternoon of November 25 these two men took Leiter to the near-by town of West Frankfort, where he boarded a train for Chicago. On their way back to Zeigler they were ambushed,

Although twenty or twenty-five shots were exchanged, no one was injured.

The attack on Platt and Browning, coming so soon after the killing of the Austrian miner, brought the state militia to Zeigler. Sheriff Stein of Franklin County telegraphed to Springfield for troops that same evening, asserting that he could not keep order; Platt and Leiter, in separate telegrams, also demanded military protection. In the absence of Governor Yates, Adjutant General Scott ordered Company F of Mt. Vernon to Zeigler; a day or two later he called out Company C of Carbondale. The following week the governor, who by then had returned to Springfield, approved Scott's action and promised that the troops would remain on the scene as long as they were needed.

For several months Zeigler resembled a battlefield. In one camp were seventy state militiamen, forty deputy U.S. marshals (whose salaries Leiter paid), and a varying number of private mine-guards and deputy sheriffs. In the other camp were several hundred striking miners, armed with everything from revolvers to shotguns.

Yet the miners were anything but a disorderly mob. Adjutant General Scott, who had visited Zeigler shortly before the attack on Platt and Browning, referred to their camp as being "under discipline of the strictest sort," and added: "I passed it without fear, and if my business had taken me into their tents I have no doubt I would have been civilly treated." Nevertheless, shooting took place almost every night, with dynamite explosions at frequent intervals.

Zeigler, under siege, had to be seen to be believed. To C. H. Leichleiter, a magazine writer who visited the town a few weeks after the militiamen were stationed there, it was an anomaly in the peaceful America of 1905. "The heavily armed men," he wrote, "and the silhouetted shadows of the soldiers, gathered perhaps about a campfire on a wooded hill or standing, silent and alert, in the shadow of the dense timber, give the impression of a beleaguered camp." A beleaguered camp, moreover, that

125

showed the scars of war. Leichleiter found them most noticeable at the pumping-station on the Big Muddy. There, because of heavy timber on the far side of the stream, attackers could approach within thirty or forty yards without being seen. As a consequence, the building was fired on practically every night, and its heavy protecting timbers were scarred and studded with rifle bullets.

Most eerie of the sights that Zeigler had to offer, and most galling to the strikers, was the company searchlight. Leichleiter wrote:

> With the first approach of darkness . . . the giant light shoots its rays over the surrounding country. Nervously it sweeps in a great circle, hesitating now and then as a suspicious object comes within its range. After a hasty reconnaissance of the immediate vicinity it turns its blinding beam upon Camp Turner, five miles away, and searches out, with curious, inquisitive glare, the conditions in the strikers' camp. Then it plays upon the pump station and scans the heavily wooded bottom of the Big Muddy River, only to return again and regard with merciless stare the woods, the hills and the valleys that surround the town. It is not to be wondered that the strikers detest and fear the light. It is something inhuman, uncanny. It is to them the evil eye, and they would, if they could, blind it with a well-directed bullet.

What did it mean, this readiness for killing, with men grim enough to use the weapons in their hands?

Joe Leiter had his answer, which he gave to a reporter in Chicago on December 5, immediately after returning from Washington, where he had attended his sister's wedding.

> Labor unions at Zeigler or anywhere else can't put a collar around my neck and give me orders what kind of labor I shall buy with my money. When I go into the market to purchase labor I propose to retain just as much freedom as does a purchaser in any other kind of a market. The union at Zeigler can't either bully, bluff or frighten me. . . .
> As to the situation in Zeigler, a riff-raff mob is trying to

terrorize the community, and as long as that condition lasts the militia will remain. Work is going steadily ahead in my properties, however, and nearly 300 men are at work under ground. There is no difficulty whatever in obtaining labor, for the country is full of unemployed men, and plenty of them do not belong to unions.

Judge Otis M. Humphrey had his answer, expressed in the federal courtroom in Springfield on August 15, 1904, when he refused to dissolve or modify the injunction he had previously granted.

Men who want to work have a perfect right to do so, and I will see that they are protected in that right in this district. The man who does not want to work has no right to interfere with the man who does. The man who owns the property has a perfect right to manage it in the way in which he sees fit. A workman has a right to sell his labor or withdraw it, but he must not interfere with other men who want to work.

And Leichleiter, summing up for both sides, came closer to expressing the conviction of the men who shivered through the winter of 1904–5 in their draughty tents than anyone else whose words are now to be found in the record.

Beneath the surface there is the knowledge, shared alike by capital and labor, that there is more in this fight than the mere failure or success of Joseph's Leiter's struggle with his striking miners. It is the realization of this fact that has made the situation at Zeigler so intense, it is this that accounts for the exceptional display of determination on the part of the opposing powers. Should the striking miners lose their battle against this persistent young man who has gone to the length of fortifying his town, and filling it with armed men and artillery and all the paraphernalia of actual war, then other operators will follow his lead, and the long-delayed, death struggle between these two great industrial forces will be a reality. . . . Today capital and labor each realize that on the outcome of the Zeigler trouble depends, to a great extent, the life or death of union labor.

Slowly, after the advent of the militia, Zeigler quieted down until the sound of shots fired in the night became a rare occurrence. Early in February 1905, the two militia companies were withdrawn, and no disturbance of any consequence followed their departure. Leiter's troubles narrowed to the difficulty of keeping an adequate number of miners on the job, for the strikebreakers he imported continued to desert after short periods of work.

Then, on the early morning of April 3, came disaster. From the mine office Leiter's mining engineer saw smoke rising from the hoisting and air shafts. Knowing that something was wrong, he started for the hoisting shaft on the run. Before he reached it there was a tremendous explosion. Smoke billowed hundreds of feet into the air, and debris in the form of shattered boards, riven railroad ties, and torn pieces of metal rained to the ground about the shaft heads.

The day shift, numbering nearly fifty, had gone down a short time before. None came up.

Women and children gathered, as they have so many times in the history of this industry which takes its toll of lives relentlessly, some weeping, some dumb and motionless, all knowing that from these shafts could come only dead bodies. The union at Zeigler offered to do what it could in rescue work, and locals in near-by towns followed its example. The company rejected all offers, and permitted only its own employees to enter the stockade. Even in disaster Leiter would have nothing to do with organized labor.

Several hours passed before a rescue party had even a slight chance to survive. Then William Atkinson, state inspector of mines for the district, John Graham, a mine examiner, and John Lindsay, Leiter's assistant manager, descended the hoisting shaft in a bucket. A second party found their bodies, and barely escaped the deadly gas with their own lives. Not until evening could anyone enter the underground workings and survive. Those who went down saw a tangled mass of wreckage—mine cars crushed against the working face, rails twisted, mules torn apart, human bodies or parts of human bodies buried under fallen rock or splattered against the sides of the entries. When all the bodies were counted—some were never found—and the mine records checked, it was established that fifty-one men, including the three of the first rescue-party, had lost their lives. In the records of Illinois mining before 1905 only one other catastrophe—the flooding of the Diamond Mine at Braidwood in 1883—had caused more casualties.

Although they refrained from making the charge directly, company officials contended that the explosion was the work of the striking miners. "We always claimed the mine was blown up by the miners," Henry R. Platt testified years afterward, "and most of us who were there have a very firm conviction that that is what occurred." To this contention the coroner's jury gave some color when it attributed the disaster to a powder explosion —a verdict that implied guilt on the part of the union miners.

The secretary of the state mining-board, on the other hand, dismissed even the possibility that the disaster could have originated with the strikers. After describing Leiter's protective measures—the stockade, searchlight, and armed guards—he asserted that it was impossible for anyone to approach the property without being detected and identified. "Notwithstanding this system of espionage the company's officials are represented as contending that some time during the night preceding the explosion, some maliciously disposed people eluded the guards, scaled the stockade, descended the mine, and exploded the powder magazine. It would seem," he concluded, "that a mere statement of the facts is sufficient to disprove such a contention without attempting any argument to further expose the patent weakness of such a defense."

Three separate investigations, in fact, agreed in attributing the explosion to gas. Immediately after the catastrophe Governor Deneen directed the state inspectors of mines and the members of the state mining-board—ten men in all—to visit the

Zeigler mine and report their findings to him. They found that the mine had been generating marsh gas, that the ventilation had been reduced far below the safety point, that powder had been stored in the mine in violation of the law, and that no inspection had been made for several days prior to the explosion. Just enough air was being pumped into the mine to make the marsh gas highly explosive. A miner's lamp touched off the first blast; a few seconds later the powder—forty-one kegs in all— blew up. These findings were confirmed in every particular by detailed investigations, also made at Governor Deneen's request, by James Taylor, one of the state inspectors of mines, and John G. Massie, a man of long experience in coal mining. The secretary of the state mining-board summarized all the findings succinctly and fairly when he wrote: "The explosion was the result of gas, which, on account of the impaired condition of the ventilating apparatus, had been allowed to accumulate in excessively dangerous quantities."

Although badly damaged, the mine was put into working condition in three months. By that time—early July 1905—Leiter had recruited a new labor force. Heretofore he had relied principally upon European immigrants—most of the men killed in the explosion of April 3 were Hungarians—but now he turned to Negroes, importing them from districts in Kentucky where work was slack. The union made little effort to interfere with his operations, but he dared not relax his vigilance. The searchlight probed the surrounding country nightly, and between a hundred and a hundred and fifty guards and deputies made sure that no unauthorized person entered the stockade.

Production mounted, and the Zeigler Coal Company finally achieved the output of which it was capable. In 1906 it brought 238,654 tons of coal to the surface; in 1907, 321,285 tons; in 1908, 522,722 tons. In 1906 it ranked twenty-eighth among the mines of the state; in 1908 only three mines stood above it.

Then, with operations going smoothly and with the future full of promise, disaster struck again. On the night of November 4,

1908, fire broke out in the hoisting shaft. In spite of all that could be done, it spread throughout the night. The next morning the management agreed with the state mining-inspector for the district that the mine should be sealed for ninety days. In that time the fire would exhaust all underground oxygen and die.

Sixty-six days later—on January 10, 1909—State Mine Inspector W. S. Burris was hurriedly called to Zeigler. Earlier that day there had been an explosion, and only one man of twenty-seven underground at the time had escaped with his life. There had been no noise, no violent eruption—only smoke drifting lazily from the hoisting shaft. When a party went down to investigate they found twenty-six bodies and one man still alive. Leiter, in Zeigler at the time, took charge of the rescue operations; his bride of seven weeks served coffee and sandwiches to the rescue teams and tried to console the wives and relatives of the men who had lost their lives.

Mine Inspector Burris quickly discovered that the mine had not been kept sealed. Holes had been drilled to the underground galleries and water, steam, and sulphur forced through them in an effort to put out the fire. Then, on January 10, a crew of men went below to clean up fallen rock, build brattices, and clean out gas. But opening the mine to let the men down also admitted air that, the inspector surmised, rekindled the smoldering fire. That ignited the gas which had accumulated, and the explosion followed.

Burris immediately called in the inspectors of three other districts. They agreed that the mine must be sealed until it was certain that the underground fire had gone out. Accordingly, on January 11 he posted the following notice:

> I have this day inspected the Zeigler Coal Company's mine and find the conditions as follows:
> Dangerous to life on account of fire. For better protection of the lives and health of the employes, would recommend the following: Both shafts be sealed up and no men be allowed therein until further orders from me.

The Zeigler management protested the closing notice. At the superintendent's request, Burris arranged for a meeting of the state mine-inspectors and mining board, and invited Leiter and his company officials to attend. None appeared. The inspectors and board members approved the closing order.

> On returning from our meeting [Burris related in his official report], I called the general manager of the Zeigler Coal Company and informed him that we could not prohibit the company from entering the mine to recover the seven dead bodies still remaining in the mine, or keep them from entering to repair the mine for operation, also that it was my opinion that it was dangerous to enter the mine, but if they did enter the mine they would have to assume all risks.

The company kept the mine sealed for three weeks. Then it sent repair crews into the workings, each man equipped with a gas helmet. On February 9, 1909, with sixteen men below, there was a sudden explosion. Three died instantly; the others, working near the main shaft, escaped. Again air had fanned the dormant fire into flame and touched off an explosion.

Word of this latest tragedy reached Leiter in Chicago, where he was recuperating from an operation. A month earlier he had met the death of twenty-six men with defiance: he would neither close his mine, he said, nor retire from the management. But this latest loss of life was too much. As soon as he could, he went to Washington to see his mother. He found her badly worried. As he recalled their conversation later, "she said she was getting old and she didn't want to be worried any more by the expectation of getting a telegram any time that the mine had blown up and that I had blown up with it. . . . She said if I didn't make an arrangement to get somebody else to run the property she was going to foreclose on it and sell it out to somebody else."

Leiter quit.

The next year, when the Bell and Zoller Mining Company took over the operation of the Zeigler mine on a royalty basis, every miner on the payroll belonged to the United Mine Workers of America.°

° *Bell and Zoller closed Zeigler No. 1, Leiter's mine, in December 1949. In its twenty-five years of operation it had given up some forty million tons of coal, and in one day in 1928 had set a record of nine thousand tons.*

When I visited the mine in the summer of 1951 I found the buildings half-demolished. Weeds obscured the postdated cornerstone. But the memory of Joe Leiter persisted. A stalwart, retired miner, the only person on the grounds, had worked there from 1906 until the shutdown—"The first mine I ever worked in, and by God the last one!" He recalled, with relish, the way in which Leiter used to walk through the machine shop, slapping the men on the back and cracking jokes. Others in Zeigler cherish memories of ten-dollar tips, of lavish parties for guests from Chicago, of Leiter's tallyho with its load of beautiful women in broad floppy hats and long, flounced dresses.

Leiter seems to have turned sour after he leased the mine. The agreement with Bell and Zoller did not include the town of Zeigler, of which he continued to be proprietor. About 1917 he made arrangements with a local contractor for the construction of a hundred houses. When pressed for specifications, he exploded: "Oh hell, build them as cheaply as possible, just one degree from a hog pen. That's all these devils need down here. They'll tear them down anyway."

8

KLANSMAN AND DICTATOR

May 1923–February 1924

●●

> It seems . . . clear that it was the pur-
> pose of the said S. Glenn Young and those
> acting in concert with him, to overthrow
> the civil authority in Herrin and in William-
> son County . . . and take upon themselves
> the task of government without any legal
> authority whatever. *Herrin Grand Jury,*
> *March 14, 1924.*

BRUSH HAD succumbed to the union; so had Leiter. A wise man
would have profited by their experience, but, as we have seen,
W. J. Lester could learn a lesson only when it was driven home
by death and ruin. As the Herrin Massacre slipped into the past,
with its participants unpunished, a new kind of hysteria threatened the community.

On the evening of May 20, 1923, an evangelist was conducting
a service at the First Christian Church of Marion. As he started
to take up the collection he was interrupted by a slight commo-
tion at the church door. Seventeen men, in masks and long white
robes, marched down the center aisle. The congregation sat in
silence, half fearful, half curious. The newcomers lined up before the pulpit while one of their number stepped forward and
handed the evangelist a letter. Then they turned, filed out,
entered waiting cars, and drove away quickly.

As soon as they were outside the church the minister read the letter to the congregation:

Rev. Scoville,
Dear Sir:

Please accept this token of our appreciation of your efforts and great work you are doing for this community. The Knights of the Ku Klux Klan are behind this kind of work to a man and stand for the highest ideals of the native-born white Gentile American citizenship which are:

The tenets of the Christian religion; protection of pure womanhood; just laws and liberty; absolute upholding of the Constitution of the United States; free public schools; free speech; free press and law and order.

Yours for a better and greater community.
Exalted Cyclops.

The token of appreciation turned out to be three ten-dollar bills. After a few seconds of silence the evangelist spoke. "That tells you," he said, "whether they are all right. They stand for something good."

In this manner the Ku Klux Klan made its first appearance in Williamson County.

Six days later the hooded Knights, two thousand strong, gathered shortly after midnight in a meadow near Marion. There, in the light of a flaming cross, they initiated two hundred candidates from Williamson and Franklin counties.

On the last Sunday in June twenty Klansmen in full regalia interrupted the evening service being held in the Methodist Church of Herrin, just as they had at Marion five weeks earlier, and presented the pastor, the Rev. P. H. Glotfelty, with thirty dollars. And late in July Klansmen to the number of four or five thousand met in a field near Carterville, burned a huge cross, and administered their secret oath to several hundred initiates.

On Sunday, August 19, by prearrangement, practically every Protestant minister in Williamson County preached on law enforcement and urged his parishioners to gather at Marion on the

following morning for a public meeting that would show the
county officials where church members stood. They responded in
force. By ten a.m., in spite of the broiling sun, and regardless of
the beginning of a new work-week, two thousand people had
congregated about a piano box in the courthouse yard. The Rev.
A. M. Stickney, pastor of Marion's Methodist Episcopal Church
South, mounted this ready-made speaker's stand to deliver a fervent eulogy of the flag. A call for the mayor met no response.
Then the Rev. P. H. Glotfelty took the stand. In a voice intended
to be heard in the near-by offices of the sheriff and State's Attorney he proclaimed that saloons and roadhouses were operating
openly, that gambling was rampant, prostitution widespread.
The county, he admitted, had a black reputation with the rest of
the world, but it was not too late to make the name of Williamson one of which the state and nation could be proud. "It's time
to show that we're one hundred per cent Americans," he shouted.

Foreigners, particularly those from Italy, were primarily to
blame, Glotfelty declared. The time had come to say to them,
and to a sheriff unwilling to disturb the bootleggers in their illegal occupation: "You must walk the line of Americanism." Williamson County, he promised, "will be cleaned up if we have to
do it ourselves."

The crowd cheered and applauded. Someone shouldered the
single American flag that had decorated the speakers' stand;
hundreds fell in behind it and paraded through the downtown
streets. Back again at the piano box another minister, the Rev.
L. M. Lyerla of Carterville, shouted a warning, grimmer, more
accurately prophetic than he realized:

"Mr. Sheriff, Mr. State's Attorney, Mr. Judge, you'd better do
your duty. If you don't, something is going to happen, and that
little mine trouble out here will be but a drop in the bucket compared to it!"

After a benediction, the meeting broke up.

That night five thousand Klansmen met at near-by West
Frankfort to initiate the largest class so far admitted to the order.

In 1923 the Ku Klux Klan was finding a welcome in many localities, but there were few in which history and current conditions combined to provide a field as hospitable as this part of southern Illinois. The Klan was Protestant. So, by a large majority, were the people of Williamson County. Theirs, moreover, was the old-style, fundamentalist Protestantism of the hill people of Kentucky and Tennessee, from whom so many of them had sprung. Their favorite denominations were the Missionary Baptist, Southern Methodist, and Disciples of Christ, denominations that, historically, had shown the greatest fondness for the revival and camp meeting, and the least willingness to depart from the literal interpretation of the Bible. No summer went by without a succession of revival meetings, with the visiting evangelist, abetted by his song leader, urging the sinners in his audience to hit the sawdust trail. That one was a believer was taken for granted, though it was understood that he might have become remiss in church attendance, and thus needed to have his spirit stimulated. Protestant affiliations were also assumed without question, for everyone knew that only foreigners were Catholics, that all Jews were clothing-merchants, and that nonbelievers were either heathen Chinese or crazy.

The liberalizing influences that were changing the character of the evangelical denominations in many parts of the United States had left Williamson County untouched. Before the discovery of coal its people had lived in isolation, almost unaffected by anything that happened more than twenty-five miles distant, and the coal era had not lasted long enough to produce fundamental changes. The son of a prosperous merchant who attended the state university or one of the state normal schools and caught there a glimpse of a world in which people were concerned with ideas or music or the other arts, rarely returned to settle down. Those who did come back were too often untouched by their "education." Early in 1924 a woman who had lived in the region for many years could write· "If there is a single teacher [in Williamson County] who believes in evolution—or understands it—

137

I venture that he or she holds that belief in the strictest privacy.
. . . What is to be expected of teachers who with rare exceptions read only the two or three books a year required for certifi-
cates? . . . Like church, like school—the Ku Klux mind is firmly
entrenched."

Coupled with emotional religion and cultural backwardness
was a fervent patriotism. These people stemmed in the main
from forebears who had lived in the New World since Colonial
days. Their ancestors had fought in the Revolution, subdued the
Indians, and peopled the wilderness west of the Alleghenies.
Some, in the Civil War, had sympathized with the South, but
since that time they had lined up with the Republican Party, and
no section of the Middle West held more firmly to the political
creed of Harding and Coolidge. In the Herrin Massacre the most
fanatical red-hunters had been unable to find evidence of either
political or economic unorthodoxy. In the war just ended the
boys of Williamson County had done their full share; so had
their parents. They may have had a tendency to confuse the
symbols of patriotism with the substance, for few meetings could
be conducted without a lusty singing of *America* and *The Star-
Spangled Banner,* yet the substance—real love of country and
unquestioned belief that the nation was worth whatever sacrifice one might be called upon to make for it—was there too.
Even to the bitter anti-Klansman, the Klan's slogan, "one hundred per cent Americanism," seemed a laudable rule of life.

Fortunately for the Klan organizers, the Italian community in
Herrin provided an easy, unresisting target. Italians, mainly
from Lombardy, had been drawn to the county as mines opened
in the nineties and early 1900's. In 1923 they and their descend-
ants constituted about twenty per cent of Herrin's population.
They had prospered from the beginning, and had been accepted
by the "Americans," yet they were Catholic, "foreign," and fond
of wine. Some, moreover, had taken to bootlegging after the
county went dry. A whipping-boy is a handy fellow to have
around, and the Italians of Herrin admirably fitted the part.

138

Williamson County already had a law-enforcement organization that the Klan needed only to make its own. The Marion Law Enforcement League had been organized by prominent citizens early in 1923 for the purpose of stamping out bootlegging and gambling. It started out to work in co-operation with the county officers, but soon reached the point where it condemned them as delinquent. and proclaimed that "as citizens we want the law enforced and . . . if our officers are not doing their duty, we must resort to such measures as will accomplish the end we desire in another way." The Klan offered the other way.

That Williamson County needed cleaning up no one can doubt. In Herrin, with the advent of prohibition, saloonkeepers simply took down their signs and sold poorer liquor at higher prices. Bars continued to operate in the small mining-towns, while roadhouses, which offered gambling as well as liquor, sprang up along the highways. Marion, older and more conservative than Herrin, was relatively free from commercialized vice, but even there conditions fell below what those who had favored the Eighteenth Amendment expected. George Galligan, elected sheriff in the fall of 1922, did little to curb the lawbreakers, partly because his force of deputies was too small, and partly because he lacked the will. A bluff, good-natured Irish Protestant, he had been opposed by the "better element" during the campaign, and shunned by it afterward. Needing companionship desperately—such was his nature—he had found it among the gamblers and bootleggers. Understandably, he was reluctant to interfere with their operations.

And Williamson County had a peculiar, impelling reason for cleaning house. Ever since the Herrin Massacre its citizens had suffered from a sense of shame. One of its cities had been an object of universal condemnation, first for cold, premeditated murder, then for its failure to punish the criminals. Hundreds of editorial writers had called the people of Herrin and Williamson County inhuman; cartoonists had pictured them as fiends whose hands dripped blood. When a resident of Herrin registered at a hotel in a strange city he usually gave a fictitious address; if he were bold enough to be truthful the clerk was likely to stare at him as if he were an escaped convict. The people of the county resented being considered a subhuman species. More than that, they were determined to prove that they did not deserve the evil reputation they had acquired. The Klan offered them an opportunity. Put the bootleggers and gamblers out of business, its leaders said, and make Williamson County "more like home and less like hell."

In the Protestant ministers the Klan had powerful proponents. Preaching on a Sunday evening in August, 1923, the Rev. A. M. Stickney compared the United States to the *Titanic*, rapidly yet unwarily approaching disaster. The iceberg that would destroy the nation was foreign immigration. The assassins of Lincoln, Garfield, and McKinley, Stickney declared, were all Roman Catholics; the great majority of newspapers were controlled by Catholic and Jewish capital. Only through the Klan could the impending calamity be averted. Another minister, preaching on law enforcement, commended "that fine body of men composing the Invisible Empire" to his congregation. And when the *St. Louis Star* quoted State's Attorney Duty as having said that he "could take a firefly on the end of a red corn cob and chase the whole damn Klan out of the county," it was a preacher—the Rev. A. E. Prince of the First Baptist Church of Marion—who publicly defended the order. He knew a great many members of the Klan, he said, and they were not cowards. He had never known of any action of the Klan which he thought needed to be investigated, but he had never seen any activity of the Knights of Columbus that was not, in his opinion, "besmirched with the stain of crime."

While the preachers fulminated from their pulpits the members of the county board of supervisors, almost all Klansmen, called for law enforcement. At its meetings in the summer and fall of 1923 the board repeatedly passed resolutions asserting that the county officials were not doing their duty; that in all sections of the county there were roadhouses where liquor was being sold, gambling taking place, and prostitutes operating; that lawless organizations were being formed to prevent enforcement and terrorize the citizens who wanted it.

After each meeting of the county board the sheriff bestirred himself and made a few raids. His activities, however, satisfied no one. The supervisors had no confidence in his sincerity and were unwilling to provide the additional deputies he said he needed. And the Klan, now numbering many thousands, was militant and impatient. It decided to carry out the promise Glotfelty had made at the law-enforcement meeting in August: Williamson County "will be cleaned up if we have to do it ourselves."

The first move was an appeal to Governor Small. A committee * went to Springfield, sat in hotel lobbies for three days, and was then told by the governor: "If you want the law enforced, go back and elect someone that will enforce the law." Rebuffed, the committee proceeded to Washington for a conference with Roy A. Haynes, Commissioner of Prohibition. Haynes sympathized with their determination to clean out the bootleggers, but admitted that his office could not be of much help. His force was limited, the demands upon it were many, and he simply could not spare enough men to do the job. If, however, the committee really meant business, and was willing to hire a private investigator to collect evidence, he would send in men to make arrests and prepare the way for prosecutions.

Somehow, in Washington, the committee met a former agent of the Prohibition Unit, S. Glenn Young, and retained him to conduct the clean-up they were determined to undertake.†

Young arrived in Williamson County about November 1, 1923. With his father-in-law, George B. Simcox, who had served sev-

---

* *Strictly speaking, a committee of the Williamson County Law and Order League. But the Law and Order League and the Klan were co-operating so closely as to be virtually indistinguishable.*
† *I have not been able to find out who recommended Young to the Williamson County Klan. In its issue of September 2, 1924, the* Herrin Semi-

eral years as a United States marshal, he began to visit the "soft-drink parlors." By the end of the month the two men had bought liquor at more than a hundred of these establishments. Fortified with this evidence of law violation, Young, John L. Whitesides, Marion Klan leader, and Arlie O. Boswell, lawyer, Klansman, and avowed candidate for the office of State's Attorney, went to Washington. There, sponsored by Richard Yates, Congressman-at-Large from Illinois, and E. E. Denison, Congressman from the Williamson County district, they appealed again to Prohibition Commissioner Haynes. This time they asked that he send an agent from his force to deputize Young and such men as he might select to raid the places in which liquor had already been purchased. Haynes agreed.

At home again, Young set out, with the utmost secrecy, to recruit his raiders. Approximately five hundred men, including most of the ministers of the county and many of the leading citizens who had joined the Klan, agreed to be deputized as federal agents for the purpose of carrying out a large-scale liquor raid. Then he telephoned to Haynes, told him that he was ready, and asked the commissioner to send the agents he had promised.

At six p.m. on Saturday, December 22, the prospective raiders assembled at the Odd Fellows Hall in Carbondale. There they found Young and the three federal agents whom Haynes had sent in—Gus J. Simons, divisional chief from Pittsburgh, and Victor L. Armitage and J. F. Loeffler from the Chicago office.

Weekly Herald, *official Klan organ, asserted that Roy A. Haynes "recommended that Mr. Young come to Williamson County." But in a telegram to the* St. Louis Star, *September 3, 1924, Haynes stated flatly: "I did not send S. Glenn Young nor have I recommended him at any time to any one." According to John Smith, Herrin Klan leader, "a Senator recommended Glenn Young to us as a man who could show us how to proceed." John Whitesides, a leading Klansman of Marion, said the committee that visited Washington got in touch with Young "accidentally." Young himself, in a statement to the Associated Press, February 11, 1924, stated: "Four years ago, while I was a federal prohibition enforcement officer, I raided Herrin and parts of Williamson County single-handed, and because the people in this county who are desirous of law enforcement were pleased with my work they sent for me."*

The men stood around laughing and chatting until Simons called for order. After giving them their instructions he said:

"Some of you may be sent home to your wives as a Christmas present, in a box. Are you ready?"

They answered with a shout. When Simons read the oath deputizing each man as a federal officer for the duration of the raid, all raised their right hands and the "I do's" rocketed through the room.

Shortly after seven o'clock the raiders left the hall in groups of five. Each group carried a federal search-warrant signed by U.S. Commissioner William W. Hart of Benton. In their own cars they proceeded a mile or two toward Murphysboro and then turned eastward to their destinations. At about eight o'clock they closed in on a hundred roadhouses and bootlegging establishments in Herrin and Marion. Everywhere they followed the same tactics, approaching stealthily, covering all doors with drawn guns, and demanding entrance in the name of the federal government. No word of the impending raid had leaked; in fact, rumor had had it that all prohibition agents in the region had been called to Chicago to clamp down on holiday festivities there, so the local liquor-sellers were operating with more than usual freedom. As a result, the raiders found evidence in almost every establishment, and soon had their cars filled with owners and bartenders under arrest.

Their instructions had been to take all prisoners to Benton for arraignment before the U.S. commissioner. The first groups arrived there while the Saturday-night shoppers were still on the streets. As the townspeople saw the occupants of one car after another dismount, guns in hand, and push their prisoners toward the commissioner's office, excitement ran high. Benton residents, including many who had already gone to bed, left their homes and headed for the public square, where by midnight between two and three thousand, the biggest crowd in the town's history, had gathered. In his office Commissioner Hart worked furiously, releasing those who could put up bail, sending the others to jail.

Long before all the raiding parties had reported the jail was full, and prisoners were being taken to the Herrin lock-up.

Two weeks later, on the night of Saturday, January 5, the raiders struck a second time. This time they met at Marion, and again federal officers deputized them. Led by Young, now a conspicuous figure in semimilitary uniform, with two forty-fives strapped to his thighs and a sub-machine gun in his hands, they arrested nearly a hundred alleged lawbreakers. Once more the jails at Benton and Herrin were crammed with those who could not give bail.

Less than forty-eight hours later 250 men, deputized by the same federal officers who had administered the oath on Saturday night, raided places in Herrin and the smaller towns of the county.

The three raids had resulted in 256 arrests, and Williamson County was in an uproar.

From the beginning, the Klan had met stout opposition. Part of it arose from the considerable number of men who had good reason to fear strict law-enforcement. In Herrin these men went so far as to form a counterorganization, the Knights of the Flaming Circle. Although it fell far short of the Klan in numbers and discipline, it was strong enough to lead many to fear an armed clash even before the raids took place. Part of the opposition also came from sober, thoughtful citizens who had no sympathy with the Protestant and nativistic platform of the Klan, and who feared the excesses to be expected when a secret organization takes the law into its own hands.

These, and many others who had assumed a wait-and-see attitude, were shocked when the full story of the mass raids seeped out. The raiders had not limited themselves to bootlegging establishments; they had invaded scores of private homes. (Doubtless it was mere coincidence that the homes were usually those of Italians who, in addition to being wine-drinkers, were also Catholics.) There were ugly stories of rough treatment, robbery,

144

even planted evidence. French nationals—there was a small colony at Johnston City—and the Italians at Herrin made so many complaints that the French consul at Chicago and the Italian consular agent at Springfield protested to the U.S. State Department. Klansmen scoffed at the charges of brutality and lawlessness, but many a troubled citizen outside the ranks of the Klan found them convincing.°

The central figure in most of the stories of robbery and brutal behavior was S. Glenn Young. It was Young—so they said—who used abusive language toward women, turned the contents of cash drawers into his own pockets, and pistol-whipped an occasional victim who failed to raise his hands above his head quite fast enough. And it was Young whose arrogant and foolhardy conduct precipitated the first crisis.

The chain of events started on December 28, 1923, when a deputy sheriff and two other officers arrested State Representative Wallace A. Bandy of Marion, an ardent dry and avowed Klansman, on a warrant issued by the State's Attorney. Bandy was held in jail for two hours, and then released on the personal recognizance of Judge Hartwell. Anti-Klansmen chortled at the fact that a bottle of liquor had been found in Bandy's home. Young claimed that the liquor was white mule that he himself had confiscated and had left with Mrs. Bandy for safekeeping.

Two days later Young and several men entered Paul Corder's restaurant in Marion and ordered coffee. Corder told them that the place was closed, but that he would make some if they would wait. While the water was heating he remarked:

° *On March 14, 1924, the Williamson County grand jury reported: "We further find that during the so-called raids by the Ku Klux Klan . . . numerous people were robbed, beaten, abused and in many instances imprisoned secretly without any legal process and wholly without justifiable cause." And on February 11, 1927, Harold G. Baker of East St. Louis, United States District Attorney, wrote of the Klan raids to the Attorney General: "There is no doubt in my mind but what the rights of citizens and the rights of property were totally disregarded in many cases." Baker was not in office in 1923–4, and had no reason for prejudice. His opinion was based on a careful study of files in his office.*

"Well, they got Bandy."

Young replied that the case was a frame-up.

"You're a smart son-of-a-bitch," Corder said.

A fight followed, and Corder took a beating. The next day he had Young arrested on an assault-and-battery charge.

A justice of the peace heard the case on January 8. A few minutes before it was called, Young and several of his followers stalked into the courtroom. All were heavily armed, and two of the group carried the portable machine-gun they used on raids. The jury retired, and emerged almost immediately to render a verdict of acquittal. The crowd clapped and cheered.

But before the case even went to the jury three companies of militia had orders to proceed to Marion with all possible speed. Sheriff Galligan, with the Herrin Massacre in mind, had wired to Adjutant General Black for troops as soon as Young and his men took their guns into the courtroom. The state authorities, who had learned their lesson in the summer of 1922, responded immediately, and General Black took the first train for Williamson County.

The next day, while soldiers guarded the courthouse and patrolled the streets, Klansmen protested vehemently to the Adjutant General. Arlie Boswell, Young's attorney in the Corder trial, spoke for a delegation which demanded that the troops be sent home at once. There had been no threats against the sheriff, he said, nor any menace to life or property. The hubbub about a machine gun in the courtroom was nonsense—the gun, dismantled, had been carried only because it would have been stolen had it been left outside. The Bandy case was a frame-up. Marion was a clean city, and the people of the rest of the county were determined that their communities should be equally clean. Since the sheriff never found any evidence in the raids he undertook, the people had had to take matters into their own hands. Sam Stearns, chairman of the county board of supervisors, and Exalted Cyclops of the Klan, told Black that all but two members of the county board were in sympathy with the Klan, and that three fourths of the people of the county wanted the clean-up to continue. Others, including the mayor of Herrin and the pastor of the Christian Church, supported their spokesmen's statements.

Black refused to be stampeded. He knew that newspaper correspondents were wiring their papers that Williamson County stood on the verge of civil war, and he could see plenty of evidence to support that estimate of the situation. The arrest of Young and four prominent Herrin Klansmen on charges growing out of the recent raids—charges filed by persons who swore that they were beaten and robbed by the raiders—pointed to trouble. So did the alacrity with which Klansmen rushed to sign the bonds of the prisoners. Ominous, too, was a telegram from W. W. Anderson, division chief of prohibition agents: "Make no further raids under present conditions."

The Klan leaders quickly concluded that persuasion would not send the troops home. Accordingly, they asked the sheriff, ill at his residence adjoining the jail, for a conference. Far into the night they argued over Galligan's demand that Young be excluded from enforcement activities, and the Klan's counterproposal that the sheriff discharge its bitter enemy and his own chief deputy, John Layman. They reached no agreement other than to meet again the following day.

Young contributed nothing to the prospect of peace by his own belligerency. "With or without federal aid we're going to continue the raids and I'm going to lead them," he told a representative of the *St. Louis Globe-Democrat*. "The sheriff's gang tried to rule me out in the conference last night, but the Klan leaders called me in and said they would stay with me to a man as long as I produced results in the clean-up and assured me fifteen thousand others in the county were behind me as well." To a reporter for the *St. Louis Post-Dispatch* he bragged: "Upon thirty minutes' notice I can gather two thousand men about me

147

to do my bidding in this drive, and in two hours I can get seven thousand from Williamson and Franklin counties, members of the Ku Klux Klan."

On the tenth the conference with the sheriff was resumed. No agreement resulted, but Galligan came to a decision: he would ask that the troops be removed when he was satisfied that Herrin, the potential trouble-spot, was quiet. On his orders Chief Deputy Layman called the alleged saloonkeepers and bootleggers to a meeting at the Rome Club. Tear down your bars, he told them, and find some other way to make a living. Young and the Klan were applying for injunctions in the United States Court, and they—the saloonkeepers—could either shut up now or be padlocked later.

Only three of the eighty-three who were present agreed to quit. An attempt to disarm the people of Herrin, where more than two hundred gun permits had been issued to Klansmen in recent weeks, failed dismally. Even when appealed to by Sam Stearns, the justices of the peace who had issued the permits refused to revoke them. The city, they argued, was under the control of the anti-Klan element, and the men who had applied for the right to carry guns were still in danger.

In spite of the failure of these moves, a compromise was reached. The mayor of Herrin agreed to discharge his anti-Klan policemen and replace them with Klan sympathizers, and Galligan promised to raid any place suspected of selling liquor. To prove his sincerity he offered to meet in private any citizen who had, or believed he had, evidence of law violation. On January 14 his deputies made eight liquor raids, and in the next several days ten more. In most of the raids arrests were made.

Satisfied with the situation, the sheriff assented to the removal of the troops. Except for a few officers, who remained as observers, the militia left on January 15 and 16.

If Galligan thought, as he apparently did, that the Klan would now leave law enforcement in his hands, he was quickly disillusioned. In the early-morning hours of Sunday, January 20, a large number of Klansmen, led by Young, raided thirty-five places, chiefly in the small mining-camps, and made sixty-six arrests. Again the county seethed with dissension.

The Klan was riding high, and had no intention of abating its law-enforcement program regardless of what the sheriff might do. As usual, the preachers spoke for the hooded Knights. Meeting on January 23, the Williamson County Ministerial Union passed resolutions denouncing "exaggerated press reports" of conditions in the county and denying that either race or religion had anything to do with the clean-up. Young, whom so many were criticizing, was "a perfect gentleman" who had the respect of every good citizen in the county. He had already effected "the most perfect cleanup that has ever been pulled off in this state," and he had done it, as he had promised, without bloodshed. "We want to say," the ministers concluded, "that all this harangue and scandal is unjust and uncalled for, and we are not willing for it to go by without our protest."

Not that Young needed advocates. On January 30, returning from a short trip to Kansas City, he gave an interview to the *East St. Louis Journal* in which he characterized Williamson County as the cleanest county in the United States, and called the police forces of Marion and Herrin the best in Illinois. Nevertheless, much remained to be done, and he promised that the raids would continue until the county was one hundred per cent perfect. They would be conducted independently of the sheriff, with whom he and the Klan would not co-operate. The next day, speaking before the Marion Rotary Club, he denied that he and his raiders had appropriated anything except illegal liquor and a few pistols, and charged that reports to that effect had been fabricated by the lawbreakers, mostly foreigners. He concluded with a pledge: "Raids will be continued monthly, semimonthly, or weekly if needed. I am making my home here and the raids will be continued until the bootleggers, gamblers, and other undesirables are driven out."

Within twenty-four hours the biggest raid of all was under

way. Between 1,200 and 1,300 Klansmen gathered at Redmen's Hall in Johnston City, where they were provided with state warrants issued by justices of the peace. At nine p.m. they fanned out over the county, but they had so many places on their lists that they continued to raid until noon the next day. Altogether, they found six stills, twenty-seven barrels of wine, fifty-four gallons of white mule, and two hundred gallons of home brew. They arrested 125 persons. These they herded into a special train, contracted for in advance, and took to Benton for arraignment before the United States commissioner. At their destination the prisoners were formed into a column, and with Young, armed with his forty-fives and sub-machine gun, at the head and armed guards on the flanks, marched to the public square. Thousands of spectators witnessed one of the most novel parades ever seen in an American city.

One week later Herrin exploded in the civil war so many had feared. The "trouble," as the local newspapers called it, started with a meeting of anti-Klansmen at the Rome Club on Friday night, February 8. Galligan learned of the meeting, and though still ill, decided to make a personal effort to prevent an outbreak. Accompanied by John Layman, he walked in on the gathering and warned those present that there must be no violence. While he was talking, a man burst into the room and shouted: "The Klan are coming!" Several men, with guns drawn, rushed for the door.

The "Klan" turned out to be two members of Herrin's new pro-Klan police force—John Ford, the chief, and Harold Crain. When Galligan and Layman reached the hallway they found the two policemen disarmed, hands up, and covered by an angry group that included Carl and Earl Shelton and Ora Thomas. Layman, fighting mad, grabbed Ford by the hair and shouted in his face:

"You damn dirty Ku Klux son-of-a-bitch, we've got you where we want you!"

Galligan ordered Ora Thomas to get the crowd back into the

150

meeting-room: he would take care of Layman and Ford. A scuffle followed, and someone fired a pistol. Layman sank to the floor, his hands over his bleeding chest. Then he struggled to his feet, and stumbled toward Ford.

"Here's the dirty son-of-a-bitch that shot me," he said. "Get him! Get him!"

Ora Thomas spoke up. "No, boys, Ford didn't shoot Layman. I have his guns."

Galligan ordered the crowd into the hall.

"Get back into the hall, hell, and get us all killed!" Carl Shelton exploded.

"No, by God!" shouted Hezzie Byrnes. "Get them machine guns and get out on the sidewalk and kill every son-of-a-bitch that comes up!"

Earl Shelton jeered: "Where's Mage Anderson [mayor of Herrin]? Go tell him here is his God damned police!"

Galligan, seeing that he had a riot on his hands, hurried the two policemen down the stairs. At the foot of the stairway they met a third officer, about to go up. The sheriff disarmed the newcomer, commandeered a car at the curb, ordered his prisoners in, and told the driver to go to Marion. There he telephoned the Adjutant General, warned him that hell was about to break loose in Herrin, and urgently asked for troops. Then, fearing a lynching, he took the Herrin policemen to the Jackson County jail in Murphysboro.

Shortly after Galligan spirited away his prisoners, the young son of Caesar Cagle, a Herrin constable who had made a quick transition from bootlegger to Klansman, passed the Rome Club on his way home from a picture show. One of the men in the crowd on the sidewalk told him that there had been a fight and that he had better find his father. He telephoned home, learned that his father was at the Masonic Temple, and went there for him. Father and son started out together, but the boy soon turned off to go home and Cagle went on alone. Near the Jefferson Hotel he met a crowd of men, twenty or twenty-five in num-

151

ber. One of them called out: "Here he is!" Three shots rang out.
The men ran, leaving Cagle lying on the sidewalk. Bystanders
carried him to the Herrin hospital, where he died within a few
minutes. John Layman, seriously wounded, had been brought in
half an hour earlier.

The news of Cagle's death spread over the county in a few

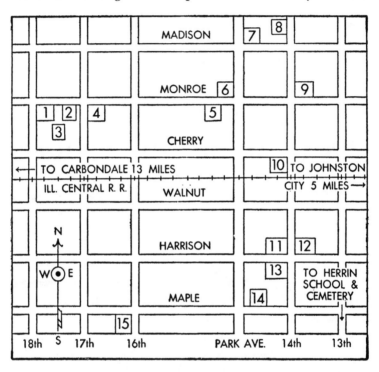

Downtown Herrin, Scene of the Klan War

1 CATHOLIC CHURCH	8 LY-MAR HOTEL
2 CATHOLIC HIGH SCHOOL	9 ROME CLUB
3 PARISH HOUSE	10 JEFFERSON HOTEL
4 SMITH GARAGE	11 MASONIC TEMPLE
5 LIBERTY HOTEL	12 BAPTIST CHURCH
6 EUROPEAN HOTEL	13 HERRIN HOSPITAL
7 CITY HALL AND JAIL	14 CHRISTIAN CHURCH
15 METHODIST CHURCH	

minutes, and armed Klansmen converged on Herrin. Young, in Marion at the time of the shooting, reached Herrin within a half hour. There he took charge, sending hundreds of men to patrol the streets and the roads leading into the city. The patrolmen stopped all cars and demanded the password of their occupants. Those who could not give it were ordered off the streets or turned back at the city limits.

Klansmen swore out warrants charging Galligan, Ora Thomas, C. E. Anderson, mayor of Herrin, and several others with the murder of Cagle. When word came that Thomas and Anderson were at the hospital with Layman, Young, followed by several hundred Klansmen, went after them. Finding the door locked, Young shouted a demand for admission. Dr. J. T. Black, the proprietor, refused to admit him. Young's followers pounded on the door and, when it held fast, fired into the panels.

As Dr. Black ran upstairs the firing became general. Windowpanes, shattered by bullets, crashed to the floor. Patients screamed. Those who could move slipped to the relative safety of the floor; the others were lifted from their beds by the doctor, the nurses, and visitors.

In an adjoining building that served as an annex to the hospital four men ordered the frightened employees, all women, into the basement. One of them said: "We're going to blow the hospital to hell and kill everybody we can get our hands on." Another told the women: "We don't want Layman; we want Ora Thomas."

The firing continued. Occasionally one of the men inside the building—the little group of those who had brought in John Layman or had come to inquire about him during the evening—risked his life by crawling to a window and firing a clip into the darkness, but that was too hazardous to attempt very often.

About three a.m. the first troops arrived. Twenty men from the Carbondale company under Major Robert W. Davis, with rifles loaded and bayonets fixed, walked into the midst of the attacking mob and ordered its members to disperse. Although they outnumbered the guardsmen twenty-five to one, they slunk away.

When dawn broke, and it became light enough to survey the damage, the floors of the hospital were found to be covered with broken glass, and bullet marks pitted every wall facing an outside window. Miraculously, not a single person, inside the hospital or out of it, had been wounded.*

On Saturday morning Herrin discovered that despite the presence of troops it was in the hands of the Klan. Armed Klansmen, wearing crude stars cut from tin, patrolled the streets and kept crowds from forming, while in the city hall S. Glenn Young, calling himself acting chief of police, heard the reports of men he had sworn in as deputy policemen, directed that arrests be made, and ordered prisoners to jail. A sentry stood at the door of the office he had pre-empted, and no one who could not give the Klan password was admitted.

At Young's direction Mayor Anderson was arrested, charged with murdering Cagle, and thrown in jail. Galligan, in Carbondale on Saturday morning, was arrested on the same charge and held there until Klansmen from Herrin called for him. In the city hall his captors led him before Young, who wore his broad-brimmed hat and pearl-handled automatics even while he sat in the city judge's chair. "I find you guilty of the murder of Caesar Cagle," Young told the sheriff, and ordered him to jail.

Young and the Klansmen behaved with incredible vindictiveness. When Galligan asked one of the jailers, a fellow lodge-member, to get him some fever medicine, he was told: "You won't need fever medicine by the time we get through with you." Harold Crain, the Herrin policeman whom he had arrested on Friday night and who had since been released, came up to his cell and said: "George, you saved my life Friday night and I'll do what I can to help you." Young, who overheard the offer, barked out: "No, we'll show no sympathy for this son-of-a-

---

* *A boy, operated on for appendicitis the afternoon of February 8, died the following morning—undoubtedly from the shock of the night's events.*

bitch." Coroner McCown, who under the law had become acting sheriff by reason of the sheriff's incapacity, demanded that
Young give him custody of his prisoner. Young refused. When
McCown asked him how it was that he had more authority than
the sheriff, he answered: "I have just as much authority as you
have."

On Sunday, February 10, the Klan made the funeral of Caesar
Cagle the occasion for a demonstration of its strength. Crowds
filled the large auditorium of the First Baptist Church long before two p.m., when the services were to begin, and thousands
stood in the churchyard and on the street. The funeral procession included a double line of men more than a block long. An
American flag covered the casket when it was carried into the
church. There a huge blanket of flowers, white except for the
green letters, KKK, was laid upon it, while at the side stood a
"fiery cross" of red roses. In his sermon the Rev. P. H. Glotfelty
referred to Cagle as a martyr in the cause of law and order, and
proclaimed that he fell in line of duty. The "liquor element" was
responsible for his death. "But these lawless actions will not de-
ter us," Glotfelty promised. "Rather must we be encouraged and
strengthened to carry out the work of good citizenship that is
before us."

At the conclusion of the service five thousand people, more
than had ever attended a funeral in Williamson County, passed
by the coffin and viewed the body.

Shortly before the Cagle funeral Galligan was removed from
the Herrin jail, and for twenty-four hours his whereabouts were
unknown. At the end of the day Mayor Anderson was still behind the bars. Though several companies of guardsmen now patrolled the streets, no one had yet interfered with the man who
held all power in his hands. That night Louis LaCoss of the *St.
Louis Globe-Democrat* summarized the situation in a dispatch
to his paper:

> Young performed his duties in the Police Department as
> usual tonight. He dined in his room in a hotel adjacent to

the City Hall and walked back without escort to his office. Two vicious-looking automatics, however, were girded to his thigh. . . . His deputized officers, none in uniform, but each provided with a telltale star of substantial proportions, still patrol the streets, and the familiar command of "keep moving" was heard tonight, both from them and the soldier squads.

9

THE KLAN WAR

February 1924–May 1924

●●

A city of fear. That is Herrin. Fear of the
neighbor next door. Fear of the man across
the way. Fear of the fellow one passes on
the street. Fear of the businessman, of the
worker, of the farmer, of the doctor and
lawyer. Fear begotten of fear. *Cleveland
News in the Literary Digest, September 13,
1924.*

IN A LITTLE more than three months S. Glenn Young had
made himself the dictator of an American county of which he
was not even a legal resident. Who, and what, was he?

Only the barest outline of his early life can be established today. He was born on a farm near the little town of Long Island,
Kansas, on March 4, 1887, and named Seth Glenn in honor of a
great-uncle. His father, a prosperous farmer, also owned an im-
plement store in Long Island. The mother died while the boy
was very young, so he spent much of his boyhood and youth in
the homes of relatives. He attended Long Island High School
and Western College at Western, Iowa—a small college no
longer in existence—but did not remain at either institution long
enough to graduate. In 1911 he decided to study medicine and
enrolled in the College of Physicians and Surgeons at Milwaukee
(later absorbed by the Marquette University School of Medicine). He married in the same year.

Evidently Young left medical school after one year and went to work as a nurse. In 1918 he became an agent of the Bureau of Investigation, Department of Justice. For several months he tracked down draft dodgers, mainly in the mountainous regions of the southern states. He made a record as an energetic, fearless, and resourceful officer.

A change in organization led to his resignation, but a year later he obtained an appointment as a special agent in the newly created Prohibition Unit of the Treasury Department, the agency charged with the enforcement of the Volstead Act. On June 25, 1920, he took the oath of office, and started to work at a salary of $1,800 a year.

Young was assigned to southern Illinois. He soon became a conspicuous figure, partly because of a striking Belgian police dog that accompanied him everywhere, and partly because of a series of flamboyant feature stories that appeared in the *East St. Louis Journal* during the latter part of August. In these he was pictured as a "noted sleuth . . . one of the youngest, nerviest and most successful of the army of secret workers which enforces government edicts." Before coming to southern Illinois he had operated for three years under the War Department—so the author asserted—and for seven years as an agent of the Department of Justice. Prior to that he had been a Texas Ranger and a deputy United States marshal in western Kansas! While serving as a government agent in the southeastern states he had made approximately 3,000 arrests, and had been forced to kill twenty-seven desperadoes.*

---

* *J. Edgar Hoover, Director of the Federal Bureau of Investigation, wrote me (December 31, 1947) that Young's services "were first utilized during the latter part of 1918 as a Special Employee and that he submitted his resignation to become effective March 5, 1919." Assuming that "the latter part of 1918" means October 1, he was actually employed for five months, or approximately 150 days. At that rate, he arrested twenty men a day, and killed a man oftener than once a week!*

I have seen no evidence, except stories inspired by Young himself, to indicate that he killed anyone prior to 1920. After that, as will appear in this narrative, he was responsible for one death, and possibly two.

Young, the feature writer revealed, had been the subject of hundreds of columns in newspapers and magazines. "Has the publicity made him egotistic," he asked, "or, in plain, everyday English, big-headed? I say absolutely no. It has had no more effect on this modest hero than a bang-up selling-talk of a live wire salesman would have with a deaf and dumb man. . . ."

The author concluded with a personal description that contrasted happily with his several columns of unwitting fiction. "The officer is five feet, seven inches tall and weighs 144 pounds. . . . He is strongly, but not heavily built, and is an average man in size only. He has slightly bowed legs, superinduced by many days spent in the saddle. His arms are long and his hands well kept, with very long fingers. His eyes are full and prominent and of a peculiar shade of bluish gray."

Young was in the prohibition service a bare four months before he became involved in serious trouble. With two Granite City police officers he raided a house in Madison, a small town near East St. Louis. They found a still, mash, and a small quantity of whisky. During the raid Young learned that Luka Vukovic, a relative of the man whom he had just arrested, lived next door, so he took one of the officers and went to investigate. According to Young's report, he saw Vukovic drinking from a milk bottle. Suspecting that the bottle contained whisky, he decided to enter in spite of the fact that he had no warrant. No one responded to his knock, so he and the police officer forced the front door.

Inside the house the officers found a twenty-five gallon keg of liquor. Suddenly Vukovic appeared, pointed a pistol at Young, and pulled the trigger, but the weapon missed fire. Young drew his gun, shot several times, and killed Vukovic.

Young was exonerated by a coroner's jury but indicted for murder by the Madison County grand jury. The Prohibition Unit suspended him on December 20, 1920, pending the result of its own investigation. On the ground that he was a federal officer at the time of the offense, the case was taken from Madison

County and set for trial in the U.S. District Court at Springfield.

A few days before the trial began, Young's wife filed suit for divorce. Her petition alleged that he was subject to violent fits of temper, that on one occasion he had thrown her down and kicked her, that his course of cruelty toward her had begun soon after their marriage, and that for a long time he had failed to support her and their twin daughters. The divorce was granted on July 1.

At Young's trial, which began on June 6, 1921, the prosecution presented only two witnesses—the deputy coroner, to identify the body, and Vukovic's widow, who testified that her husband had had no gun, that Young had shot him in cold blood, and had then planted one of his own guns beside the dead body. Young took the stand and claimed self-defense. The case went to the jury on the evening of June 10. After an hour's deliberation, it brought in a verdict of not guilty.

Young was a free man, but any elation he may have felt at his acquittal must have been dampened by the knowledge that he had no job. Two weeks earlier he had been dismissed as a prohibition agent, with the dismissal dated December 10, 1920, when he had been suspended.

His discharge was the result of an investigation, conducted by two special agents, that the Prohibition Unit initiated after he killed Vukovic. In that case the agents concluded that Young had acted in self-defense, but that he did not exercise the caution and discretion to be expected of a government officer when he entered the house without a search warrant. In other instances of alleged improper or unlawful conduct the agents found Young guilty. He had, as charged, presented a fictitious claim for auto hire; he had inspired the *East St. Louis Journal* articles, which were held to be "improper newspaper publicity"; he had continued to represent himself as a prohibition agent after his suspension.

In the course of their investigation the government agents uncovered irregularities beyond those specified at the outset. They learned that, in August 1920, Young had confiscated a roulette wheel, 500 poker chips, and $157.50 in cash from a gambler at Tamms, Illinois, and had never turned the property over to the agent in charge, although repeatedly ordered to do so. They learned that while he was acting as a Department of Justice agent he had borrowed four hundred dollars from a woman who lived in Aiken, South Carolina, and had never paid the debt. And they learned that while he was in the active service of the Prohibition Unit he and a young woman had frequently registered at hotels as man and wife.

The only conclusion in Young's favor that the special agents arrived at came as the result of their review of a rape charge on which he had been arrested in early December 1920. In that episode the local grand jury had refused to bring an indictment. The investigators also found the charge baseless.

But one favorable verdict could not offset half a dozen adverse ones. Young had been in trouble constantly by reason of his lack of discretion and good sense.

> This opinion [the special agents concluded] is strengthened by our personal observation of Agent Young, having found him to be of a belligerent nature, prone to make threats of violence, unwilling to accept advice and apparently convinced that he is a law within himself. Agent Young is of a boastful and garrulous disposition, officious and in no sense lacking in his efforts to impress others with his official importance. . . . The evidence overwhelmingly shows Agent Young to be not only entirely unfit to be in the government service but a distinct and glaring disgrace to the service.

While the investigation was in progress dozens of Young's supporters—district attorneys, U.S. commissioners, ministers, Anti-Saloon League officers, and lay workers in the cause of prohibition—appealed to the prohibition commissioner in his behalf. He was "unostentatious in bearing and diligent in the performance of his duty," "admired and trusted by all law-abiding people," "faithful and efficient," "a terror to evil doers." And so forth.

The testimonials had no effect, but when Young himself, after his dismissal, complained to the commissioner that the agents who had investigated him were prejudiced, that official reopened the case. Two other agents reviewed the evidence and interviewed the original investigators. In September 1921 they reported that Young's charges were without foundation and recommended that the case be closed.

Six months later Richard Yates, Congressman at Large from Illinois and an ardent dry, asked the prohibition commissioner, a new appointee, to reconsider the Young case. A Congressman is not to be disregarded, so the commissioner pulled out the file and went through it. He could find no reason, he informed Yates, for reopening the investigation.[*]

Thus the man who, on the evening of February 10, 1924, ruled Williamson County in the name of law enforcement and good government bore on his official record black marks for recklessness, dishonesty, boastfulness, arrogance, and immorality.

In Herrin, troops were still disembarking as late as Monday, February 11, almost three days after the first Klan bullets shattered the windows of the hospital. In all, 1,700 soldiers patrolled the streets and manned machine guns at strategic corners. The ranking officer of the Illinois National Guard, Major General Milton J. Foreman, was in command.

As his first official act General Foreman issued a proclamation prohibiting all except duly authorized officers of the law from carrying firearms. The order continued: "Only such persons as are legally elected or appointed will be permitted to exercise the functions of deputy sheriff, police officer or other peace officer and all appointments of special deputy sheriffs and special peace officers heretofore made are revoked and annulled." Young,

---

[*] *From the time of his dismissal from the Prohibition Unit until he was employed in Williamson County, Young made a living by conducting private investigations for sheriffs in various Illinois counties, among them Iroquois, Champaign, and Massac.*

Foreman told newspaper correspondents, had no official standing. "We do not understand that Young occupies any position
justifying him in administering law and order in the State of
Illinois."

Nevertheless, Young continued to occupy the office of the
chief of police until February 12, when John Ford returned to
resume the position.

By this time the regular authorities were emerging from the
various jails in which they had spent the weekend. Ford and
Crain, whom Galligan spirited away on the night of the 8th,
were turned loose at Belleville. Galligan and four deputies came
to light in the Champaign County jail at Urbana; Acting Sheriff
McCown and a detail of guardsmen brought them back to
Marion. Mayor Anderson of Herrin was freed from the county
jail at Marion.

The release of the mayor and twenty-three others resulted
from the verdict of the coroner's jury in the inquest over the
death of Caesar Cagle. After examining fifty-four witnesses the
jury concluded, on February 13, that "Caesar Cagle came to his
death . . . by gunshot wounds at the hand of one Shelton,
described as tall and slim, and one Shelton, described as heavy
set and sleepy eyed." With the verdict, all those whom Young
had jailed on the charge of murdering Cagle were released. The
two Sheltons—Carl and Earl—were not in custody.

While the coroner's jury was still hearing witnesses, General
Foreman initiated a movement that he hoped would bring peace
to the troubled community. In conferences with officials and
other leading citizens he urged them to take the lead in rescuing
the county from disgrace. Good-hearted men, he told them,
must dispel the antagonisms and hatreds that had brought
about virtual mob rule. A county couldn't be run with rifles and
machine guns, and it wasn't the state's business to do it even if
it could be done.

As the result of his plea, a group of representative citizens met
at Marion on the 13th and constituted themselves the Citizens'

Committee. The next day the members, thirty-five or forty in number, spent several hours in separate conferences with Klan leaders and Sheriff Galligan. Their deliberations took on urgency from the call that Judge E. N. Bowen of the Herrin City Court * issued for a special grand jury to investigate the events of February 8 and 9. "It's about time the real citizens of this county ran things," the judge asserted. "Far more important than any faction's desires or ambitions is the right of law-abiding people of Herrin to enjoy peace and quiet, to have in this city a decent place in which to live and bring up families. . . . This is not something for Williamson County to do, or for the State of Illinois and its troops to do. It's our task, and we're going to do it." The Herrin post of the American Legion, the Rotary Club, and the Lions Club all promised their co-operation.

But difficulties appeared at once. The grand jury then in session returned a number of indictments against prominent Klansmen for alleged offenses committed during the recent raids, and their arrest did not allay the prevailing tension. Even worse, in its effect, was the public controversy over Young's status. By what authority, newspaper correspondents wanted to know, had he conducted the wholesale liquor-raids? They had the statement of the assistant prohibition commissioner that Young had not been connected with the service since his dismissal in 1920, and a denial by the director for the Illinois district that he had any authority from the government for the Williamson County raids. On the other hand Arlie Boswell, Young's lawyer, insisted that the raider had full authority for what he had done, although Boswell refused to reveal from whom that authority stemmed. On one point there was no longer

---

* *Herrin had taken advantage of that provision in the Illinois statutes which permits a municipality to set up a court having jurisdiction concurrent with that of the circuit court, the highest court of original jurisdiction in an Illinois county. The city court, however, can take cognizance only of those matters originating within the limits of the city for which it has been established.*

mystery: Young was being paid, and handsomely, by a number of leading Klansmen. Those who should have known stated that he had received between five and seven thousand dollars for his services since early November, and his admirers had also given him a Lincoln touring car. Law enforcement under Klan auspices, it is evident, was more lucrative than being a prohibition agent at $150 a month.

Would Young continue as the Klan's enforcer? He himself announced that his work was "finished temporarily," and that the county was now "fairly dry." He intended to go to Washington to help frame injunctions against the bootleggers whose places he had raided, and then he planned to reside permanently at Marion. The decision to withdraw from the enforcement crusade, though apparently his, had actually been made for him. Sam Stearns and the other Klansmen who had put up the money that he had received were shocked by his recklessness, and had notified him privately, after the mass raid of February 1, 1924, that he would no longer be paid for his work. They declined, however, to repudiate him publicly, and when anti-Klan leaders, conferring with the Citizens' Committee, tried to make his dismissal one of the conditions of peace, Stearns and other Klansmen issued a manifesto in which they declared that he continued to enjoy their confidence. "S. Glenn Young has the support and good will of every law-abiding citizen of Williamson County," they asserted ". . . and we recommend him to the world as a perfect gentleman, honest, true and upright in all his dealings, but a terror to all law violators."

The insistence of anti-Klansmen that Young be dropped was matched by the Klan's demand that Galligan resign as sheriff. He refused. "I will co-operate," he declared, "with any body of citizens looking to the establishment of peace and orderly government in Williamson County. I will compromise. I will agree to any reasonable suggestions as to the management of my office and the enforcement of law, but I will not resign."

In this impasse the Citizens' Committee could do little except issue pious pronouncements calling on the populace to abstain from violence. Even so, General Foreman decided that the prospect justified the release of most of the troops. On February 15 all except five companies were sent home. A few days later the two factions effected a compromise. By its terms, the war against the bootleggers would be conducted by the sheriff in the future. On his part Galligan agreed to replace his field deputies with new men nominated by the committee, the understanding being that neither Klansmen nor Knights of the Flaming Circle would be approved. The county board promised funds for the two additional deputies whom the sheriff insisted he needed, and for raising the salaries of the new appointees to a decent level.

Galligan immediately appointed the men who had been agreed upon, and then telegraphed to the governor requesting that all troops, except one company to be stationed at Herrin for the time being, be recalled. The governor complied.

On March 3 the special grand jury summoned by Judge Bowen held its first session, but its deliberations were eclipsed by the greater spectacle that opened in the United States District Court at Danville the same day. There more than two hundred residents of Williamson County, all arrested in the wholesale liquor raids, prepared to stand trial. Long before court convened the defendants, their friends and relatives, Klansmen, and curious spectators filled the courtroom and the corridors of the federal building. Deputy marshals kept a close watch for guns, but the crowd was orderly. Only Young, daily more arrogant, raised a disturbance by throwing an epithet at Charlie Birger, one of the more notorious defendants, when he met him in the corridor. A deputy marshal prevented trouble. And when the Klan leader tried to enter the courtroom wearing his automatics he discovered that in a federal court he was no exception to the rules.

As soon as court convened the defendants, in a long line, passed slowly before Judge Walter C. Lindley. Special Prosecutor Lawrence T. Allen, assigned to handle the liquor cases in place of District Attorney W. O. Potter, who was known to be violently anti-Klan, read the specific charges to each defendant and asked him whether he pleaded guilty or not guilty. Usually the response was not guilty. The few who entered guilty pleas were fined from fifty to three hundred dollars.

After the first day the court settled down to the tedious business of selecting juries, presenting evidence, and awaiting verdicts. Interest waned, to be aroused only when the case of some conspicuous defendant was decided. Thus there was gratification in the Klan camp when Ora Thomas, reputed to be head of the Knights of the Flaming Circle, pleaded guilty and drew a fine of five hundred dollars and a four months' jail sentence. There was even greater satisfaction when Judge Lindley passed the stiffest sentence of all—fines totaling $2,500 and one year in jail—on Charlie Birger. By the end of the term Special Prosecutor Allen had brought 178 defendants to trial, and had convicted the great majority. Most of the violators were fined $200, $250, or $300, and some were also sentenced to a month or two in jail.

But before the liquor trials at Danville ended Herrin had resumed its place as the focal point of interest in the Williamson County "trouble."

On March 14, after a nine-day session, the grand jury of the Herrin City Court presented its findings to Judge Bowen. In connection with the killing of Caesar Cagle and the attack on the Herrin hospital it returned ninety-nine indictments. Ninety-five involved men who had participated in the hospital riot. Leading the list was S. Glenn Young, whose offenses against the peace, the grand jury found, included parading with arms, false imprisonment, conspiracy, kidnapping, assault with attempt to murder, assault with deadly weapons, falsely assuming an office, robbery, larceny, riot, and malicious mischief. No other person was charged with quite so many infractions of the criminal law, but it appeared that a goodly number of Herrin's prominent citizens would be headed for jail if the indictments resulted in convictions.

From the ranks of the anti-Klansmen the grand jury picked two men—Carl and Earl Shelton—and indicted both for the murder of Caesar Cagle. In addition, it returned indictments against Carl Shelton for assault with a deadly weapon and assault with attempt to murder.

The grand jury concluded its work by adopting a scathing report. Characterizing the events of February 8 and the days which followed as a "Reign of Terror" resulting from acts of "oppression and persecution by the so-called Ku Klux Klan" it paid its respects to that organization and its hired law-enforcer in biting phrases. The attack on the Herrin hospital, "entirely unlawful and without any justification whatever," was "the most amazing display of mob violence" the jurors had ever known. Young was a usurper, who could not have acted legally as Chief of Police because he had not resided in the state and county one full year, as the law required. "It seems . . . clear," the jury concluded, "that it was the purpose of the said S. Glenn Young and those acting in concert with him, to overthrow the civil authority in Herrin and in Williamson County, seize and imprison the Sheriff and Mayor and take upon themselves the task of government without any legal authority whatever."

The grand jury's action infuriated the Klan. To show their resentment, members of the order staged a protest parade. At nine o'clock on the morning of March 17 some three thousand people gathered at the Christian Church in Herrin. The Protestant ministers stepped out in front, then came veterans of the Civil War in automobiles, and after them a band. The rank and file followed—professional men, merchants who had closed their stores for the morning, women pushing baby buggies, others carrying small children—"all," as the *Marion Republican* put it, "marching with determined step and each with a small American flag in their button hole or pinned on their dresses." In the rear rank marched S. Glenn Young, John L. Whitesides, and Arlie Boswell, the color guard of a huge American flag.

The paraders, calling their demonstration a "religious protest" against the "unrighteous verdict" of the grand jury, marched and countermarched through the business district. From a window in his office Judge Bowen watched impassively.

The parade over, many of the marchers dashed to the City Hall to sign the bonds of the men under indictment. Guardsmen with fixed bayonets—now an accepted feature of Williamson County courtrooms—looked over all who entered to see whether they carried pistols. As man after man pushed his way to the judge's table—Young, Stearns, Carl Neilson, John Ford, Abe Hicks—the crowd cheered. It was understood that the bonds might total four million dollars, and men whose property aggregated three times that sum came forward to pledge their lifetime savings.

Late in the afternoon, with the business of signing bonds still far from finished, Judge Bowen announced that there would be a recess until March 20. Young mounted a chair and barked to those who were present:

"I want all you fellows to be here Thursday, so we can finish this up!"

The response, "We'll be with you, Glenn!" was almost smothered by cheers and handclapping.

Noting the enthusiasm, amounting almost to hysteria, an observer would have said that S. Glenn Young had reached the climax of his career. Yet anyone who came to that conclusion would have been wrong. In sober fact, the man's position was anything but enviable. The Klan leaders who had been paying him from their own pockets determined to put into effect their tentative decision of a month earlier, and cut off his salary. Cheers are sweet, but they do not obliterate for long the imminence of a dozen criminal prosecutions or the fear of a jobless future.

There is reason to think that Young was downright desperate. On the night of April 15 someone in a fast-moving automobile fired into the home of Sam Stearns. Stearns and his family escaped injury, though Ross Lizenby, his bodyguard, was hit in the leg. Months later two of Young's henchmen, then serving jail sentences for bank robbery—of such were the legions of the Lord composed!—confessed to Lizenby that Young had framed the shooting in an attempt to force his own rehiring, and that they had fired the shots from Young's car. Even Stearns believed that Young instigated the attack.

But Young was soon provided for. Certain members of the Klan in East St. Louis had been proved guilty of acts of extortion in connection with Klan-supported liquor raids, and in consequence state officers of the order revoked the local charter. Young, who had joined the Klan during the spring—he had not been a member at the time of the big liquor-raids—was put in charge for the purpose of re-establishing the district's respectability. Accompanied by four Williamson County ministers, he drove to East St. Louis on April 25 to take over the duties of his office. To the 1,400 Klansmen who greeted him he announced: "East St. Louis is a rotten city and has a bad reputation all over the state. It is run by a bunch of corrupt politicians. I am still a resident of Williamson County, and that county is the cleanest in the entire state now." To which the mayor of the city replied, in an interview published on the same day: "If the city is rotten it is because of the Klan and not the city officials being corrupt. . . . As for cleaning up the city, I think he [Young] will only get it dirty."

Young's departure should have brought peace to Williamson County. The Klan, however, was too sure of its righteousness. In the primary election of April 8, 1924, its candidates had swept the field. The next night thousands celebrated the victory by staging a motor parade that visited Herrin, Johnston City, and Dewmaine, and returned to Marion to burn a huge cross—the first such demonstration in almost a year. Four days later ten robed Klansmen marched into the Marion Methodist Church, knelt in silence while a young woman who accompanied them sang a stanza of "The Fiery Cross," and then presented the pastor with twenty-seven dollars and a letter commending him for his good work. On May 1 several thousand attended a Klan barbecue at Herrin, burned two crosses, and initiated two hundred men and women. Three weeks later, crowds thronged to a "Klantauqua" at Marion, and for three days listened to Klan orations relieved by entertainment in the Chatauqua manner.

The pattern was that of the summer of 1923—silent visitations upon churches, ghostly gatherings in the light of flaming crosses, new recruits by the hundred. But in the late spring of 1924 there was this difference, best stated in the words of George Galligan:

> The chief figures on both sides were never away from their guns. I slept, performed my duties and ate my meals with my pistols always within reach. There were always riot guns and high-powered rifles available to repel a possible Klan attack on the jail, and there were men awake at all hours acting as sentrymen. Hand grenades and machine guns, both of the hand operating variety and those to be fired from heavy tripods, were brought into the county by both sides.

10

DEATH IN A CIGAR STORE

May 1924–January 1925

●●

Don't pull that gun, Ora!
S. Glenn Young, January 24, 1925.

TWENTY-FIVE YEARS ago the motorist traveling from Marion to East St. Louis drove northward until he came to an improved east-and-west road known as the Atlantic-Pacific Highway, which he followed to his destination. The highway crossed the Kaskaskia River a few miles beyond the little town of Okawville, traversing a stretch of country dreary even in springtime. Tangled trees and underbrush lined both sides of the road, and backwater from the river lay stagnant in the ditches. No one lived there.

On May 23, 1924, Young, accompanied by his wife—he had married again after his divorce—was driving to East St. Louis in the big Lincoln car that had become almost as well known as he was. As he entered the lonely road through the Kaskaskia bottoms a Dodge that had been following him started to pass on the left. When it drew abreast its occupants poured a volley of shots into the Lincoln. Mrs. Young slumped forward. Young skidded to a stop and jumped from the door to fire at the Dodge, now speeding into the distance. Instead, he collapsed. He had been hit in the knee, and one leg was useless.

In a short time a passing motorist found the wounded couple

and took Mrs. Young to St. Elizabeth's Hospital in Belleville. Young followed in his own car, with another man driving. Mrs. Young, hit in the face by shotgun pellets, was in serious condition; Young's knee had been shattered. Surgeons operated at once. Both patients would recover, they announced, although Mrs. Young would certainly lose the sight of one eye, and perhaps of both.

Word of the attack flashed through southern Illinois. In Williamson County, Klansmen swore that the outrage would be avenged. During the evening of the 23rd a report reached Herrin that Young's assailants were on the way to that city. A member of the city police force hastily "deputized" a large number of Klansmen, who took up posts on the roads at the edge of town. Throughout the night and the following morning they stopped and searched all cars.

About ten a.m. word came that a side-curtained Dodge touring car had just passed through Carterville at high speed and that it was headed in the direction of Herrin. The "deputy police" on the Carterville road were warned to be on the lookout. In a few minutes the car came in view. The road guards, pistols in hand, signaled it to stop. The occupants responded with a burst of speed and a volley of shots, which the Klansmen answered. An instant later the Dodge crashed into another car on the road. Two men crawled from the wreckage and ran. Klan pistols brought both to the ground. One died at the Herrin hospital a half hour later; the other, not seriously wounded, was held there under guard.

The dead man was identified as Jack Skelcher. He had been arrested for bootlegging during the Klan raids, and was under indictment for assault with a deadly weapon at the time of his death. His companion was a hoodlum named Charles Briggs. Several months earlier Briggs had been indicted, with Bernie Shelton, a brother of Carl and Earl, for highway robbery.

A coroner's jury held that Skelcher had come to his death at the hands of parties unknown.

The murderous assault in the Kaskaskia bottoms and the quick vengeance visited on one of the reputed assailants brought Young into the headlines as never before, and the injuries to his wife, an innocent sufferer, aroused much sympathy. Bulletins came from the sickrooms in St. Elizabeth's Hospital as regularly as if the patients had been royalty. Other reports indicated that Young's arrogance, recklessness, and egotism had, if anything, been heightened by the attempt on his life. A small coterie of Klansmen were standing guard around the hospital, a Catholic institution, and the raider's pistols lay within his reach. The man would not remain silent. On June 12, for no apparent reason other than to keep himself in the public eye, he released the text of a letter he had written three weeks earlier to W. W. Anderson, head of the federal prohibition forces in Illinois. There he charged that hundreds of saloons and stills were oper-ating in Madison and St. Clair counties, and threatened that if the officials did not act soon, he and Klansmen under his leader-ship would clean them up. The laxity of U.S. District Attorney Potter, he implied, was primarily responsible for the deplorable situation. Copies of the letter were sent to Illinois Congressmen, ministers, and others active in "law enforcement."

Potter replied by pointing out that Madison County was not in his district, and citing the record his office had made in con-victions for violation of the liquor law. Stung, Young issued a wild statement from the hospital in which he charged that Potter had been "fixed" by the bootleggers, that those who had been arrested were allowed to plead guilty and were let off with light fines, and that the district attorney "had done everything within his power to obstruct the officers in the enforcement of the Eighteenth Amendment in Williamson County."

Within two weeks Young made another public display of bad judgment. This time the occasion was a hearing before a justice of the peace at Carlyle, the county seat of Clinton County, in which the assault on him and his wife had taken place. Early in June he had sworn out warrants for attempted murder not only against Briggs but also against Carl and Earl Shelton, who, he charged, were the other occupants of the car from which assassins' bullets were fired on May 23. The two brothers voluntarily surrendered to the sheriff of Clinton County and were admitted to bail. On June 26 they were to appear at the county seat for a preliminary hearing.

The biggest crowd in Carlyle's history gathered for the event. The courtroom was packed, and hundreds were turned away. Fifty deputies, each armed with a shotgun, stood guard. Shortly after two o'clock Young arrived, not alone, or with a small escort, but accompanied by thirty autoloads of Klansmen. Most of the cars were decorated with American flags. Many of the Klansmen carried arms, which the sheriff compelled them to leave in his office.

It was a spectacular performance, but many saw it as a brazen effort to give notice that the Klan meant to see its own concepts of justice carried out.

The hearing took little time. Without any show of doubt Young identified Briggs and the Shelton brothers as members of the party that attacked him and his wife on May 23. The justice bound the three men over to the November grand jury, and then released them on bond.*

No matter how much Young's swaggering, brash behavior pleased his Klan followers in Williamson County, the practical

---

* *The case was never prosecuted. According to Art Newman, a bootlegger and gambler of East St. Louis who will appear again in this narrative, Carl, Earl, and Bernie Shelton, Jack Skelcher, and Charlie Briggs were the ones who ambushed Young and his wife. Newman claimed that the Sheltons told him the story. This is the account he gave to Roy Alexander, who printed it in the* St. Louis Post-Dispatch *of January 31, 1927:*

Young had left Herrin to go to East St. Louis and even before he took out of Herrin that peckerwood began to brag.

He stood on the running board of his Lincoln in Herrin and when a crowd gathered around, he said: "Boys, I'm going up to East St. Louis now. We've cleaned up Williamson County. Watch what we do in East St. Louis."

The Sheltons heard him make that foolish crack, they told me, and they took out after his car. . . .

Carl told me they almost burned the Dodge up after the Lincoln, but men who headed the statewide organization knew that they could no longer retain him as an official and employee. In early June, as soon as he was permanently discharged from St. Elizabeth's,* he was dismissed from his position in East St. Louis. At the same time the Grand Dragon for Illinois, Charles G. Palmer, wrote a public letter to District Attorney Potter in which he stated that Young's intemperate charges did not represent the official attitude of the Klan and apologized for his "exhibition of impetuosity."

Nor was this the only blow. Ever since spring Young had been trying to have the cases pending against him as the result of the liquor raids—robbery, assault, and so forth—transferred to the United States District Court on the ground that he was a deputized federal officer at the time the alleged offenses occurred. Potter, of course, tried to block the move, but he did ask the Attorney General for instructions. That officer and his assistants

---

finally they caught up with the Youngs in the Okaw Bottoms. . . . They pulled up alongside the Lincoln, with Bernie driving the Dodge, and opened up on Young and his wife with pistols and a 30–30 rifle. . . .

The cars, traveling pretty fast, caught together for a minute and then the Lincoln plunged away and ran down a bank at the side of the road. The door fell open on the driver's side and Young fell out.

"The dirty louse crawled under the machine," Carl told me later, "but we sure got him. He looked like his whole head was shot off."

When Newman told this story he had become the Sheltons' bitter enemy. I have heard a prominent citizen of Williamson County, whom I am not at liberty to name, say that one of the attackers told him that when they drove away they were certain they had killed both Young and his wife. My informant would not name the man.

* *In the fall of 1928 a Belleville collection-agent was still trying to collect the hospital and medical bills that Young and his wife had incurred. They were itemized as follows:*

St. Elizabeth's Hospital	$473.70
Physicians	650.00
Drugs	8.55
	$1,132.25
5% interest, 4 yrs. & 3 mos.	226.45
	$1,358.70

The Department of Justice, to which request for payment was made, disclaimed responsibility on the ground that Young was not a federal employee.

were no more anxious to defend the Illinois troublemaker than the District Attorney, but they made a thorough investigation of the merits of his contention. Gus J. Simons reported that he deputized Young for the raid on December 22, 1923, but that —and this was contrary to statements given out at the time— he had not deputized him for the raids that were staged on December 31, 1923, January 5, 1924, January 14, or later. Since the alleged offenses had been committed during the later raids, Mabel Walker Willebrandt, Assistant Attorney General, decided that Young's defense was not a responsibility of the Department of Justice. Accordingly the District Attorney moved that Young's cases be remanded to the state courts, and Judge Lindley, sitting in East St. Louis, ruled in Potter's favor on all except two indictments. These, growing out of the raid of December 22, could be tried in the federal courts; all others in which Young was a defendant would have to be heard in Williamson County, where both judges—Bowen and Hartwell—were definitely hostile.

From this time on Young acted with complete abandon. Two performances in quick succession were typical. One took place on July 31 at East St. Louis, where he had been summoned to appear for a preliminary hearing on an attempted-murder charge. Young arrived with an escort of hundreds of Klansmen, who proceeded to take over the Labor Temple. Instead of appearing in court he sent for the justice of the peace to come to the Temple for the proceedings. That official supinely obeyed. After being bound over to the grand jury, Young ordered the corridors of the building cleared while he made out his bond, and his followers sprang to do his bidding. Then he emerged to receive the cheers of his private army.

The other incident occurred in Marion two weeks later. Learning that a charge of carrying concealed weapons had been filed against him there, he appeared, late in the afternoon, to give bond. Three carloads of his henchmen, armed with pistols, rifles, and a portable machine-gun, accompanied him; he himself wore his pearl-handled automatics. The group strode into the clerk's office as if they were officers of the law. When Young saw that the information against him was sworn to by Ora Thomas, he cursed the clerk for issuing the capias. The violent argument that followed attracted a score of spectators, who watched in fascination even as they looked for cover in the event that someone pulled a pistol.

The next morning Young and his gang appeared again. As the little caravan circled the public square Galligan leaned from the window of his office and called out derisively: "Hello, Young!"

Young stopped his car and yelled back: "Come out here and say that, you dirty crook!"

Parking near the sheriff's office, he exchanged profane epithets with Galligan for several minutes. Again a cluster of bystanders watched expectantly for an outbreak of gunfire.

Tension, in fact, had reached a point that made everyone fearful of another eruption. The primary cause, aside from Young's inflammatory antics, was the session of the Herrin City Court scheduled for August 18. Twelve cases growing out of the killing of Cagle and the riot that followed were set for trial at that time.

During the first days of the term, several cases against Klansmen were dismissed, and in one or two the defendants were acquitted. Then, on August 25, the judge called a larceny case in which Young was one of three defendants. His attorneys asked for a continuance on the ground that he had gone to Atlanta, Georgia, for medical treatment, and supported their motion with affidavits from two physicians of that city. State's Attorney Duty, prosecuting, contested the motion. Judge Bowen found for Duty and ordered Young's bonds, totaling thirty-nine thousand dollars, forfeited.

The tension tightened. Klansmen sent hundreds of telegrams to Governor Small urging him to intervene in Williamson County. The sheriff, according to many of those who sent wires, had deputized a large number of gunmen so as to dominate the Herrin court while Young's cases were being tried. Small made a blanket reply in an interview at Springfield: it was the sheriff's duty to preserve order, and the State of Illinois had already spent as much as it intended to in the turbulent county.

But the Klan had other ways of exerting pressure. One of these was tried in late August, when the Klan held a big picnic at the county fairgrounds. The day of festivity came to a close with a parade consisting of floats, bands, a ladies' drum corps, and hundreds of cars decorated with flags and white crosses. The parade over, five thousand people assembled to listen to the speakers and to participate in initiation ceremonies for both men and women.

Galligan, infuriated by the performance, gave out a bitter interview:

"It's a shame that the Ku Klux keep stirring up trouble. . . . Instead of letting things get quiet they stir up trouble with this parade. Two men can't get together on the street but what they start talking about the Klan. This business is ruining our lodges, it's hurting the churches, it hurts neighborhoods—even brothers won't speak to each other because of this Ku Klux business. Until the Ku Klux Klan is forgotten there will be no peace in Williamson County."

On the day this interview was published the case of the *People* vs. *Carl and Earl Shelton* for the murder of Caesar Cagle came up for trial. By midmorning of the next day the jury was completed. But instead of introducing testimony, Duty moved that the case be dismissed. He took this course, he explained, because the sole witness who had connected the Sheltons with the Cagle killing had disappeared, and therefore the state had no case. Besides, Tim Cagle, father of the dead man, had become convinced that the two defendants had nothing to do with the murder of his son.

As soon as Duty finished Tim Cagle rose and addressed the court. In a voice trembling with emotion he said that he ap-

179

proved what the State's Attorney had done. Then he pleaded for peace among the warring factions. He recalled the days of the Bloody Vendetta, in which he confessed that he had been involved. The participants in that long-drawn-out feud had been good men; so were many of the principals in the Klan war. But the fighting must stop. "Let's get it settled," the old man begged. "We have a great country here and my God, let's be great in it!"

Judge Bowen granted the State's Attorney's motion, and the Sheltons walked from the courtroom free men.

Half an hour later Galligan, special deputies "Bud" Allison and Ora Thomas, the Shelton brothers, and other enemies of the Klan drove to John Smith's garage in Herrin, stepped out of their automobiles, and entered the establishment. All were armed. They intended to recover the Dodge car that Jack Skelcher had been driving on the day of his death, and that Smith had been holding ever since. Now that the murder charge against the Sheltons had been dismissed, the car would not be needed as evidence. The show of force was called for—so Galligan thought—because the garage was a Klan gathering-place.

Galligan asked for Smith. When told by one of the several men who were loafing around the place that the garage owner had gone home to dinner, Galligan said that he had come to get the Dodge, and demanded that it be produced. An attendant started to comply with his demand, but with infuriating slowness. Galligan ordered him, profanely, to get a move on. The attendant replied, also profanely. Someone in the sheriff's party undertook to quicken the garageman's dragging steps by punching him in the ribs with the barrel of a pistol. A scuffle followed.

The noise attracted a passerby named Chester Reid. Stepping inside the garage door, and seeing that a fight was about to break out, Reid called to the men to put up their pistols. Two or three of the sheriff's men, coming up to talk to the newcomer, noticed a car passing slowly and ran out to stop it. Recognizing the riders as Klansmen, they jerked them out and ordered them to line up on the street.

Someone fired. An instant later volleys rang out inside the garage and on the street in front of it. When the shooting stopped six men were dead or dying, and several others were bleeding from wounds.*

Three of the dead men were Klansmen—Green Dunning, Dewey Newbold, and Charles Wollard. Reid, the peacemaker, lost his life; so did Otto Rowland, another innocent bystander. Allison, the sheriff's special deputy, was the sixth casualty. Herman Phemister, one of the sheriff's friends, was badly wounded; Carl Shelton was shot in the hand.

Galligan and the surviving members of his party placed the dying and wounded men in cars and took them to the Herrin hospital. That done, the sheriff telephoned to the Adjutant General and asked that troops be rushed to the city. Fearing an attack on the hospital, he ordered special deputies from all over the county to report there as soon as possible. At the same time, the Klan was mobilizing at the Methodist Church two blocks away. Fortunately, forty men of the headquarters company of the 130th Infantry arrived in trucks from Carbondale before the two groups clashed. As soon as their machine guns were set up on the hospital grounds the danger of open civil war ended. That evening a full company from Salem reinforced the first militiamen. On the surface Herrin was quiet, but the bulges of concealed weapons showed in the light summer clothing of many men.

The presence of troops gave assurance that for the moment at least there would be no gunplay, but not even soldiers can keep people from talking. So the battle of the Klan continued with words. From Atlanta, Young wired to John Smith: "If the boys need me I will come, if I have to come on one leg." "We've fooled with these Klansmen long enough," Galligan told a *St. Louis Post-Dispatch* reporter, "and you can say for me we're

---

* *The stories told by participants in the Smith garage fight are hopelessly at variance. All are demonstrably wrong in many particulars. I have limited my narrative to the established facts.*

ready to fight it out." The Rev. I. E. Lee, Herrin Baptist minister, told the same reporter that the election of a new State's Attorney and a new sheriff offered the only solution of the county's trouble. Calling on Duty for a comment on Lee's statement, the reporter noticed that the State's Attorney shook hands with his left hand while he tried, unsuccessfully, to conceal his automatic behind his back. All the county needed, Duty said, was a thorough cleaning-up by the National Guard. If the commanding officer would seize the four arsenals of the Klan in Herrin, the principal source of trouble would be eliminated. Not to be left out, the Ministers' Association of Williamson County issued a long statement, reviewing the history of local law-enforcement, or the lack of it, and concluding with a prescription similar to that of the Reverend Mr. Lee:

> The imprisonment of innocent men upon unfounded charges must cease. The persons guilty of these outrages must be brought to justice without favor or partizanship. Honest witnesses must not be so cowed that they will fear to give evidence. The courts must dispense justice, punishing the guilty and protecting the innocent. To do that we need a States Attorney who will enforce the law and a Sheriff who will apprehend the real criminals. We have neither.

Duty, shown this pronouncement, made the kind of comment that always infuriated the crusading preachers: "Every time they get up in their pulpits they ring in the Klan. They stir up trouble and hatred, and the people who listen to them come out inflamed."

In a courthouse guarded by militiamen armed with automatic rifles and hand grenades, a coroner's jury held its inquest on the deaths of those killed in the Smith garage riot. Witnesses contradicted each other. Charles Denham, Herrin merchant, swore that while the riot was in progress Duty, Judge Bowen, and Jane Lassiter, the coroner's secretary, drove past the Smith

garage and that Duty and Bowen fired into his car. Miss Lassi‑
ter swore that at that time she and Duty, in the latter's car,
were well on their way to Marion. Mrs. Chester Reid identified
John Smith, the garage owner, as the man who shot her hus‑
band; others swore that Smith did not arrive at the garage until
fifteen or twenty minutes after the shooting. Dr. Black, some
witnesses testified, fired at the rioters; others asserted that he
drove up hastily and immediately began to work with the men
who had been shot.

The jurors, impressed by Mrs. Reid's testimony in spite of
contrary evidence, found that Smith killed Reid. They also con‑
cluded that Allison and Dunning killed each other. The other
three men met death at the hands of parties unknown. Smith
was ordered held for the grand jury.

The implication of Smith in the murder of Reid made Klans‑
men boil with anger. So did the appearance of Ora Thomas at
the Herrin hospital four days after the riot, even though he
came only to pay a visit to the wounded Phemister. As word of
his presence spread, groups of Klansmen formed, and the out‑
look became ominous. Captain H. L. Bigelow, commanding the
sixteen militiamen who remained in Herrin—all others had
been sent home two days earlier—learned what impended and
ordered Thomas to leave the city. Thus a clash was averted. But
passions had no chance to cool. On September 4 word came
from Danville that a federal grand jury had just indicted Young
and nine other Herrin residents on charges of impersonating
federal officers. On the same day, in Herrin, Galligan, Ora
Thomas, Carl, Earl, and Bernie Shelton, and other members of
the sheriff's faction were put under bond to await the action of
the next grand jury in connection with the Smith garage riot;
so were nine prominent Klansmen. Herrin seethed with appre‑
hension.

Young did not help matters by returning from Atlanta. On
September 12 he and his wife registered at the Ly-Mar Hotel in

Herrin; immediately afterward, accompanied by a large party of Klansmen, he drove to Benton to give bond under the federal indictments.

The next day he was formally expelled from the Klan. (In the action taken against him in the summer he had only been relieved of his position as a Klan employee.) Charles G. Palmer, Illinois Grand Dragon, gave notice of Young's expulsion in the *Illinois Kourier,* the official Klan paper. Young, Palmer asserted, had an "inordinate craving for personal publicity," a fondness for "ostentatious displays of firearms and braggadocio," and a tendency to take the law "into his own hands, shoot at the drop of a hat, and give utterance to the most incendiary thoughts." He had performed "splendid service" in Williamson County, but even there he had been well paid for his work.

Young's expulsion from the order had little effect on his popularity with the rank and file of Williamson County Klansmen. That became evident a few weeks later when he appeared, unannounced, at a Klan meeting in Marion. Wild cheers broke out as he hobbled to the platform on two canes, and applause rocketed through the auditorium again when he declared that for the first time in his life he was going to vote Republican. "If you want to have the illegal sale of liquor, disreputable women, and disorder in the county," he told the audience, "vote the Democratic ticket on election day. If you want law enforcement, vote the Republican ticket." Hundreds rushed up to shake his hand when he finished.

Three days before Young's dramatic appearance Galligan announced that he had dismissed the deputies whom he had appointed by agreement with the Citizens' Committee. One of his new appointees, he revealed, was Ora Thomas, who would take the place of Allison, killed in the Smith garage riot.

If Galligan had lain awake nights to devise means of driving the Klansmen to fury—and perhaps he had—he could have thought of no better way than to give Thomas a permanent appointment. The hatred they bore the new deputy made their animosity toward the sheriff a pale emotion. A resident of the county since boyhood, Thomas had worked in the mines until the United States entered the first World War. He saw service in France, and was wounded in action. After the war he went back to coal mining, but soon drifted into shady occupations. The fact that he was with "Whitey" Doering, a convicted mail-robber and member of Egan's Rats, a notorious St. Louis gang, when Doering was killed in November 1923, gave rise to the report that he too belonged to that unsavory mob. Klansmen believed him to be the organizer of the Knights of the Flaming Circle, and he was certainly a leader of the violent anti-Klan faction. Caught in two of Young's big raids, he had only recently been dismissed from jail after serving one of Judge Lindley's stiffer sentences. As late as October 4—ten days before his appointment—he had been indicted for murder in connection with the Smith garage riot. In fact, thirteen indictments stood against him at the time Galligan made him a permanent deputy.

Thomas's record, not a good one for a law-enforcement officer, contrasted strangely with his appearance. Slender and under average height, he carried himself with none of Young's swagger. To his friends he showed a quiet joviality; to his enemies he was taciturn, hard, and unrelenting. His sparkling black eyes shone from a sensitive face, the natural pallor of which was accentuated by a heavy shock of curly hair. And his long dextrous fingers seemed out of place on the trigger of a blunt automatic.

Whatever Thomas's enemies said of him, none ever questioned his courage.

Within a few days Galligan sent his new deputy on an errand that baited the Klan to the limit of endurance. In Herrin, Young, though still on crutches, became involved in a fight between members of the two factions. After the fracas one of the principals swore out a warrant charging him and two other Klansmen with assault to commit murder. Galligan applied to Captain

Bigelow for two squads of guardsmen, and then gave the warrants to Thomas to serve. When Young and the two other men who had been placed under arrest were taken to the courthouse to post their bonds, the soldiers had to clear a pathway with bayonets. Only the rifles of the militiamen prevented an outbreak.

And only the rifles of militiamen, stationed at all the polling-places in Herrin, kept peace on election day in early November. At that time the Klan swept the field, putting Arlie O. Boswell into the State's Attorney's office and electing all other candidates it supported. But the result of the election raised the temper of the public to such a pitch that Galligan asked the governor to supplement the militia on the ground, now numbering seventy, with another company, and the commanding officer joined him in requesting that there be no parade or demonstration by the victorious faction.

Young, however, could not be repressed. Late in the afternoon of the day following the election he drove up to the courthouse and parked his car opposite the main entrance. A number of his constant followers accompanied him. Seeing Adron Smith, one of Galligan's new deputies, on the steps, he called out tauntingly:

"Well, Adron, I understand they've let you out."

(The reference was to the refusal of the county board, a day or two earlier, to pay the salaries of the sheriff's new appointees.)

"Who wants to know?" Smith replied.

An argument followed, and one of Young's men kicked Smith down the steps. Word of the fight spread instantly, and men ran from all directions for the showdown they expected. Fortunately, several deputies, hastily summoned from the jail, arrived in time to prevent an outbreak, and when Sam Stearns induced Young to leave, serious trouble was once more averted.

By this time Young's behavior had become so reckless that the Klan leaders concluded his mere presence could no longer be tolerated. The man was constantly browbeating everyone who opposed him in the slightest degree, and resorting to violence far too often. The performance he put on at the office of the *Herrin News,* about this time, was typical. Stomping into the front office with three armed guards, he cursed out the people there, and then went back to the composing-room. There he served notice on a little Irish linotype-operator that the next time he saw his name in print he would come in and clean up the entire force. The operator, a new employee unawed by Young's reputation, made a reply that angered the insolent visitor. Young swore, and broke one of his walking-sticks over the man's head. The Irishman landed a punch in Young's face, ran, and was never seen again.

To induce the troublemaker to leave, the Klan leaders tried persuasion. Young answered that although he had planned to spend the winter in Florida he had changed his mind, and would not leave Williamson County so long as Ora Thomas served as deputy sheriff. Moreover, he saw that the local press published his decision. The Klansmen tried a different kind of inducement, with better effect. In return for one thousand dollars, which they themselves contributed, Young promised to leave the county and stay away. Shortly afterward, he disappeared.

Three weeks later he returned to Herrin. He was engaged, his friends said, in writing a book about his exploits. Now and then he participated in small liquor-raids, but his former associates took steps to prevent even this activity, once so much to their liking. The Herrin chief of police refused to receive the prisoners Young brought in, on the ground that he had no authority to make arrests, and State's Attorney Boswell informed him that his office would not bring prosecutions because of the lawless methods to which he resorted. A few fanatical followers gave him money to live on.

On the surface he was now a harmless figure. Weeks passed without a disturbance, the troops departed, and Herrin seemed to be well on the road to permanent peace. But those who came to that decision ignored certain ominous facts. Young and Ora Thomas hated each other. They lived in the close confines of a town of ten thousand, they met frequently, and every meeting served to keep their enmity at the flash point.

The encounter that took place in the late afternoon of January 24, 1925, followed a well-established pattern. Thomas, on his way to supper, met Young and a number of his satellites. The gang blocked the sidewalk and proceeded to abuse the deputy. Thomas replied in kind. During the argument Young taunted:

"I wish you had killed my father, you yellow bastard!"

The remark was intended to prompt one of his party, Mont Wollard, whose father had died in the Smith garage riot, to attack the man before them, but Wollard made no move. Thomas threw another epithet, then pushed his way through the group and proceeded to his home.

After supper he returned to the Herrin City Court, where he had charge of a jury that was still deliberating. About seven p.m. it brought in its verdict, and court adjourned. With several others, he left the courtroom. As the group reached the street, a bullet struck a concrete pillar near their heads. The men scurried behind parked automobiles and awaited developments. A moment later Young and his henchmen drove up, located the spot where the bullet had hit, then drove away.

When nothing else happened, the men in hiding dispersed. Thomas walked to the European Hotel, where he often found a taxi to take him home. From the cigar store in the corner of the building he heard voices in angry argument. With his hand on the pistol that he carried in the pocket of his overcoat he opened the door and entered.

In the corner of the little room, with his back to the door, Young was violently upbraiding a coal miner for having spread word that he had once been a strikebreaker. Several men stood about, absorbed in what was taking place. After a moment one of them turned, saw Thomas, and hastily slipped out a rear door. Young swung around. As he backed toward the door he said:

"Don't pull that gun, Ora."

Thomas's pistol flashed from his pocket. In an instant the noise of gunfire and crashing glass filled the room. Then there was silence. Smoke drifted slowly into the hotel lobby.

Several minutes passed before those who heard the shooting dared enter the cigar store. When they did they found four bodies on the floor. Young and Ora Thomas were dying. So was Ed Forbes, one of Young's constant guards. Homer Warren, another guard, was dead.

That night no member of the Herrin police force had courage enough to appear on the street. Klansmen patrolled the city, stopping all cars that attempted to enter. At two a.m. the first troops arrived. As their first act they disarmed the Klan patrolmen and sent them to their homes. The town was quiet.

Thomas was buried on the afternoon of January 27. His little home was too small for even the simplest funeral, so the casket was placed on the front porch. Under a gray sky thousands shifted from foot to foot in the snow while the Rev. John Meeker, pastor of the Presbyterian Church, conducted the service.* Galligan, surrounded by grim-faced deputies, stood in the crowd.

At the conclusion of the service the funeral procession—a thousand marching miners, hundreds of automobiles, two truckloads of flowers—made its dreary way to the cemetery. There the minister said the final prayer as the casket was lowered into a grave only a short distance from the weed-grown plot where the victims of the Herrin Massacre had been buried. On the other side of the burial ground, workmen were finishing the imposing mausoleum in which Young's body was to lie.

---

* *Thomas was not a church member. Mrs. Thomas, a Baptist, refused to ask her minister, the Rev. I. E. Lee, to conduct the services because of his close Klan affiliations. The Presbyterian minister, though in sympathy with the Klan's objectives, had not become involved in its activities.*

Few cities, large or small, have ever seen a funeral like that of S. Glenn Young. No one knows how many people viewed his body during the three days it lay in state; estimates ran as high as seventy-five thousand. By noon on the day of the funeral— January 29—out-of-town visitors jammed the streets. The conservative *Post-Dispatch* computed their number at fifteen thousand; local papers placed it at forty thousand. Only a fraction of the crowd succeeded in entering the Baptist Church, where the service was held. Thousands found places at overflow meetings in the Christian Church, the Methodist Church, and the Masonic Temple; but most of the visitors were compelled to stand on the streets.

Those fortunate enough to file before the casket saw that the body was clothed in the purple robe of a Kleagle of the Klan. After all had taken their seats a soloist sang "The Rosary." The Twenty-third Psalm was followed by a prayer. Then another solo, "Somewhere a Voice is Calling," the reading of Young's obituary, and "Beautiful Isle of Somewhere." The Rev. J. E. Story, First Christian Church, spoke on "His Early Life"; the Rev. William Carlton, Baptist Church, Marion, on "S. Glenn Young, the Raider"; the Rev. I. E. Lee on "Young's Work in Williamson County: A Backward Look"; the Rev. P. H. Glotfelty on "A Forward Look." The hymn, "Day is Dying in the West," brought the service to a close.

Through it all, the blind wife of the dead Klansman sat at the head of the open coffin, stroking his face.

The funeral procession formed in heavy twilight. At its head three men carried American flags. Two hundred Klansmen, all robed and hooded, followed on foot, and the six pallbearers in Klan regalia rode horses that also were robed and hooded. Mrs. Young and her relatives rode in the bullet-riddled Lincoln. Carloads of flowers and five hundred automobiles followed the hearse.

At the cemetery Carl Neilson, Exalted Cyclops of the Herrin Klavern, read the Klan burial ritual in the light of a burning cross. The Rev. Robert Evans of St. Louis pronounced another eulogy. A bugler sounded taps.

As the procession turned back to Herrin, twelve armed Klansmen took their positions around the mausoleum, the first of those who were to stand guard nightly until all fear that the grave would be desecrated had passed.

11

THE KLAN LOSES

January 1925–July 1926

●●

It may not all be over yet. *Hal W. Trovil-*
lion in "Persuading God Back to Herrin."
The joints were bad, but I don't believe it
was worth what it has cost to get rid of
them. *Herrin businessman in St. Louis Post-*
Dispatch, February 8, 1925.

MAYOR ANDERSON of Herrin was in Chicago when Young
and Thomas killed each other. To a reporter who obtained an
interview he predicted:

"This will wind up the trouble in Williamson County. With
the leaders of both the Klan and anti-Klan factions dead . . .
from now on there will peace and quiet in Herrin."

Galligan, in Marion, found the prospect equally hopeful.
Announcing that in an effort to restore harmony he would not
appoint a successor to Ora Thomas, he pleaded:

"Let us try more brains and fewer bullets. I invite the co-
operation and advice of all who have heretofore opposed me,
and trust that the lives of those sacrificed in the recent tragedy
may be an added incentive to peace, more friendly relationships,
and higher regard for human life and property."

The outlook was so promising that on January 29, 1925, only
five days after the shooting, all troops in the county were ordered
to their homes.

192

Yet in forty-eight hours two events brought on a new crisis. The coroner's jury found that Young and Thomas killed each other, and that Forbes and Warren met death at the hands of parties unknown. Klansmen, who by this time had convinced themselves that Young's two guards had been shot by persons outside the cigar store while the fatal duel was in progress, were infuriated by the jury's failure to reach the same conclusion and to name the murderers.* The second inflammatory episode was an altercation between Herrin Police Chief Matt Walker and a pro-Klan member of his force. When the chief ordered the officer to turn in his star hot words followed, and the rumor spread that the Klan intended to make an issue of the dismissal.

Galligan, in panic, telegraphed to Adjutant General Black:

DEEPER TROUBLE NOW ON AT HERRIN. MYSELF AND CHIEF OF POLICE WALKER AT HERRIN FULLY BELIEVE THAT MARTIAL LAW IN CITY OF HERRIN IS THE ONLY SOLUTION OF THE TROUBLE. QUICK ACTION IS NECESSARY, AND ONLY MARTIAL LAW WILL AVAIL ANYTHING.

Justifying his telegram, the sheriff said that at least five hundred Klansmen in Herrin still carried arms. If troops would come in and disarm them, he and his deputies, with the police, could keep order. But if the Klansmen continued to carry guns, there would be more bloodshed.

The Adjutant General replied with a blunt refusal.

That same night a drunken man staggered into the lobby of the Ly-Mar Hotel, brandishing a revolver. When a policeman attempted to disarm him he resisted, and another policeman shot and killed him. Ugly rumors flew: the stranger had been seen with City Judge Bowen a few hours earlier; he was a killer in Galligan's pay—this because the hat he wore was stamped

---

* I have found no one in Williamson County who believes that Young and Thomas killed each other. Former Klansmen contend that friends of Thomas, outside the cigar store, shot Young; while men who knew Thomas believe that he was killed by one of Young's men who hid behind a counter until Thomas had emptied his pistol.

with the sheriff's name. Herrin immediately developed a bad case of nerves, and fingers itched for triggers.

Fortunately, the truth came out quickly. The dead man turned out to be a ne'er-do-well from a near-by town, unconnected with either faction. His hat had been stolen from Galligan a few days earlier, and had no significance. The only inference that could be drawn from his behavior was that Herrin was a poor place for a man in his cups to flash a pistol.

Though the killing almost led to a riot, its result was salutary. Realizing how narrowly another disaster had been missed, the responsible members of the county board decided that a solution for the county's troubles was imperative.

For two days the supervisors listened to leading citizens, Boswell and Galligan among them, and wrangled with one another. Then they decided to send a committee to Springfield in an effort to induce the governor to remove the sheriff from office. Governor Small listened to the delegation and turned down their demand: Galligan had given no cause, under the law, for which he could be removed. Then the governor called in Attorney General Carlstrom, Adjutant General Black, and Galligan (on hand to argue his own case if need be) and tackled the job of effecting a compromise. Five hours later an agreement was reached. It provided:

1. That Galligan would turn over his office to one of his deputies, Randall Parks, who would have unrestricted authority.

2. That Galligan would leave Williamson County at once and remain away "until and unless, after conference with the Governor of the State of Illinois, it is agreed conditions are such as to permit his return."

3. That the sheriff would receive his full salary for the remainder of his term.

4. That the county board would take steps to revoke all gun permits and to induce citizens with arms in their possession to surrender them.

5. That in the future all raids should be made by regularly constituted or elected county officers.

All who were present signed the document embodying these provisions.

Back in Marion, the supervisors met to ratify or reject the work of their committee. They invited the public to attend the meeting and the public accepted—widows whose husbands had been killed in the feuding, men who had argued the questions at issue with a pistol in each hand, graybeards who had participated only to the extent of talking endlessly on the courthouse square. And the public let its feelings be known. Abe Hicks, the Herrin justice of the peace who had issued pistol permits by the wholesale, wanted to know what assurance of protection law-abiding citizens would have if they turned in their arms. Klansmen objected to Randall Parks on the ground that he was a second cousin to Delos Duty. The payment of Galligan's salary during his absence rubbed many the wrong way. "I don't care if Galligan goes to Niagara Falls and jumps off," one objector said. "I don't want him to go to Cub-y and drink that Cuban whiskey at the taxpayers' expense. I don't want him to go to Hi-waya or any of them places!"

In the end it was a speech by Attorney General Carlstrom, who had come down from Springfield for just such a contingency, that was decisive. After everyone had spoken he took the floor. Deferentially, but with impressive earnestness, he told his audience:

"I hope we can go back to the day when confidence is placed in the courts and processes of the law. Only then can we remove the necessity of an armed camp in this county. I don't want to be understood as making a threat, but if it should be necessary to declare martial law here values of property will go down below the present level and the county must bear the cost. Martial law would bankrupt Williamson County."

In spite of his disavowal it was a threat, and the supervisors knew it. They retired, argued for a seemly interval, and returned to announce that they had ratified the agreement unanimously.

A few days later Galligan departed. Before leaving he gave a statement to the newspapers: he had signed the abdication agreement in good faith and intended to live up to it, but if the other party failed to keep its word he would consider himself relieved of all obligations and would return.

Three months later, without advance notice, he walked into the county jail and announced that he was resuming his office. He had missed his friends, he told startled reporters, and wanted to come home. Yes, he said in reply to inquiries, he had seen the governor a few days ago, and had encountered no serious objection to his return. For his part, he believed that the recent township and municipal elections (in which anti-Klan candidates had been successful) proved that the people were tired of strife and that there would be no more trouble.

Galligan's return might easily have touched off another explosion had it not been for the fact that Herrin was about to turn to a familiar but neglected help in time of trouble—the old-time religion.

For several weeks Harold S. Williams, a young evangelist whom "Gypsy" Smith had converted only two years earlier, had been conducting a series of revival meetings at Cairo. The Rev. John Meeker, who had heard of his phenomenal success, asked him on what terms he would come to Herrin. Williams made only one stipulation: that he should have the full co-operation of the other ministers. Meeker assured him that that would be his as a matter of course. Yet when the minister returned to Herrin and talked with his fellow preachers, he found them apathetic.

Then Hal W. Trovillion, editor and publisher of the *Herrin News,* intervened.

If your Bible has all the pages in it, [he wrote in a letter to the evangelist], if the Commandments are there intact, if Paul's great essay on Love is there, if the Sermon on the

Mount is there and you preach these things—come on to Herrin posthaste. . . . If you can accomplish only a few little things, you will have done great good to Herrin— make us believe that God is Love—that we should really love our neighbors, not hate them nor carry guns to kill them with, if you can only get people who have known each other for ten and twenty years to simply greet one another when they pass on the streets with a brief "good morning," surely you will have accomplished a thing which we have all failed to bring about with long and patient effort.

Trovillion reinforced his plea with a check and the promise of the full support of his newspaper. Williams agreed to come.

The first of the revival meetings took place on the evening of May 24, 1925. On behalf of the thousands who packed the gymnasium of the Herrin High School, Mayor McCormack welcomed the evangelist and his party. Williams won his audience immediately. Three of the four Protestant ministers—all except Story, who was absent—pledged their support. The manager of the Hippodrome and Annex theaters offered the Annex for noonday prayer-meetings.

For the next six weeks practically every business house in Herrin closed daily for prayer meetings, many of which were held in stores. A big poster advertising the revival, hanging from a coatrack in the European Hotel cigar store over the very spot where Young fell, indicated the spirit that permeated the town. At the evening services more than a thousand citizens, including a sprinkling of gunmen, feudists, gamblers, and bootleggers, declared themselves ready to embrace Christ's way of life. Even Galligan attended frequently. On one of his visits Williams asked those who were present—and they numbered some five thousand—to recognize the sheriff as the symbol of law and order in Williamson County. The audience rose and cheered, and several hundred men, including some of Galligan's inveterate enemies, pressed forward to shake his hand.

While the revival meetings were in progress, State's Attorney Boswell made a contribution to the growing wave of good feel-

ing by asking that 145 pending cases, all of which had originated
in the activities of S. Glenn Young, be stricken from the docket.
To support his motion he pointed out that in several of the cases
that had already been tried juries had been unable to arrive at
verdicts, and admitted that in those which remained the evidence was so flimsy that convictions could not be expected. His
motion was granted.*

Another event that had a mollifying effect was the suspension
of the *Herrin Herald*, Klan newspaper. As the revival drew to a
close the *Herald's* creditors forced it into bankruptcy, and the

---

* *These cases were striking evidence of the cleavages brought about by
the Klan warfare. At the time of his death Young was under seventy-three
indictments. The charges included: falsely assuming an office, robbery,
larceny, assault with intent to murder, assault with a deadly weapon, kidnapping, false imprisonment, conspiracy, riot, malicious mischief, and
parading with arms. In two indictments he was the sole defendant, in all
others a codefendant.*

*Ora Thomas, when he died, was under thirteen indictments, including
riot, murder, assault with intent to murder, and conspiracy.*

*Eleven indictments, charging riot and assault with intent to murder,
stood against Arlie Boswell. Delos Duty, as State's Attorney, had drawn a
number of indictments in which he himself was charged with rioting and
murder. One of his codefendants on several counts was Judge E. N. Bowen.
Galligan was a defendant in ten indictments charging malfeasance in
office, rioting, robbery, conspiracy, and murder. C. E. Anderson, Mayor of
Herrin during most of the Klan trouble, was named in three indictments
for assault with intent to murder. Seventeen indictments stood against
Harry Walker, Herrin policeman; Ross Lizenby, also a Herrin policeman,
was under six indictments for false imprisonment, kidnapping, and conspiracy.*

*Ten charges of assault with intent to murder hung over Otis Maynard,
member of the county board of supervisors and uncompromising enemy of
Galligan. In seventeen indictments Sam Stearns, chairman of the board,
was charged with malicious mischief, riot, assault with intent to murder,
and conspiracy. Harry Herrin was under sixteen charges, including false
imprisonment, riot, parading with arms, and assault with intent to murder.*

*Coroner George Bell, who had been elected with Klan support, was a
defendant in nineteen indictments. John Ford, former Herrin Chief of
Police, was named in seven. Ten charges stood against Police Magistrate
Abe Hicks; twenty-nine against Carl Neilson, Exalted Cyclops of the
Herrin Klan; twenty-five against John Smith, Klan leader; and twenty-
three against Brady Jenkins, constable. St. Louis Post-Dispatch, February 6,
1925.*

sheriff—with relish, one may be sure—attached the property.

After the last of Williams's services, when cool judgment had supplanted emotional fervor, all appearances indicated that the revival had accomplished its purpose. Local citizens, even Klan leaders, assumed that the Klan was dead. Hal W. Trovillion, taking stock, expressed the belief that "we are now set well back on the road," and that "the church houses are rechristened once more as the House of God." A group of Illinois legislators came to the opinion that the Golden Rule had replaced the blue-steel pistol as the arbiter of honor. And a staff correspondent of the *New York Herald Tribune,* visiting Herrin to investigate the remarkable transformation that had been reported as having taken place there, concluded that Williams had really worked a reformation—that he had "taken the guns out of Herrin's hip pockets and replaced them with clean handkerchiefs," and had put a "kindly smile" on the faces of people who had worn "grouchy frowns" for years.

Yet those who knew Williamson County best had reservations. Its people held grudges. A resident still had to be careful of what he said about the Bloody Vendetta, although half a century had passed since that feud had come to an end. Even Trovillion, justly proud of his part in arranging the Williams revival, inserted a warning in the pamphlet, "Persuading God Back to Herrin," that he published to record the community's attempt at regeneration: "It may not all be over yet—the volcano may not only send up smoke from time to time but it may again spout destruction and death. . . ."

The volcano did, in one final, convulsive eruption.

The occasion was a series of elections held in April 1926. The first, for township officers, took place on the 6th; the second, for members of the Herrin school board, was held four days later. In both, the results proved that the Klan had come to life and had succeeded in electing members or sympathizers to almost every office. By the 13th, when candidates for county and state officers were to be nominated, the old familiar tension was again

199

apparent. Klansmen strutted about Herrin with chips on their shoulders; anti-Klansmen sullenly oiled automatics and filled cartridge belts.

On election day tempers were taut, nerves jumpy. Nevertheless John Smith, a watcher at one of the polls, recklessly challenged a number of Catholic voters, including a nun who had lived in Herrin for twenty years. Anti-Klan watchers objected violently, then fists flew. Special deputies rushed up and separated the disputants, and Smith retired from the polling-place to his garage.

Commenting on the incident in its afternoon edition, the *Marion Post* asserted that the fight had aroused little excitement in Herrin, and that no further outbreaks were expected. But it warned: "There is a funny feeling in the air . . . and we advise people to stay away from the crowds that swarm after a little excitement during the pitch of election battle. Both Klan and Anti-Klan are reported heavily armed now for any new developments."

The involvement of John Smith gave reason for apprehension. Somehow this garage owner, a relative newcomer—he had lived in Herrin since 1918—had attracted to himself the same fervent hatred that the anti-Klan forces had lavished on Young. Yet he was a man of altogether different mold. Smith was mild-mannered where Young swaggered, cheerful where Young was dour —his bright blue eyes twinkled with almost every word—facile and pungent in his soft Kentucky speech, and neither a church member nor an advocate of prohibition on principle. The only qualities he shared with Young were stubbornness and the ability to inspire loyalty. He knew himself to be a marked man, and for months had had armed guards stationed in his garage night and day.

Early in the afternoon Smith made his second mistake of the day—he left his garage for the street. As he emerged, a car filled with anti-Klansmen drove past. One of its occupants—"Blackie"

Armes, a known gangster—fired at him. The bullet grazed Smith's neck, and he ran back to the garage.

As if the pistol shot were a signal, firing began from the direction of the European Hotel, two short blocks away, and bullets shattered the windows and chipped the walls of Smith's building. Armed men deployed from cars parked near by. Others worked their way up on foot, all the while pouring a steady rain of bullets into the garage. Now and then a shot was fired in reprisal, but the defenders—Smith's guards—were too badly outnumbered for effective counterfire.

After fifteen minutes the attackers stopped shooting. Those who had come in cars drove away with motors roaring, those on foot ran. Not a whole pane of glass remained in the building, the outside woodwork was splintered and torn, and many cars in storage were badly damaged. Miraculously, no one had been hit.

Shortly after the attacking party withdrew, twenty guardsmen arrived from Carbondale by truck. (Someone had called for troops as soon as the first shot was fired.) The soldiers, with rifles loaded and bayonets fixed, formed in line before the garage.

The militiamen had hardly taken their positions before the gunmen returned to the attack. Parking their cars a block or so away, they started forward on foot. When they saw the troops they hastily re-entered their automobiles and drove off.

This time, however, they proceeded only as far as the Masonic Temple, where one of the polling-places was located. The drivers stopped in the middle of the street, keeping their engines running. Men armed with rifles and pistols stepped out and walked toward the poll watchers and loungers, mostly Klansmen, who stood on the Temple lawn. Approaching John Ford, one of the newcomers said to another:

"Here's one of the sons-of-bitches we're going to kill."

He fired and missed, although he was so close that the powder of the charge burned Ford's face.

A burst of gunfire answered the initial shot. The gunmen,

knowing that the troops would arrive in a minute or two, ran to their cars. In seconds they were out of sight.

All the cars, that is, except a Buick coupé. Its driver lay limp against the steering-wheel, dead; the man beside him was mortally wounded. Four others, all dying, lay on the lawn. Three of these were Klansmen—Mack and Ben Sizemore, brothers, and Harland Ford, John Ford's brother. The fourth was a gangster named Noble Weaver, from West Frankfort. In the Buick were Orb Treadway, of Harrisburg, and the same Charles Briggs who had escaped with a minor wound when Jack Skelcher was killed. Both were enemies of the Klan.

The day after the riot John Smith told a reporter for the *St. Louis Post-Dispatch* that he was about ready to give up. Twenty-four hours later he made the decision.

"They would get me next time," he said. "I'm going to leave, to keep from getting killed, and to keep from killing anyone.

"In all the liquor raids," he added, "I never shot anyone. The raiding ended more than a year ago, and today I wouldn't start a raid if they put a saloon next door to me. But the liquor gang has kept after me, and today my business is ruined, for people are afraid to come to my place to trade."

That same day he sold his business and left for Florida.

Automatically, Herrin tendered the three dead Klansmen the same flamboyant funeral that had been the last reward of their predecessors who had lost their lives in the "trouble." Once more there was an overflow crowd, a profusion of flowers, flag-covered caskets, and crosses of red roses. And once more one minister after another proclaimed that the dead men had fallen in line of duty and exhorted the living to carry on the fight for the rigid enforcement of the Eighteenth Amendment.

This time, however, neither the funeral dramatics nor the exhortations of the ministers had any inflammatory effect. The coroner's inquest, begun on the day the riot victims were buried, caused no ripple of excitement. A reporter for the *Marion Republican* noted the absence of ominous signs with some wonderment: nothing indicated "that three days before, the bustle of traffic on the streets had been punctuated by the crack of pistol shots and the moans of dying men." His story continued:

> School children with their books under their arms passed without so much as a casual glance at the armed militiamen who slowly stalked the principal streets. Women were downtown shopping early, dressed in their spring attire. The bright spring sunshine glistened on the polish of the automobiles that slipped through the traffic of trucks and pedestrians. Everywhere there was a stir as if the city had awakened from a period of lethargy. There was hardly parking place for automobiles downtown. Crowds gathered on the street corners, clerks rushed across the streets bareheaded, smiling and waving to friends passing by. There was everything to indicate, on the surface at least, that peace and rejoicing had come to Herrin with the springtime.

Even a resumption of raiding was taken in stride. Perhaps the spectacle of Boswell and Galligan conducting raids jointly, as they now proceeded to do, stunned the entire populace.

Early in May the grand jury met to investigate the election-day riots. Its members had before them the verdict of the coroner's jury: "Death by gunshot wounds at the hands of parties unknown." After remaining in session for more than two weeks the jurors came to the same conclusion. Not one of three hundred witnesses could or would name a single living participant in either the Smith garage battle or the Masonic Temple riot. The grand jury found no indictments, and adjourned.

Six weeks passed without the hint of a disturbance. Then Judge W. W. Duncan of the Illinois Supreme Court, who lived in Marion, called a meeting of the mayor and aldermen of Herrin, the county officials, and every factional leader of consequence. He had the promise of the state authorities, he informed them, that the troops who had been on duty since election day would be kept in the county until he was satisfied that peace had been established permanently. He was convinced that that time had come, but before notifying the governor of his decision he demanded that all who were present pledge their word that they would use every effort to control the troublemakers. All promised.

The governor responded to Duncan's notification by sending a telegram to every newspaper in the county. If, he warned, local officials failed to maintain order, and if it became necessary to send the militia in again, he would declare martial law.

Two weeks later, on July 16, 1926, the one company that had been on duty piled its machine guns and equipment into baggage cars and left for home. The Klan war was over.°

No war, however, ends with the firing of the last shot, or even with return to normal living. Costs always exceed gains, leaving a balance for the future to pay.

On the surface, the Klan cleaned up Williamson County. Open liquor-selling, open gambling, open vice were stamped out. It was soon to be demonstrated, however, that the bootlegger was still in business, though operating more warily and in the face of greater hazards than before. For this partial victory, twenty lives and a maiming-for-life were only a down payment. Long friendships had been broken, and the common ties of church, lodge, and labor union broken. Reunion, moreover, would come with agonizing slowness. Galligan wrote with prescience when he predicted: "The old hatreds will live on, through this generation, and into the next, for Williamson's blood is liberally tempered with the old mountaineer stock and Williamson's people are slow to forget, loath to forgive." Even today in Williamson County a man is more likely to be described as a "Klucker" or

---

° *The Klan still had a duty to perform. On August 8, 1926, three state officers of the Klan visited Herrin and Marion to pay the debts of the Williamson County Klan. At that time it was revealed that prominent local Klansmen had borrowed between $15,000 and $20,000 to finance the clean-up. The note had been reduced by substantial payments, but balances of $4,000 at two Herrin banks, and $3,400 at two Marion banks, remained unpaid. These were paid in full with funds from the Klan's national treasury.* Marion Republican, *August 9, 1926.*

"anti-Klucker" than as a Republican, or a Methodist, or a Mason, and the terms still carry a residue of animus or approbation.

Years would pass before the Italians of Herrin would consider themselves a part of the community in which they had formerly been at home. From the beginning of the crusade, the Klansmen denied, with some truth, that they were primarily anti-Catholic or anti-foreign. Yet, since most of the Italians were winemakers, and many of them bootleggers as well, they suffered the same consequences they would have if the Klan had been moved by religious or racial prejudices. The result was resentment and a cleavage that seriously retarded their amalgamation with the older stock.

Two and a half years of almost constant turmoil bred an abnormal degree of recklessness and lawlessness. "The joints were bad," a Herrin businessman said shortly after Young's death, "but I don't believe it was worth what it has cost to get rid of them. I would hate to have my boy conduct, or frequent, such places—but I would hate even worse to have him become a gun-toter, and a potential gun-fighter and murderer." Boys did become gun-toters, and some became murderers, who might have gone straight had the county kept its sanity.

Worst of all was the effect of the Klan warfare on the hard core of lawbreakers who had constituted themselves the gun-fighting opposition. Constant conflict gave this group solidarity, discipline, and contempt for orderly living. These qualities, in these men, would soon exact a heavy price.

12

GANG WAR

June 1926–January 1927

●●

What is Charlie Birger going to do? Will
he stand for the killing of his men? Is his
reply to be a pitched battle with the Shelton
crowd . . . or are his men to make reprisals
only where they can find single Shelton
gangsters? . . . *St. Louis Post-Dispatch,
October 27, 1926.*

TWO MONTHS after the election-day riot, coal miners on their
way to work found the body of a young man beside a country
road north of Herrin. Blood still seeped from a bullet wound in
the jaw. Evidently the dead man had been taken by surprise, for
the revolver he wore had not been fired. No one could identify
the body, and the murderer was never discovered.

A few days later a resident of Herrin was assailed as he sat in
his parked automobile and clubbed into unconsciousness.

One night during the first week of July a waiter at the Jefferson Hotel was badly beaten after an argument with a patron.

Mayor McCormack ordered the Herrin police to arrest all gunmen found in the city and throw them into jail unless they could
show some means of support. "We are at present having trouble," he announced, "with a gang of undesirable citizens who are
striving to keep up a reign of terror by beating up some respectable citizens without warning." And the State's Attorney filed an

information against Earl and Bernie Shelton and three of their followers—Ray Walker, Harry Walker, and "Blackie" Armes— charging them with assaulting the Jefferson Hotel waiter.

The mayor's threat and the State's Attorney's action accomplished nothing. Within a week a notorious character known as "Oklahoma Curly" was killed in a roadhouse on the outskirts of the city. Four days later three unmasked gunmen held up a gambling establishment in the basement of the European Hotel and robbed the patrons of watches, rings, pistols, and three thousand dollars in money. On the last day of July an eighteen-year-old Herrin boy was shot four times while taking part in the robbery of a local roadhouse.

"Keep calm," a local newspaper admonished its readers. "There may be a few roadhouse killings, because where there is wine, woman—and pistols—there is liable to be a little friendly argument any time." But as for calling in the troops again— unthinkable!

There were more roadhouse killings. On a Sunday night late in August Harry Walker and an ex-convict named Smith shot each other to death in what appeared to be a personal quarrel. Some of the townspeople, however, thought it ominous that one of the Sheltons and "Blackie" Armes should have been interested spectators at the coroner's inquest. Yet, in spite of the fact that Walker had been a Herrin policeman and the son of a former chief of police, another local paper shrugged off the killing as "a war among kindred tribes . . . just like the feuds in the larger cities. Unless new developments take place in which a general clean-up is staged between the feuding factions, there will be no further disturbance."

New developments soon took place. On the night of September 12 "Wild Bill" Holland, Mack Pulliam, and Pulliam's wife left a roadhouse near Herrin. As they entered their car two men opened fire from the shadows. The three victims slumped in their seats, unconscious. Someone drove the automobile with its bleeding passengers to Herrin and parked it in front of the hospital. When the occupants were found Holland was dead and Pulliam in serious condition. Both men were friends of Walker and Smith and adherents of the Sheltons.

Two days later Pulliam's family, apprehensive about his safety, decided to take the wounded man to a hospital in Benton. His mother rode in the ambulance with him, his wife followed in another car. A short distance south of Benton an automobile filled with armed men passed the ambulance at high speed, then swung across the road so as to block it. After ordering the men in the Pulliam party to line up with their hands in the air, the gunmen forced their way into the ambulance. Pulliam's mother, frantic, threw herself across her son's body and refused to move even when prodded with gun barrels. Finally one of the invaders grunted at the wounded man: "Well, we don't intend to kill a woman to get you." So they beat him into unconsciousness with gun butts and drove away. Later, in the hospital, Pulliam declined to comment on the affair, and no one in his party could or would identify the assailants.

Not even the local editors, anxious as they were to play down anything that might revive Williamson County's notoriety, could ignore the fact that the Holland killing and the attack on Pulliam signified that a gang war was in progress. With the defeat of the last remnant of the Klan in the election-day riot, bootleggers and gamblers had proliferated with hothouse luxuriance. Roadhouses had sprung into existence overnight until their number was larger than before the clean-up. Each was a gathering-place for actual or potential criminals—gunmen who had been drawn to the region during the Klan warfare, or local boys who had come to hold the law in contempt. Now the outlaws were fighting among themselves. Why they were fighting was not yet clear. The gangsters were shooting, not talking.

The mystery, however, did not last long. One day early in October loiterers on the streets of Marion noticed a big truck as it passed through the town and headed east. In place of the usual truck body it was equipped with a steel tank resembling those used by farmers for watering troughs. By itself, that would not have been unusual, but the tank was filled with men who made no effort to conceal the rifles and submachine guns they carried.

Near Harrisburg the men in the truck found the object of their search—Art Newman and his wife, driving westward on the highway. They fired a volley. Mrs. Newman was hit, but not hurt seriously; Newman escaped uninjured. Before the cumbersome truck could be turned around he sped away to safety.

Newman was a gambler, bootlegger, and former friend of the Sheltons who had recently broken with them. In Harrisburg he had been visiting Charlie Birger, also a former associate of the brothers and now, according to rumor, their bitter enemy. Apparently, the feud was between the Sheltons on the one hand and Birger on the other.

The alignment was confirmed a few days later when several carloads of armed men shot up a Shelton roadhouse north of Herrin. The place had not been occupied for several weeks, but on this particular night lights had been seen inside the building. The attacking party fired several rounds, then battered in the door, smashed the fixtures, and riddled the interior with bullets. Soon afterward, carrying their guns, they swaggered into the lunchroom of the Jefferson Hotel. "If anybody wants to know who did the shooting," one of the men bragged, "tell them that Charlie Birger did it." A few days later Birger himself urged a St. Louis reporter to visit the ruined roadhouse. "Look it over," he said, "and see what these babies"—pointing to his machine guns—"can do."

Within two weeks—on the early morning of October 26—the body of a Birger follower known as "High Pockets" McQuay was found on an old dirt road between Herrin and Johnston City. A bullet-riddled Ford coupé stood near by. On the same day the body of Ward Jones, one of Birger's bartenders who went by the inevitable name of "Casey," was discovered in a creek near Equality in Saline County, thirty-five miles east of the spot where McQuay had been killed. Birger claimed both men as his own, charged the Sheltons with the killings, and swore vengeance.

By all signs, a pitched battle was imminent. The day before the bodies of his two henchmen were discovered Birger and several of his men paid a call on Joe Adams, a great lump of a man who combined in his person the somewhat incongruous callings of roadhouse operator, Stutz dealer, and mayor of West City, the small town on the edge of Benton in which he lived and operated. Birger had heard that the Sheltons had left the steel tank of their truck at Adams's garage for repairs.

"You old son-of-a-bitch," Birger told the mayor, "you give me the top to that armored truck, or I'll drill you so full of holes people won't know your corpse."

Adams refused. An argument followed, which Birger ended with an ultimatum and another threat:

"It's almost midnight now, and if you'll deliver that half a truck, right side up with care, at 'The Hut' before five a.m. you'll save yourself a lot of trouble with undertakers and caskets, if you know what I mean."

At a near-by barbecue stand, where the gang stopped before leaving West City, Birger became even more explicit:

"If that tank isn't delivered to me before five o'clock tomorrow morning, we're going to kill that double-bellied son-of-a-bitch, and the God-damned Franklin County law isn't big enough to stop us!"

Instead of complying, Adams called on the county authorities for protection. When they refused it he appealed to the Sheltons, who had been his friends for years. With a number of armed men they fortified the garage and waited for Birger and his gang to return. The State's Attorney learned of the presence of the mayor's allies and ordered them from the county. They left.

Early on the following morning a farmer who lived beside a roadhouse, reputedly Birger's property, near Johnston City, saw fifteen or twenty men stealthily emerge from the near-by woods and open fire on the place. In a few minutes it caught fire. The men laughed and talked as they watched the flames. Passing motorists slowed down, but none dared stop. As dawn broke, the attackers slipped back into the woods, where they had parked their cars, and drove away.

> The old tenseness, the just-before-the-battle feeling, has returned to Williamson County [the *St. Louis Post-Dispatch* reported]. Where men meet on the street corners the talk is of the gang war. What is Charlie Birger going to do? Will he stand for the killing of his men? Is his reply to be a pitched battle with the Shelton crowd, perhaps along the Williamson County roads or in one of the towns, or are his men to make reprisals only where they can find single Shelton gangsters by themselves?

Newspaper reporters decided that the best answer to these questions could be had from Birger himself. Their usual procedure was to drive out to his roadhouse halfway between Marion and Harrisburg and park at a barbecue stand that served as an outpost of the main establishment. One of the several men who always lounged there would go to Birger's headquarters—a large cabin on the edge of a grove a hundred yards from the road. When the messenger returned, four or five heavily armed roughs, all young, would escort the visitor to the gang leader.

The cabin, known usually as "Shady Rest" but sometimes called "The Hut," had been built in 1924. By way of amusement it offered not only bootleg liquor and gambling, but also cockfights and dog fights. During the day, when patronage was light, liquor runners from Florida lay over there so that they could make the last leg of the trip to St. Louis after dark. Though notorious throughout southern Illinois, "Shady Rest" was never molested by the authorities.

Now, its patronage frightened away by the gang war, the place had been put in shape to stand a siege. Its foot-thick logs were practically bulletproof, and the deep basement would be a safe place even during an attack. Rifles, sub-machine guns, and boxes of ammunition lined the walls; cases of canned goods assured plenty of food. A truck with an open body sheathed with steel plate—Birger's answer to the Sheltons' mounted tank—stood in the yard. Floodlights, supplied with electricity generated on the grounds, prevented surprise after dark.

Visitors meeting Birger for the first time were invariably impressed by his attractive appearance and pleasant greeting. Dark skin, prominent cheekbones, and heavy black hair suggested his Russian Jewish parentage, but he spoke with no trace of accent. His handshake was hearty, his smile quick. The riding-breeches, puttees, and leather jacket that he customarily wore were neat and clean. Just under six feet tall, he carried himself with military erectness, and looked younger than his forty-four years. He usually wore two guns in holsters, and often cradled a submachine gun in one arm as he sat and talked.

By his own account, he had been born in New York City. While he was still a young child his parents, recent immigrants, moved to St. Louis. There, as he always related with pride, he had first gone to school. After a few years the family removed to Glen Carbon, a coal town near East St. Louis. That was his home until the outbreak of the Spanish-American War. Though under age, he enlisted in the Regular Army, served his full term in a cavalry regiment, and was honorably discharged. On his return he found life in Glen Carbon insufferably dull and escaped it by going to South Dakota, where he worked for three years as a cowhand. Back in southern Illinois once more, he drifted into saloonkeeping and gambling. After prohibition, he became a bootlegger.

In the fall of 1923 Birger achieved sudden notoriety when he killed two men in three days. The first was a youth of seventeen —Cecil Knighton by name—who had worked for him as a bartender. Police, called as soon as shots were heard, found Knighton dead, and Birger standing over him with a shotgun in his hands. The next day a coroner's jury brought in a verdict of self-defense. His second victim was a St. Louis gangster named

"Whitey" Doering, under sentence on a federal robbery-charge but out on bail pending an appeal. According to Birger's story Doering called him out from his roadhouse, then fired at him as he stepped from the door. Birger fired back. Doering was mortally wounded; Birger, hit in the arm and lung, recovered. Again he was exonerated on a plea of self-defense.

The next year he made news by drawing a fine of $2,500 and a jail sentence of a year for violation of the prohibition law—the heaviest sentence passed by the court in the trials arising from the Klan clean-up.

Yet many people chose to see Birger as a public benefactor rather than as a killer, bootlegger, and ex-convict. In Harrisburg, where he lived with his fourth wife and two small children of former marriages, he had helped many a person in need. One severe winter he had canvassed the town and sent coal to all the destitute families he could find. On another occasion he had bought schoolbooks for the children whose parents could not afford to buy them themselves. He let it be known that he would not permit a resident of Harrisburg to patronize one of his gambling tables—"you can't win in a professional game." He claimed, perhaps with justification, that he had forestalled several robberies in his home town. With the outbreak of the gang war he assumed the role of public protector, assuring his fellow townsmen that "in Harrisburg, his home, where he was educating his children," no one would be harmed. Even on the public highways they would be safe "because a gangster's bullet in this instance will be aimed at an enemy gangster."

To the reporters who questioned him about the causes of the gang war he talked freely. He had first met Carl Shelton in the fall of 1923, when he was in the Herrin hospital recuperating from the wounds he had received in the Doering affray. The two men became personal friends and business associates in bootlegging and the slot-machine racket, which they practically monopolized in Williamson County. In all the Klan fighting they stood together against the clean-up forces.

Birger admitted that he was resentful when the Sheltons, as he charged, skulked the last battle with the Klan in April 1926, while three of his own men were killed, but the real break with his former partners came as the result of his determination to protect the people of Harrisburg from harm and robbery. In late August, according to his story, "Blackie" Armes and several Shelton gangsters—none of the brothers was in the group—robbed a Harrisburg businessman of a valuable diamond ring that they intended to hold until he redeemed it with cash. Birger forced them to return it.

After that it was war, though as yet undeclared. "The Shelton gang just began to shoot up roadhouses where I had been," he said, "and I knew what that meant. Every time I would visit a place, 'Blooey,' a few minutes later the Sheltons' armored truck would go by and pour in the lead.

"Now," he told a *St. Louis Star* reporter, "I'm out to get Shelton or any of his men, because if I don't get them they'll get me."

He continued with no more emotion than most men would display in discussing a business transaction:

"I showed what I'd do to them when we caught Mack Pulliam, one of Shelton's friends, on the road in an ambulance a few weeks ago. His mother was sitting beside him, and they had some sort of a procession . . . to make it look like a funeral and fool us. But I and my men drove up and conked that fellow until he fainted away. We showed him."

His gang, he always emphasized, had been formed only for protection. Where the Sheltons were a crowd of "red hots"—"professional trigger-pullers and roughnecks"—his boys were simple coal-miners, farmers, and clerks, brought together by their friendship for a man in a tight spot. Yet he would match them any time against his enemies. "The boys would be tickled pink to have it out on the open road," he told Roy Alexander of the *St. Louis Post-Dispatch*. "We don't want to have a shooting scrape in any of the towns where someone might get hurt, but we're glad to meet the Shelton crowd any time.

214

"And," he concluded soberly, "it's likely we will."

The Sheltons were natives of southern Illinois. Their father, as a young man, had come from Kentucky to settle in Wayne County, where he had married a local girl. He was a sober, God-fearing farmer who worked hard but without much success. He and his wife were the parents of numerous children, but for practical purposes, in the twenties, "the Sheltons" meant three of the five brothers—Carl, born in 1888; Earl, two years younger; and Bernie, born in 1899.

The boys had been brought up on the farm, but from early youth they had shown an aversion to farm work. Carl and Earl took to leaving home for months at a time to drive taxicabs in St. Louis or East St. Louis. When he was old enough Bernie followed their example. All had an aptitude for trouble. In the fall of 1915 Earl was convicted of compounding a felony—a charge arising from a holdup in which he had participated some months earlier in Wayne County—and was sent to the Illinois State Penitentiary at Pontiac, where he served eighteen and a half months. About the same time Carl, in St. Louis, pleaded guilty to a charge of petty larceny and was sentenced to a year in the workhouse. Bernie was arrested in a stolen car while Earl was still in prison, sentenced to a year in the workhouse, but paroled.

After Carl and Earl had served their terms they worked in Illinois mines, but about 1920, with Bernie, they located again in East St. Louis. Prohibition gave them their chance. They ran gambling houses and bootlegging establishments in East St. Louis and its environs, but the coal counties to the south and east offered a field too tempting to be ignored. John Bartlow Martin describes what happened:

> Each coal town had its own gang of local toughs, gamblers, and bootleggers. The only things needed to weld these into a monopoly were brains and guns. Birger and the Sheltons had both. They allowed the local boys to continue to operate, but only under their protection and selling their liquor. . . . The advantages of this orderly

215

system were quickly apparent to many law-enforcement officers—it reduced local rivalries that made trouble and it increased the amount and certainty of the payoff to the officials. . . . Some sheriffs cooperated for money, some "as a matter of survival"—the gangsters became so strong that the remaining honest officials could not cope with them. Soon the Shelton boys were in command.[*]

The Shelton brothers were hardly—as Williamson County legend today would have it—wild but essentially good boys who were driven to lawlessness by the persecution of S. Glenn Young and his fanatical Klansmen. They were men with criminal records who fought the Klan because if it succeeded in cleaning up Williamson and other counties it would put them out of a very lucrative business.

Now, as the Sheltons fought again for survival, newspaper men sought their story of the feud with Birger. Having no fixed headquarters, they were harder to find than their enemy; found, they were less loquacious, but the reporters had some success.

A representative of the *St. Louis Star* located Carl Shelton at his home in East St. Louis. Armed men filled the parlor; women and children occupied the rear rooms. The gang leader—tall, dark, heavily built—spoke slowly and softly until the reporter told him that Birger had charged him with the possession of stolen cars. Then he flared up:

"So Birger says I have hot cars, and that I'm a bootlegger, does he? Well, let me tell you, I'll run a list of the registry numbers of my cars in the newspapers any day, and that's more than he'll dare do.

"I'll admit I'm a bootlegger," Shelton continued, "but he is too, and the people in Williamson County have known that about both of us for a long time."

The Shelton brothers, he said, had left Williamson County for

---

[*] *"The Shelton Boys," copyright 1950 by the Curtis Publishing Company, included in* Butcher's Dozen and Other Murders (*New York: Harper, 1950*), p. 109. Quoted by permission.

good, but he implied that they had no intention of leaving the territory to Birger.

"I can prove enough on Birger," he promised in ending the interview, "to make him Uncle Sam's boarder for a long, long time, and I'm going to do it."

Earl Shelton, ill with malaria in an East St. Louis hospital, was more expansive. The Sheltons, he told a *Post-Dispatch* reporter, were not given to boasting like that "coward" Birger.

"He's got himself all hemmed in with armor and machine guns, and whenever you see a man hiding behind a fortress, that means he's afraid to come out in the open.

"He talks about wanting to meet us on the highway. . . . If we didn't know he was only blowing, we might get excited and go up there to see what it's all about, but we know Birger and aren't taking his loud talk very seriously."

The first disagreement with Birger, Earl said, came when he and his brothers refused to help smuggle some of Birger's Russian relatives into Florida. The real difficulty, however, had its origin in the slot-machine partnership. Under their agreement, the Sheltons and Birger were to split the profits on a fifty-fifty basis. After a time the brothers learned, by underworld channels, that Birger had held out three thousand dollars. Confronted with the charge, he claimed that he had spent it for protection. Whereupon, Earl snorted, "we banished him."

What about the Shelton "gang"? the reporter asked.

"Our so-called gang," Earl replied with an air of innocence, "consists of friends, all natives of Williamson County, who took common cause with us in our fight against the Ku Klux Klan. We were not robbers or gunmen, but we never ran away from trouble. We don't know whether any of our friends are in the fight against Birger, but if they are, they will take care of themselves. We're out of it."

Despite the talk of their leaders, neither gang moved toward a pitched battle. The in-fighting, however, continued. On a Saturday night early in November 1926, a shady character named

Milroy was riddled with machine-gun bullets as he left a roadhouse near the mining town of Colp. The mayor and chief of police, called from another roadhouse near by, were shot from the darkness as they stepped out of their car. The mayor was fatally wounded; the chief, who ran at the first shot, escaped with a shattered hand. Both officers, rumor had it, were in the bad graces of the Sheltons.

A few days later someone tossed a homemade bomb from a speeding car near Birger's roadhouse. Intended for the barbecue stand by the roadside, it was thrown too soon and missed its mark. Birger's place was unharmed, but an innocent farmer, two hundred yards away, was terrified and suffered a considerable loss in shattered windowpanes.

The bomb was thrown about two o'clock on the morning of November 10. At the same hour, on the 12th, machine gunners, supposedly Birger gangsters, shot up Joe Adams's home in West City. Hours later, in full daylight, an airplane flew low over Shady Rest. After circling the woods around the cabin it returned at a higher altitude. Several of Birger's men, watching apprehensively, saw three bundles leave the plane in quick succession. One fell apart in the air, but two plumped to the ground near the cabin. They turned out to be bombs constructed of sticks of dynamite bound around bottles of nitroglycerine, but so crudely made that none exploded. The attack was attributed to the Sheltons, repaying Birger for shooting up the home of Joe Adams, their ally.

The following week a dynamite bomb, thrown from a passing automobile, exploded in front of Adams's house. It damaged the porch, blew off the front door, and shattered the windowpanes. Had the bomb fallen ten feet closer to its mark, Adams, his wife, and brother—all in the house at the time—might have been fatally injured. As it was, they escaped harm.

But not for long. On a Sunday afternoon in mid-December Mrs. Adams answered a knock on the front door. Two young men asked whether Joe was at home.

"Won't I do?" she asked.

"Tell him we have a letter from Carl," one of them replied.

Mrs. Adams left. A moment later her husband, eyes heavy with sleep, lumbered to the door. One of the boys handed him the note. While he read both drew pistols, fired them into his huge fat body, and ran. He lived long enough to whisper to his wife that he did not recognize either of the men who shot him.

The next day, at the coroner's inquest, Mrs. Adams placed the blame for her husband's death on Charlie Birger. During the last several weeks, she testified, he had telephoned repeatedly, sometimes as often as three times a day. Once, in Joe's absence, he had asked:

"Mrs. Adams, have you got much insurance on Joe's life?"

"No, not very much," she replied.

"Well," Birger said quietly, "you'd better get a lot more because we're going to kill him, and you'll need it."

Gus Adams, the mayor's younger brother, and Arian, his fourteen-year-old daughter, corroborated the widow's statements. Arian, moreover, remembered the occasion when Birger had demanded that her father turn over to him the tank with which the Sheltons had armored their truck. Standing on the sidewalk, she had heard Birger say: "We're going to kill you, you big fat son-of-a-bitch." The girl brought out the ugly word without hesitation.

Birger, questioned about the murder, told a correspondent for the International News Service:

"I don't know who killed Adams, but I'm certainly glad he was killed. Everyone comes to me to ask who did this and that. What am I—a detective force for southern Illinois? What the hell does anyone care who killed Adams?"

The gang war moved toward a climax. To many people in the community, and elsewhere, that point was reached on the early morning of Sunday, January 9, 1927. About midnight a farmer who lived a short distance from Shady Rest was awakened by five or six shots that seemed to come from the vicinity of the resort. He had no more than dropped off to sleep again when an explosion, apparently at the same location, aroused him. Rushing to the window, he saw the cabin fall apart, and felt his own house tremble on its foundation from a second blast. Flames flickered tentatively for a few minutes, and then lighted the countryside as they consumed the logs of the resort.

When dawn broke, and curious spectators thought it safe to approach close enough to see what had happened, they found only ashes, burning embers, and the remains of four bodies charred beyond recognition.

A body blow by the Sheltons, everyone said, and one that would undoubtedly end the gang war. Birger was no fool. Surely he would realize that he was beaten, and that if he attempted to continue hostilities he would lose his life as he had lost his stronghold.

The analysis was sound as logic but inaccurate as prophecy.

One of the most frequent visitors at Shady Rest was a state highway patrolman named Lory Price. Rumor had it that he worked with Birger in the stolen-car racket—that Birger's men would steal a car, hold it until a reward was posted, then park it in some out-of-the-way spot and tip off the officer. Price would "find" the automobile and divide the reward with the gangsters.

Whether that was true or not, it is certain that Price was on intimate terms with Birger and several of his men. Moreover, he was known to have stopped at Shady Rest only a few minutes before the first of the explosions that destroyed it, and he was one of the first persons to visit the ruins on the following morning. At the inquest into the death of the victims he gave important testimony. On the night of January 8, he said, he had stopped at the Birger resort after attending a motion-picture show at Marion. Steve George, the caretaker, greeted him at the door of the cabin and asked him to come in to meet his wife. While there he noticed a man whom he had never seen before sitting, half-intoxicated, beside the fireplace, and George had shown him a boy whom he called Clarence dead drunk on a cot in an adjoining room.

"When this man leaves," George said, pointing to the stranger, "I'm going to bed."

By his own testimony, Price remained a few minutes only and then returned to Marion. There, seated at a lunch counter, he heard the two explosions that signalized the destruction of Shady Rest.

One week after Price appeared before the coroner's jury, his stepfather, who lived near his home on the outskirts of Marion, became concerned over the fact that he had seen neither the highway officer nor his wife for two full days. When his knocks brought no response, he telephoned the sheriff's office. Deputies forced the door. Price's uniform lay on a chair, his pistol and cartridge-belt on the dining-room table. Although the bed was rumpled, Mrs. Price had not retired—her nightgown, neatly folded, was still on the coverlet. The fact that her hat and coat were missing, and that telephone wires leading to the house were cut, pointed to a kidnapping.

Or a murder. Perhaps two murders.

13

MURDER—AND MORE MURDER

January 1927–July 1927

•••

> I don't know what in the hell's the matter
> with me. . . . Every time I kill a man it
> makes me sick afterwards. I guess it's my
> stomach. *Charlie Birger, January 17, 1927.*

FROM ALL appearances, Birger was finished. Shady Rest was
gone, the men of his gang had dispersed, his rivals had taken
over his bootlegging business, he himself was under suspicion of
murder.

Actually, Birger's round was coming up.

During the fall of 1926, foreseeing, perhaps, that the Sheltons
might win a war of guns and dynamite and armored cars and
aerial bombs, he had resorted to finesse. Almost two years earlier—on January 27, 1925—a post-office messenger at Collinsville, Illinois, had been robbed of a mine payroll amounting to
twenty-one thousand dollars. So far the crime was unsolved.
Birger hunted up a postal inspector, told him that the Sheltons
had pulled the job, and convinced the officer that he knew what
he was talking about. Early in November a federal grand jury
returned secret indictments naming the three brothers. One by
one they were arrested and released on bond.

Their trial opened in the United States court at Quincy on the
last day of January, 1927, with Judge Louis Fitzhenry presiding.
Since both Newman and Birger were expected to testify, interest

ran high. The authorities, fearing gunplay, scattered deputy marshals and detectives around the courtroom; spectators were searched as they entered.

Newman, the government's first important witness, held the stand—and the spotlight—for three hours. Small, trim, dapper, hard, he sat in the witness chair with legs crossed and hands clasped over one knee, an embodiment of self-assurance. Whenever he mentioned the Sheltons in his story of their former friendship his voice dripped with contempt.

Early in January 1925, he related, Carl Shelton had asked him if he wanted in on a good thing.

"I said sure, but when he told me it was a mail robbery, I backed out."

He heard nothing more until the morning of January 27, when Carl telephoned him at his home in East St. Louis. That was the day Ora Thomas was to be buried, and Shelton wanted Newman to drive him and his brothers to Herrin for the funeral. Newman demurred.

"I told him I was tired and that he would get in trouble going there."

"Well," Shelton answered (so Newman said), "we pulled that Collinsville job this morning and we must have an alibi and it's up to you to give it."

Newman yielded, and started for Herrin with the brothers in his car. At Marion, however, Delos Duty dissuaded them from continuing. In the afternoon they loafed around the county seat and then returned to East St. Louis. Late that night Newman dropped in at Shelton's saloon. There, in a back room, were Carl Shelton and Charlie Briggs, with bundles of money on a card table before them.

"See you later, Art," Carl said in a greeting that was a command to leave. Newman left.

The witness swore that it was at least nine a.m. before he took Shelton's telephone call, and that the party had not started for the funeral before nine thirty or ten. The Collinsville robbery had taken place at seven a.m. Since Collinsville is only ten miles from East St. Louis, the Sheltons had plenty of time to make their way to the latter city, even by a devious route.

Newman was followed on the stand by a weak-chinned, ferret-faced ne'er-do-well named Harvey Dungey, who was actually one of Birger's liquor runners, although that fact was not known at the time. Dungey testified that in January 1925 he was driving a taxi in East St. Louis, and that on the early morning of the robbery he took several passengers to Collinsville. At about six thirty, while approaching his destination, he saw a stalled Buick. Carl Shelton was looking at the engine, Bernie sat at the wheel.

Dungey's testimony was of critical importance, since he was the only witness to place the defendants near the scene of the crime at the approximate time it was committed. But the crowd in the courtroom paid only perfunctory attention to what he said. They had come to see and hear Charlie Birger.

The gang leader entered with the nonchalance of a veteran actor. Instead of his outdoor costume he wore a freshly pressed gray suit, and his wavy black hair was carefully brushed and parted. Ignoring the Sheltons, he bowed slightly to the jury, took the oath, and then awaited interrogation with a faint but confident smile on his swarthy face.

"Did you have any conversation with the defendants about the Collinsville robbery?" District Attorney Provine asked.

"Yes, sir, I did," Birger replied. "It was in January 1925, at Nineteenth and Market streets, in East St. Louis. Carl said he had been thinking about starting to haul whisky up from Florida. He had a payroll job in Collinsville, he told me, and when he got through with that he was going to start hauling whisky."

"And the next time?"

"That was at my house five or six days after Ora Thomas's funeral," Birger continued. "Carl, Earl and Bernie and Charlie Briggs split $3,600 in my dining-room. When I looked in, Carl said: 'This is some of Uncle Sam's money, but we won't need you for an alibi because we were at Ora Thomas's funeral.'

"I asked Carl how much they got," Birger went on, "and he said about $21,000. He told me Bernie drove the car up to Collinsville, and that he and Earl and Briggs went up with him. Briggs got out and grabbed the sack, and fell down getting back into the car.

"That," the witness concluded, "was about all they ever said about the job."

After twenty minutes, his story unshaken by cross-examination, Birger walked from the courtroom, again without even glancing at the defendants.

The Sheltons denied all the assertions made by the government witnesses. The day after the appearance of Birger and his henchmen, Carl, tall, taciturn, soft-spoken, took the stand in his own defense. When asked by his attorney whether he had any connection whatever with the mail robbery at Collinsville he replied in a level, emotionless voice:

"No, sir."

"Mr. Shelton," came the next question, "did you ever talk to Art Newman about any robbery?"

"No, sir."

"Were you ever in the dining-room of Charles Birger's home at Harrisburg, Illinois, when a robbery was discussed and the proceeds of a robbery talked about or divided?"

"No, sir."

"Are you friendly with Charles Birger?"

"No, sir."

One phase of the District Attorney's cross-examination relieved the tension of the proceedings. When asked where he lived in East St. Louis Shelton leaned back in his chair, studied the ceiling, turned to smile at the judge, then stared at the floor. Finally his lawyer came to his rescue with an objection, which the court sustained.

"How long have you lived in East St. Louis?" he was asked.

"About one year. Since December 1925."

"What is your present business?"

225

After a long pause Shelton replied:

"Collection agency."

Guffaws from the spectators disrupted proceedings for several minutes.

Earl and Bernie, following Carl on the stand, corroborated his testimony. So did a succession of other witnesses—Joe McGlynn, an East St. Louis lawyer who had accompanied the brothers on the morning of January 27; Delos Duty, who confirmed their statement that they had called at his office in Marion before noon; an East St. Louis taxicab operator who denied that Harvey Dungey was in his employ at the time of the robbery; Mrs. Mack Pulliam, who created something of a sensation when she related that Birger had told her husband, in her hearing, that he intended to pin the robbery on his former friends. And defense attorneys, in their closing arguments, hammered on the obvious animus of Birger and Newman.

The jury, however, preferred to believe the accusers. Five hours after receiving the case the jurors brought in a verdict of guilty. The defendants took it without the twitch of a facial muscle; their wives, seated in the spectators' section of the courtroom, were equally stoic.

The next day the three Shelton brothers were sentenced to twenty-five years in the federal penitentiary.

The proceedings at Quincy threw light on many aspects of the gang war; others were clarified, more or less, by Art Newman's "inside story," which the *St. Louis Post-Dispatch* ran simultaneously with its reports of the Shelton trial.*

Newman dated his acquaintance with the Sheltons from the

* Late in January 1927, Sam O'Neal, then a Post-Dispatch *reporter and now a public-relations counselor in Washington, received a telephone call from Art Newman at Gillespie, Illinois. Newman asked O'Neal to meet him there as soon as possible. At Gillespie, O'Neal found Freddie Wooten and Connie Ritter, both Birger gangsters, as well as Newman. The three men proposed to sell their story of the gang war to the* Post-Dispatch. *O'Neal arranged for them to meet O. K. Bovard, the managing editor, the following day. Bovard agreed to buy the series, but wanted Birger's name also. As O'Neal remembers it, the three gangsters were to receive $1,500 each in any event, $2,000 each if Birger would permit the use of his name, and*

time when S. Glenn Young and his wife were shot in the Okaw Bottoms. On the representation of a friend that the brothers were "high-class boys" who were broke and in trouble, he gave them free board and room at the Arlington Hotel, the disreputable East St. Louis establishment of which he was then proprietor. Despite some friction, all remained on good terms until Newman shot and killed a friend of his three free boarders in a barroom brawl. (He was acquitted on the usual plea of self-defense.) After the killing he spent a year in Memphis. When he returned he discovered that the Sheltons were still his enemies, so he joined forces with Birger.

(Ironically, it was Carl Shelton who had introduced him to Birger in the first place. "Boys," Carl had said to Newman and Freddie Wooten, "I want you to meet a high-class man. If you ever need any help in Williamson County he's the one who can give it to you.")

The first killings in the gang war had taken place before Newman returned to Illinois, but he told the reporters what he had heard about them. Walker and Smith, who died in August 1926, were killed by a gangster whom he refused to name, "but that wasn't hardly a gang shooting—it was just a drunken brawl." On the other hand the attack on Holland and Pulliam, in which one was killed and the other wounded, was the work of Birger's men, who expected to find Carl Shelton in the company of the two victims. The Sheltons retaliated with the murder of "High Pockets" McQuay, Birger's bartender, and "Casey" Jones.

Newman still sorrowed over the death of Jones. "We gave him a mighty fine funeral," he assured the reporters. "It cost $498. Charlie Birger paid for it because Casey was a good man and

---

Birger would be paid either $3,000 or $4,000. Birger, approached later, refused.

O'Neal, John Rogers (now dead), and Roy Alexander (now managing editor of Time) spent two or three days talking with Newman, Wooten, and Ritter in a hotel at Carlinville. The series was written by Alexander, since O'Neal and Rogers were covering the Shelton trial by the time it appeared. So O'Neal wrote me on April 6, 1951.

Charlie issued orders that he was to have plenty of flowers."

Newman admitted that the Birger gang had threatened Joe Adams and that they had taken $750 in a raid on his roadhouse, but he knew nothing about the murder. On the afternoon the corpulent mayor was killed, he and Connie Ritter were in Marion, Birger was at Shady Rest, Wooten at East St. Louis.

"Of course," Newman said, "we didn't shed any tears about Adams getting killed. We all had a drink on it and if we had known who shot him we would have bought them a drink too."

With the arrest of the Sheltons for mail robbery, and the death of Joe Adams, Birger concluded that the war had ended in his favor. He no longer needed to keep an armed garrison at Shady Rest. The men left, and thus only Steve George, the caretaker, and his wife were at the resort on the night it was destroyed. (Four bodies, in fact, were found.)

The three gangsters told Sam O'Neal that they planned "to get the hell out of these parts" as soon as the Shelton trial was over; that was why they were willing to tell their story.

The verdict in the Shelton trial caused a sensation; so did the revelations of Art Newman. But the biggest sensation of all made headlines on February 5. The body of Lory Price had been found.

That morning a farmer walking across a field near Dubois, a little town in the southeastern corner of Washington County thirty-five miles north of Herrin, had come across a partly clothed dead body. Several bullet-holes were visible. Evidently it had lain there for several days, since animals had gnawed the hands away. County officials, summoned at once, identified the dead man as the missing state policeman.

Reporters broke the news to the Sheltons, in jail in Quincy awaiting removal to Leavenworth. Bernie said: "Oh"; Earl was silent; Carl asked whether they had also found the body of Mrs. Price.

"I hope she's living so she can tell who did it. That's what I hope."

228

The remark seemed to be significant, and the reporter pursued it.

"Have you any idea who killed Lory Price?" he asked.

"Well, this is my theory. You know he used to hang around Charlie Birger's place, and the papers said he was there a few nights before it was burned down, and Birger, you know, is always suspicious of spies. I always figured he did away with Price on the theory that Price was spying to inform those who destroyed it of a good time to do it. I never had any trouble with Price, and I don't know his wife."

Art Newman, still in touch with the *Post-Dispatch* men, would say only that "Slim"—the dead officer's nickname—"was a friend of our crowd and the Shelton gang must have got him."

Birger could not be located.

Southern Illinois simmered with speculation about the murder of Price and the fate of his wife, but nothing happened. Nothing, that is, except a trial—strictly speaking, two trials—to which few, in the prevailing excitement, paid much attention. The principals were only minor hoodlums charged with robbery, and neither their status nor their crime was important enough to attract notice.

In January Sheriff Oren Coleman had raided a whorehouse in Herrin, where he found several articles that had been stolen in two separate robberies not long before. He arrested the proprietor, a young woman who went by the name of Jackie Williams; Pearl Phelps, a girl who was present; and three young hangers-on of Charlie Birger. A fourth was picked up subsequently.

The four men were tried at Marion early in March for one of the robberies, and freed when the jury failed to reach a verdict. The next day three of them went on trial for the second offense. This time they were convicted, and sentenced to ten years in the penitentiary.

The principal witnesses for the prosecution were the two women. At the time of their arrest they had been on intimate terms with two of the defendants, but during the weeks they

spent in jail—the sheriff had held them on a liquor charge—
they became convinced that their lovers had thrown them over.
On the stand they testified with venom. They swore that the defendants had brought the stolen property to Jackie's place and
left it there, that they had forced them at gunpoint to indulge in
abnormal sexual practices, and that they had threatened them
with death if they ever revealed what had happened. The second
jury believed them.

One of the defendants thus convicted was Harry Thomasson,
nineteen years old. With five brothers he had been orphaned at
an early age, and had spent his boyhood in orphanages and foster homes. A year before his conviction, he and his brother Elmo,
two years his senior, had become attached to Birger, who took
them into his gang when he assembled it. Harry had not seen
Elmo since the night Shady Rest was destroyed, and by the time
of his trial he had become convinced that his brother was one of
the four people whose bodies were found in the ruins.

While Thomasson was being held in the Williamson County
jail awaiting trial on the robbery charges, State's Attorney Roy C.
Martin of Franklin County, in which Joe Adams had been killed,
worked on a clue. In his possession was the note that the murderers had handed their victim before they shot him. It read:

Friend Joe: If you can use these boys please do it. They are
broke and need work. I knew their father. C. S.

To Martin the sentence, "I knew their father," indicated that the
boys were brothers. Presumably, the writer of the note would
have foreseen such an interpretation and have avoided any
wording that might give rise to it, yet even the wiliest criminals
slip occasionally. At any rate, the clue was worth following.

Martin soon established the fact that the only brothers in either gang who could be called boys—and the killers of Adams
were indubitably young—were Harry and Elmo Thomasson. As
his next step, he arranged to have Mrs. Adams see Harry in the
jail without being seen. She identified him positively as one of

the two young men whom she had met at the door the afternoon her husband was killed. Elmo, presumably dead, she identified from photographs.

In sentencing Harry after the robbery trial the judge had decreed that because of his age he should serve the first two years of his term in the Pontiac Reformatory rather than in the penitentiary. Martin gave the young convict several weeks in which to brood, and then went to Pontiac. With him he took John T. Rogers of the *Post-Dispatch*, who had an uncanny ability to make criminals talk. Between them they convinced young Thomasson that they knew he and his brother had killed Adams, and that he would fare better if he confessed and pleaded guilty than if he stood trial. By this time Thomasson had come to believe that Birger himself had fired Shady Rest, and was thus responsible for Elmo's death; he also blamed the gang leader for failing to help him at the time of his own trial. The boy cracked, told his story, and agreed to plead guilty and testify in open court whenever called upon.

On April 30, 1927, loiterers in the circuit courtroom at Benton saw the bailiff lead in a slight young man clothed in a rough, ill-fitting, prison-made suit. State's Attorney Martin presented him to Judge Charles H. Miller:

"This is Harry Thomasson, who is one of several Birger gangsters under indictment for the murder of Joe Adams. He wishes to plead guilty."

The spectators—few in number, since no word of what was coming had leaked out—came to attention as the judge reminded the prisoner of the seriousness of the charge and the possible consequences of his plea. Then he asked:

"Do you wish to plead guilty?"

"I do," Thomasson answered.

The court appointed two lawyers who happened to be present to act as counsel for the defendant, the clerk read the indictment, and Thomasson started to tell his story. After a few sentences Judge Miller interrupted.

"Why are you so insistent on pleading guilty of murder?"

Thomasson answered quietly and without any of the arrogance that had characterized his behavior when he was on trial before:

"Because Charlie Birger, Art Newman, Connie Ritter, and Freddie Wooten blew up Shady Rest cabin and killed my brother."

He proceeded:

"On the morning of the murder, one of the Birger gang called me at my home in West Frankfort and told me to come to Shady Rest. I got in a car and went to Shady Rest where my brother Elmo had stayed the night before. Birger, Newman, Ritter and Ray Hyland were there. They gave Elmo a .38 and me a .45."

Hyland, Thomasson continued, drove the two boys to West City. Newman and Ritter, in another car, followed them as far as Marion, and arranged to meet them after the killing.

"When we reached West City," the prisoner related, "Elmo and I went to Adams's house, leaving Hyland sitting in the car. We knocked on the door and then Adams came. Elmo handed him the note, and while he was reading it, I shot him twice with the revolver which I had hidden up my sleeve. Elmo then shot him once. We then ran back to the car where Hyland was waiting, and drove away. That night, Elmo went back to Shady Rest and stayed there all night, but I stayed in a hotel in Harrisburg.

"The next day," Thomasson concluded, "I went back to Shady Rest and they paid us $150, fifty dollars for each shot fired."

Martin, State's Attorney, joined with the prisoner's counsel in asking for mercy.

"I shall sentence you to life imprisonment," the court responded.

Thomasson walked from the courtroom without faltering. Outside he asked to see Gus Adams, the dead man's brother, and when Adams came up, offered his hand. Gus took it.

"I'm sorry I killed Joe," Thomasson said. "I never knew him

and he never did me any wrong. I had to do it. I'm sorry for you. My own brother was killed too."

Tears blurred his eyes as he was led away.

In the Franklin County jail Birger, who had been arrested the day before and charged with murder in anticipation of Thomasson's confession, denied that he had had anything whatever to do with the killing of Joe Adams.

Thomasson's testimony was not the only blow Birger had to parry. The day before the gang leader was arrested Edmund Burke, one of the lawyers for the Sheltons in their trial at Quincy, filed a motion in the United States court at Springfield asking that they be granted a new trial. To support the motion he produced an affidavit that Harvey Dungey, witness for the prosecution, had made in his office on the previous day. Dungey swore that he had perjured himself when he testified that he saw Carl and Bernie Shelton near Collinsville on the day of the mail robbery. Birger and Newman, he said, had threatened to kill him unless he testified as he did. Now, conscience-stricken, he had decided to admit his guilt.

Another blow came a few days later, when a Williamson County grand jury indicted four former members of Birger's gang for the murder of "Casey" Jones. Word spread that the grand jury acted on evidence showing that Jones was killed at Shady Rest in Birger's absence, that his body was allowed to lie outside the cabin all night, and that early in the following morning it was taken twenty miles away and dumped into the creek in which it was found. Named in the indictment were Rado Millich, a Montenegrin whom Birger had formerly employed as a caretaker, and two local boys not yet twenty, Clarence Rone and Ural Gowen. (The fourth person was not named.) Millich, Rone, and Gowen were already serving sentences for other offenses.

To add to Birger's troubles the Shelton brothers were granted a new trial and released on bond.

These adversities, however, could not approach the catastrophe that struck the gang leader early in June.

Ever since the murder of Lory Price the chief of the Illinois state police and several of his men had been quietly working on the case. They had started on the presumption that Price had been abducted by Shelton gangsters, but from a former Birger follower, whom they tracked down in Ohio, they received information that led them to believe Price was killed by members of the Birger gang because he knew too much about their operations. Their problem, then, became that of finding the influential Birger gangsters still at large. Late in May 1927, they located Art Newman in Long Beach, California, where he was working as a private detective under an assumed name. Local police arrested him and charged him with murder. The governor of California honored a request for extradition, and Sheriff Pritchard of Franklin County set out to bring the prisoner back for trial.

With the sheriff went John T. Rogers of the *Post-Dispatch,* hoping to induce Newman to tell his story as he had induced Thomasson to tell his. Somehow, on the long ride from California to Illinois, he succeeded. Arriving in Benton, Rogers handed Newman's confession to State's Attorney Martin as the sheriff locked the prisoner in his cell. Martin turned it over to the State's Attorney of Washington County, in which Price's body had been found. That official called a special grand jury to meet at Nashville, the county seat, on June 11. Newman, brought into court there, swore that the confession he had made on the train was true in every respect, and was indicted—along with Birger, Connie Ritter, Ernest Blue, Leslie Simpson, and Riley Simmons—for the murder of Lory Price.

Newman began his story by saying that on the day Price and his wife disappeared Birger called him to Harrisburg and informed him that the gang intended to question "Slim" (Price) about "snitching" to the Williamson County authorities. The men started to Price's home in midafternoon, but found no one there. They returned in the evening, saw that there were visitors, left and returned again. It was almost midnight before they were certain that they would find the highway officer and his wife alone.

All the men, seven in number, went to the door. Price answered their knock. Birger, with loud profanity, asked who blew up Shady Rest. When Price said he didn't know, Birger ordered him into Newman's car, parked in front of the house. At the same time he seized the officer's pistol.

"Are you going to hurt me, Charlie?" Price asked.

"No," Birger promised, "I just want to talk things over with you."

Birger pushed his captive into the back seat and sat down beside him; Wooten took the place next to Newman at the wheel. As the car started Birger called to the men in the second automobile:

"Take that woman out and do away with her!"

"Charlie, please don't hurt Ethel," Price pleaded.

"Never mind," Birger snapped. "Shut up!"

Birger ordered Newman to keep driving. Then he began to berate the policeman—for trying to find out who killed Joe Adams, for being at Shady Rest the night it was destroyed, for carrying tales to Sheriff Coleman. With every mile he became more vituperative.

Newman stopped at Birger's home in Harrisburg, but the gang leader stayed there only a minute or two. Re-entering the car, he named as their destination a part of the county where there were several abandoned mines.

"I've got a notion, Price," he said, "to knock you off and throw you in one of these mines."

Then he changed his mind and headed for the site of Shady Rest.

"I want to show this Price what has happened to my cabin on account of him," he announced.

The party arrived at the barbecue stand about two a.m. Price, thoroughly frightened, whispered to Newman:

"Art, can you help me now?"

Birger overheard. "I'd like to see somebody try to help you now," he blustered. "Come on in here."

Inside the stand he faced Price in wild rage. When the officer denied, once more, that he had double-crossed the gang, Birger fired. Three shots passed through Price's body, and he pitched to the floor.

At this moment the second car came up.

"You've played hell now," Wooten told Birger. "Here's the car with that woman."

"Don't worry about the woman," one of the newcomers said. "We killed her."

"What did you do with her?" Newman asked.

"We shot her and threw her in a mine shaft near Carterville."

"All right," Birger broke in. "We'll put him with her."

"We can't," came the reply. "We filled up the place with tin and timbers."

Birger thought for a moment. "I know another old mine near Du Quoin," he said. "Throw this man in Newman's car."

Newman protested. "I'll be damned if you do. Put him in that Buick."

Birger flew into a rage, pointed his machine gun at his worried, hesitant followers, and shouted:

"Everybody will go through this with me or I'll wipe you all out!"

They put Price, still alive, in the back seat of Newman's car, and Birger, machine gun in hand, sat on his body. Near Carbondale the gangster ordered a stop. Stepping to the roadside, he vomited violently.

"That's too much for me," he said when he was able to speak. "I can kill a man, but I can't sit on him. I don't know what in the hell's the matter with me. It isn't my nerves. Every time I kill a man it makes me sick afterwards. I guess it's my stomach."

Birger told Connie Ritter to take his place. After a few miles Price regained consciousness.

"Connie, I'm an innocent man," he managed to say.

"Shut up, you bastard, or I'll turn this machine gun on you," Ritter responded.

A few more miles and Price spoke again. This time his voice was barely audible.

"Connie, you'll live to regret this."

By this time Ritter, too, had had enough, so another of the gangsters took his place astride the body of the wounded captive. Birger ordered a stop at an old coal-mine, and then saw a watchman on duty. The cars moved on to a schoolhouse. There he hoped to dump the dying policeman and burn both building and body, but rain, now falling hard, thwarted the plan. Farther on, near Dubois, he stopped by the roadside and directed the men in the first car to carry Price into the adjacent field.

"Art," the officer moaned, "I thought you were my friend."

"By God, I am, Lory, but I can't help this," Newman replied.

Shots rang out, and a moment later Birger and the others who had dragged Price away returned to the cars. On the way back to Shady Rest one of the men who had abducted Mrs. Price told Newman that they had taken her to an abandoned mine, shot her, and thrown her body to the bottom of the shaft. Then they covered it, to the depth of many feet, with timbers, stone, and debris. No one would ever find her.

Thus Newman's confession. Was it true?

If it was, Mrs. Price's body would be found where it had been hidden five months earlier. As soon as the gruesome story was made public, a crowd gathered at the old mine-shaft. Many were miners with picks and shovels. They worked in relays, passing the dirt to the surface by a bucket line. After dark the lamps on their caps twinkled like fireflies. Campfire Girls and Red Cross workers set up a canteen and served coffee and sandwiches.

The diggers worked the following day, and the day after that until noon. Then they came to the dead woman's body. Art Newman had told the truth.

With public opinion inflamed by a revelation of brutality even more savage than had been imagined, Rado Millich and Ural Gowen went on trial for the murder of "Casey" Jones. (Charges against Clarence Rone, also indicted, were dismissed when he turned state's evidence.)

On June 24 the defendants were arraigned before Judge Hartwell in the old Williamson County courthouse. They made a strange pair—Gowen a slender, diffident boy in shirt sleeves, looking more like a young farmhand than a gangster; Millich twice Gowen's age, dark-skinned, with glittering black eyes in a deep-lined face, an abnormally long nose, and a head that tapered toward the top like a blunt-nosed bullet. He spoke in broken and halting English, but when asked by the judge whether he could understand the language he answered: "Yes, sir, very well." Neither defendant had counsel, so the court appointed two lawyers to defend them.

State's Attorney Boswell built his case on the testimony of former Birger gangsters. All agreed that on the day of Jones's death Birger was absent from Shady Rest. Jones and Millich, then the caretaker, quarreled over the question of who had charge. In the course of the argument Millich shot Jones.

This much the defense admitted. They contended, however, that Millich fired in self-defense, and that Gowen was an innocent bystander who did nothing more than help drag the body to the bear pit, where it lay until the next day when Birger, having returned, gave orders that it be thrown into Saline Creek.

Oral Gowen, thirteen-year-old brother of Ural, gave damaging testimony in behalf of the prosecution. He was plowing in the vicinity of Shady Rest, he related, on the day the murder took place. When he heard shots he ran to the cabin.

"Who was the first person you saw when you got there?" he was asked.

"My brother," he replied.

Harry Thomasson, now serving his lifetime sentence in Menard Penitentiary, testified that on the day of the killing he was at the barbecue stand when he heard shots from the direction of the cabin. Running there, he came upon Jones, face-down on the ground. Gowen, standing over the body, had Jones's machine gun in his hands; Millich was near by. Several others came up, saw what had happened, and returned to the stand. Thomasson went with them. Once he looked around, saw Gowen and Millich dragging the body by the heels to the rear of the cabin. Shortly afterward he heard two more shots.

When asked why he did not do something for Jones while the dying man lay bleeding on the ground, he answered with a flash of his old defiance:

"I don't generally get mixed up in killings that aren't my own."

Millich took the stand in his own defense. In his halting English he told a straightforward story. On the day of the killing he was walking from the barbecue stand to the cabin when Jones, behind him, called out: "Rado!" As he turned, Jones opened fire with a machine gun. Millich pulled the trigger of his own rifle. Jones missed, Millich did not. That was all there was to it, except that Ural Gowen had had no part in the shooting.

The jury, after pondering the evidence for fifteen hours, found both defendants guilty. Gowen's punishment was set at twenty-five years in the penitentiary, Millich's at death.

In the first murder case arising from the gang war the prosecution had won two convictions and one death penalty. Charlie Birger, in his cell, had something to think about.

Ten days after the verdict Judge Hartwell overruled a motion for a new trial and announced that Millich would be "hanged by the neck until dead" on October 21, 1927. The condemned man stood before the bar, impassive, until the judge finished. Then he asked permission to speak.

"I had no fair trial," he said. "The evidence was framed against me by Mr. Boswell. I never killed the man because I wanted to but because he forced me to. I tell the truth."

The sheriff led him to his cell.

14

THE HANGING
OF CHARLIE BIRGER

June 1927–April 1928

■■

It *is* a beautiful world.
Charlie Birger, April 19, 1928.

J U N E 11, 1927, was a memorable day in the history of the gang war. That afternoon Art Newman revealed the revolting story of the murder of Lory and Ethel Price. In the morning Charlie Birger, now fighting for his life, met his first setback.

The occasion was a hearing on a motion for a change of venue. Birger entered the crowded courtroom on the heels of a deputy, jaunty and confident, took a chair at the side of his pretty young wife, who had previously found a place inside the rail, and clasped her hand. While his lawyers contended that local newspapers had prejudiced the general public against their client, and that the publication of Harry Thomasson's confession had heightened the prevailing animosity, he listened intently. When the judge denied the motion he showed no sign of disappointment, but he twisted and squirmed with impatience during an argument over the date of his trial. As soon as that was settled he turned to the sheriff and said abruptly: "Are you ready?" After a brief good-bye to his wife he fell in behind the officers and marched, ramrod-stiff, from the room.

On the 6th of July, as a Williamson County jury was about to decide the fate of Rado Millich, jailers led Birger, Newman, and Ray Hyland into the bare courtroom of the Franklin County courthouse to stand trial for the murder of Joe Adams. Arguments on motions took up the first two days. After that came the tiresome business of selecting a jury. All the defendants paid close attention to the questioning, the State's Attorney trying to ascertain each talesman's attitude toward capital punishment, the lawyers for the defense feeling for reactions to insanity and alibis.

One morning, before court convened, an incident revealed how bitterly Birger and Newman had come to hate each other. In response to a question from a reporter, Newman said something about Birger's connection with a bank robbery some months earlier. Birger overheard.

"Why, that guy's crazy!" he exploded. "I didn't even know him then. Look at him sitting over there. Anybody can tell he's crazy."

Facing his codefendant, he continued:

"You dirty, woman-killing son-of-a-bitch, you ought to be ashamed to ask for a trial. You ought to ask the people to hang you."

"That's enough of that," Newman growled.

One of Birger's attorneys quieted him. As he subsided he remarked for all to hear:

"If Newman gets out I want to hang."

Although the interminable questioning of prospective jurors was a dumb show to the spectators, they jammed the courtroom from morning to night. Whenever the sweltering heat and sheer boredom drove someone to the open air, newcomers waiting outside at the head of the stairs would jostle each other for his place. If they could hear little of what went on, and make little out of what they heard, there were the defendants to gape at— Birger by the side of his wife, his two daughters on his knees; Newman, dapper and nonchalant; Hyland of the swarthy complexion, thick lips, sloping forehead, and sinister joviality. Since the courtroom was small, only a few of those who sought admission managed to squeeze inside. Others, by the hundred, stood in the courthouse square, forced to be content with a brief glimpse of the prisoners as they were led to and from the jail.

A week passed before a jury was completed—a jury of miners, farmers, and clerks, all with such "American" names as Fisher, Gunn, Knight, and Simpson. Then the lawyers made their opening statements, and the State's Attorney began to call the witnesses for the prosecution.

Following time-tested tactics, he worked slowly to the testimony by which he intended to prove his case. Two days went by before he introduced the widow of the victim. Dry-eyed, she spoke in short, toneless sentences, with no striving whatever for dramatic effect.

> "The two young men knocked on our door. I got up and went to the door. They asked me if Joe Adams lived here. I said he did. They asked me if he was home.
>
> "I said yes, but he was asleep. I asked them if I would do. They said they wanted to see Joe personally. They said they had a letter from Carl Shelton. I went back and got Joe. I walked beside him to the door."
>
> "What did they do then?" the State's Attorney asked.
>
> "They shot him."

Clarence Rone, serving a term in the Williamson County jail, tightened the case against Birger. The boy was seriously ill, and spoke in such a low voice that the jurors strained to hear him. He had been at Shady Rest, he related, on the night before Adams was killed. He saw Harry and Elmo Thomasson come in, and he watched them enter a closed room with Birger, Newman, Ritter, and Hyland. An hour or so later Harry left; the others stayed all night.

The next afternoon, Rone continued, he saw Connie Ritter hand a pistol to Newman, who in turn gave it to Hyland.

"Take the bullets to the basement," Ritter ordered, "and dose them with poison."

Then he scribbled a note that he read aloud, sealed, and handed to Elmo.

Rone was at Shady Rest when the gang gathered there after the killing. Birger was elated.

"That was fine work you boys did," he said to the Thomassons. "I won't have to worry about that big son-of-a-bitch any more."

Harry Thomasson, however, was the witness on whom Martin relied for clinching his case. Staring sometimes at the floor, sometimes at the three defendants, the young convict told the full story of the crime.

On the night of December 11, 1926, Birger, Newman, and Ritter called him and his brother into a room at Shady Rest and closed the door.

"We've got a job for you two boys and it's got to be done tomorrow," the gang leader announced.

Art Newman asked Harry if he had ever killed anyone.

"No," the boy answered, "I never had enough against anyone to kill them."

Birger broke in. "You are the boys to kill Joe Adams. He don't know you and the law won't suspect you. What I want you to do is this. Go to West City and leave your car about a block from Joe Adams's house. Then go up to the front door and knock. If Carl Shelton, Joe Adams, or Ray Walker come to the door, shoot, and don't stop to ask questions. If anybody else comes to the door, ask for Joe. If they say he's not there, stick around in the neighborhood and watch the house."

They sent for Ray Hyland. "Jew," Birger said, "we want you to drive a car tomorrow."

"Why, that Jew ain't got guts enough to kill anybody," Newman taunted. "He wouldn't even drive the Chrysler that bombed Joe Adams's house."

"What do you say, Jew?" Birger asked.

Hyland laughed. "I don't know, Charlie. I'll think it over."

Harry wanted to go home that night. Birger objected, but finally allowed him to go to Benton, where he stayed with Pearl Phelps.

The following morning, Thomasson continued, Elmo and Hyland came after him and the three drove to Shady Rest. He described, as Rone had, the poisoning of the bullets and the writing of the decoy note. In the remainder of his testimony, he repeated, substantially, the confession he had made in April.

As Thomasson left the stand, after a futile effort by the defense to shake his testimony, Hyland smiled. Newman's face was expressionless. Birger yawned, but those close to him heard him mutter, "Damn," and saw that beads of sweat stood out on his forehead.

On the morning after Thomasson's appearance the state completed its case and the judge declared a recess until afternoon. Attorneys for the defendants used the time for a conference. Again Newman showed the depth of his animosity toward his former friends. He would have nothing to do with his codefendants, he announced, and he would not confer with their attorneys for the purpose of making a joint defense.

Although upset by Newman's attitude, the lawyers for the defense proceeded, after the recess, to make their opening statements prior to putting the defendants on the stand in their own behalf. R. E. Smith, representing Birger, asserted that his client had not stopped at Shady Rest on the night of December 11, and that his peregrinations on the following day, when Adams was killed, were for the sole purpose of tracking down Carl Shelton. Hyland had driven the car for the Thomasson brothers, his lawyer admitted, but had not even an intimation that they planned to commit murder. Newman, according to W. F. Dillon, whom he had retained, was implicated only because he had met the killers after they had done their work. The meeting, he asserted, was accidental—Newman had run into them by chance while he was delivering gin to one of Birger's customers.

At the conclusion of the opening statements, Newman told his attorney that he wanted to speak to him in private. The two men retired. Dillon soon emerged, obviously perturbed, and called a conference of his colleagues. He related what Newman had just revealed to him—that the little gangster intended to take the stand and tell the full story of the Adams killing. Newman had added that his testimony would be corroborated by a confession that he had made to John T. Rogers on the way back from California—a confession that Rogers, by agreement, had kept secret.

One of Birger's lawyers immediately filed a motion for a continuance, contending that the gang chief's counsel should have time to prepare to meet the statement that Newman was expected to make.

The following day Birger's lawyers supported the motion with heated arguments. The State's Attorney resisted with equal vehemence. Judge Miller denied the motion. Then he called on Birger's counsel to introduce their witnesses. Afraid to put the gang leader on the stand until they knew what Newman would say, they announced that they would waive evidence in chief but reserve the right to introduce evidence in rebuttal, thus saving Birger's testimony until the other defendants had given theirs. Hyland's lawyer made the same announcement. So did Newman's.

Again the judge asked the attorneys for the three defendants to present their evidence; again all waived. The case, therefore, would go to the jury on arguments only. Art Newman was satisfying his hatred of Birger at the risk of his own life. Spectators who had expected to hear the gangsters testify against each other stared in amazement as they watched the defense lawyers try to wriggle out of the net that the state had thrown around the prisoners. Observers saw, or thought they saw, fear in Birger's eyes; Newman's face semed to take on added hardness. Only Hyland maintained the smiling bravado that had characterized his manner from the beginning.

Thus the trial became a battle of words. In that contest Assistant State's Attorney Glenn made the opening move. Fearful that the defense might waive arguments, as it had waived the right to present evidence, he set out to summarize the entire case of the prosecution. For ninety minutes he paced back and forth before the jury box, waving his arms, pleading, shouting. Long before he had finished, his shirt was wet with sweat, his collar a sodden rag.

Repeatedly Glenn emphasized the fact that the Thomassons were boys.

"Think of it, gentlemen," he thundered, "Newman thirty-eight years old and Birger forty-four years old forcing two orphan boys, one seventeen years old and one nineteen years old, to go out and do murder for them! They thought the boys would go out and take the fall for the murder, and that the law would never find out who planned it.

"Who could be more guilty of murder," he wanted to know, "than these men who made two orphan boys do the killing instead of doing it themselves?"

Reminding the jury that a witness had testified that Newman had said to Elmo Thomasson: "You do this and the law can't take you from under the arm of Charlie Birger," and that Elmo had died at Shady Rest, Glenn shouted:

"If that orphan boy who had no mother, no father, who depended upon Charlie Birger, gave his life, and let Birger send his soul to hell, what are we going to do with men like this?"

That question he answered himself: "Hang the conspirators by their necks until they're dead!"

Following Glenn, two of Birger's lawyers spent the entire afternoon attacking the credibility of the state's witnesses. On the next day, however, Hyland's counsel, H. R. Dial, took a new tack.

"Is it blood you want?" he asked, facing the crowded courtroom. Turning to the jury he said quietly: "I know that back under the old Mosaic law it was a tooth for a tooth and an eye for an eye, but even in those days they didn't take three lives for one.

"If you find these men guilty of crime," he continued, "why

do you have to hang them? Won't confinement in the penitentiary satisfy you? Do you have to have blood? I thought we were trying to stop the shedding of blood in Franklin County and Williamson County.

"When I finish," Dial concluded, "nothing more can be said for Ray Hyland. . . . Gentlemen, I ask you to deal with him according to your human judgment, and then trust your God, your Judge, to deal likewise with you."

That afternoon Dillon made a dramatic appeal, on Newman's behalf, for leniency. After assailing young Thomasson's testimony as that of a man motivated by hatred, he tried to break the force of the plea he knew the State's Attorney would make.

"He is going to dope you gentlemen," he warned the jurors, "into signing a death warrant for these men to hang until they are dead, dead, dead, until their tongues stick out of their mouths, and they hang suspended in the air."

Hanging, Dillon pointed out, had been abolished by the Illinois legislature at its last session, and hereafter men who committed capital crimes would be electrocuted. But the penitentiary offered an even more humane form of punishment.

"If you have to find these men guilty," he begged, "give them some humane punishment, so that when the end of time comes, and the lightning strikes, the hills crumble, and the fire rages, as the pearly gates open we may meet these men, take them by the hand, and say that we have forgiven them."

R. E. Smith, Birger's chief counsel, concluded for the defense. Thomasson and Rone, he charged, were perjurers; the defendants were their victims. Then he, too, made a plea for leniency.

"Thomasson didn't hang," he shouted, "and he is the confessed murderer!

"If I hand you a pistol," he asked, facing the men in the jury box, "would you kill Birger as he sits there? If you wouldn't, would you ask the sheriff to do it? In the county to the south of us they hang men, and hang men, and hang men, and more and more murders are committed."

Smith turned to Birger and held out his hands. "Charlie, in a few minutes your life is going to be taken from my hands and given to these twelve men."

Then to the jury: "Gentlemen, Birger's fate rests with you."

It was Saturday morning when State's Attorney Martin rose to conclude the case. He reminded the jurors of their admitted willingness to administer the death penalty, and warned them against the pleas for sympathy that counsel for the defense had made. With Smith's attack in mind he defended Thomasson, the prosecution's star witness, but declared that without one word from him all three men would have been convicted of the Adams murder.

Then he swept into his conclusion:

"I ask you, and the people of the state of Illinois are asking you through me, that you return a verdict of guilty in the case of Charlie Birger, and fix his punishment at death. And I ask of you the same verdict as to Art Newman and Ray Hyland.

"I see in your verdict the passing of the rule of the machine-gun gang and the establishment of the rule of the law. I know you men will say that the gang war has no place in this part of the state of Illinois, and that the gunman and gangster has no place in Franklin County."

Early in the afternoon the case went to the jury.

Twenty-four hours later word spread through Benton that a verdict had been reached. Boys and girls, men and women, all in unaccustomed Sunday clothes, headed for the courtroom and filled it to capacity before the judge called for the jury. As the twelve men filed in, eyes red from lack of sleep, their set faces and their unwillingness to look at the defendants forecast the verdict they were about to announce: death for Birger, life imprisonment for Newman and Hyland.

The three gangsters sat silent and impassive. As the verdict for Birger was announced, his sister uttered a faint cry. (Mrs. Birger and the children were not present.) Mrs. Newman sighed and appeared to be relieved. At first no one seemed to be concerned with Hyland, but when the three men were being led from the courtroom, a large woman pushed through the crowd, threw her arms around him, and burst into tears.

"Mother, you shouldn't have come," Hyland said.

The guards moved rapidly with the prisoners to prevent a repetition of the scene.

Birger's attorneys lost no time in filing an appeal for a new trial. In denying it Judge Miller read the condemned gang-chief a lecture in which he pleaded with him, for the sake of his children and in atonement for the evil he had done, to help the authorities clear up the crimes as yet unsolved. Then he sentenced him to die on the gallows between the hours of ten a.m. and two p.m., October 15, 1927, concluding with the ancient formula: "May God have mercy on your soul."

Birger gulped, blanched, and asked permission to say a few words. Speaking almost incoherently, he denied that he had ever aspired to be a gang chief or that he had wanted to kill, and blamed Art Newman's perjuries for his plight. His attorneys announced that they would appeal to the Supreme Court.

Newman and Hyland, glad to have escaped the death penalty, began serving their sentences. In mid-August, while Birger sat in his cell awaiting the outcome of the legal maneuvering that could prolong his life, if not save it, Sheriff Coleman of Williamson County announced the solution of one of the crimes to which Judge Miller had referred.

Almost a year earlier the charred body of Lyle Worsham, known as "Shag," had been found in the ruins of an abandoned house fifteen miles south of Marion. According to a statement by Coleman (and at the subsequent trial of Dungey, Booher, and Thomasson the prosecution's witnesses gave similar testimony, although the three were acquitted), Worsham had been seen a few hours earlier at a resort in Zeigler in the company of Fred Thomasson, an older brother of Harry and Elmo, Joe Booher, and Harvey Dungey—all Birger gangsters. Coleman had been hunting for Thomasson and Booher ever since. Now he had them in the Williamson County jail, and could reveal the story.

On the last night of Worsham's life the three gangsters had taken him from Zeigler to Shady Rest, where Dungey accused him of talking too much to Carl Shelton. Worsham denied the charge. Dungey, insisting that he could prove it, forced Worsham to re-enter his car, and with the two others, started toward Marion. Birger followed in a second car, accompanied by Connie Ritter, Steve George, and others of the gang.

The two cars passed through Marion to the western part of the county and then turned south until they came to a lonely spot where thick timber bordered the road. There, Coleman said, Dungey stopped, pushed Worsham out, and ordered him to run for his life. A spotlight followed him. Suddenly he was hit by revolver fire from Dungey's party. As he stumbled, two machine guns from Birger's car, which had stopped behind the first automobile, cut him down.

Dungey, Thomasson, and Booher tossed the body into the weeds beside the road, still according to Coleman's statement, and drove away. Birger, given a moment to think, became furious and cursed the machine-gunners in his own party for their recklessness—the noise and shells would show that this was a gangster killing. The men turned around, bundled Worsham's body into one of the cars, and drove to Marion, where Birger bought five gallons of gasoline. After that they proceeded to an abandoned house they knew about, put the body inside, poured out the gasoline, touched a match, and fled.

The story, which Coleman declared had been corroborated by independent witnesses, would do Charlie Birger no good in his effort to escape the death penalty.

Early in October, however, it became evident that he would not pay that penalty on the 15th of the month, the date set by Judge Miller. On the 5th his attorneys filed a petition for a writ of error with the state Supreme Court, alleging that the verdict was contrary to the law and the evidence; on the 7th the court granted a stay of execution until it could review the case.

This was reassuring, but the developments in the case of Rado Millich, Birger's former henchman, were not. Two motions for a new trial, the second filed under instructions from the Serbian Consul in Chicago, were turned down during the summer and early fall. Finally, four days before the date of the execution, the consul appealed to the governor for a stay, and at the same time asked the State Department to intervene. The governor referred the case to the State Board of Pardons and Paroles, which recommended that no stay be granted.

Shortly before ten o'clock on the morning of October 21 Millich was led to the scaffold. While his arms and legs were being bound he stood in silence. Then he began to read, in broken English, from a paper that Sheriff Coleman placed in his hand. His statement began with the assertion that he had killed Ward Jones in self-defense.

"None of you people," he continued, "would have hung for killing him. . . . My lawyers, they say they do all they can for me. Charlie Birger was to hang October 15th, but he's still alive. . . ."

The man about to die tore the paper to bits but kept on talking.

"I want to say to you people that the man sending me to the gallows, Arlie O. Boswell, is the man who had Lory Price and his wife killed, and some day you will know that I tell the truth. And that when Charlie Birger's cabin was burned, Charlie Birger himself was in the front line."

Turning to the sheriff, Millich said quietly: "Thank you very much. Go ahead." Coleman sprang the trap.

That afternoon, in his cell, Birger commented on Millich's statement: "The last shot of a poor dumb fool at the man who sent him to die."

While Birger's appeal to the Supreme Court was pending, Boswell brought Dungey, Booher, and Thomasson to trial for the murder of "Shag" Worsham. Ural Gowen and Clarence Rone, both of whom had ridden in Birger's car on the night of the murder, corroborated the story of the crime that the sheriff had made public in August. The defendants, however, offered alibis, and the jury brought in a verdict of acquittal.

"Lucky boys!" Birger snorted enviously. "They sure got a break."

Toward the end of February 1928, Birger heard the bad news. The Supreme Court had denied his appeal, and had directed that the original sentence of death be carried out on Friday, April 13. The decision seemed to come as a relief. He would rather be dead, he remarked, than live through another ten months in jail.

A month later R. E. Smith, who had managed his case from the beginning, filed another petition for a rehearing. This, too, the Supreme Court denied. But the lawyer had not yet reached the end of his resources. On April 12, the day before his client was to hang, he presented a plea for a stay of execution to the Board of Pardons and Paroles, and supported it by an argu· ment to the effect that while Birger, accused only of plotting the murder of Joe Adams, had received the death sentence, the active killers had been let off with life imprisonment.

To the amazement of everyone, Arlie Boswell turned up at the hearing and urged that Birger's plea be granted. Only the day before, he said, he had visited the condemned man, and had learned that he was willing to tell what he knew about the murder of Lory and Ethel Price. The Williamson County State's Attorney wanted that evidence to use in the prosecution of the Price cases, and asked that the execution be delayed so that he could secure it.

Boswell's performance aroused State's Attorney Martin. He charged that Boswell had known for months everything that Birger was willing to tell about the Price murders.

"A majority of the people in Williamson County," he added ominously, "do not believe that Boswell wants to prosecute Birger or any of his gang."

After Martin's argument the board announced its decision: no clemency, no stay of execution.

Smith left Springfield, where the hearing was held, as soon as the decision was announced and rushed to Benton. There, in the name of Nathan Birger, a nephew of Charlie's, he filed a petition for a sanity hearing. Martin, anticipating the move, was in court to oppose it. When the judge indicated that he intended to allow the petition, the State's Attorney demanded that the hearing be held immediately. The court, however, set Monday, April 16, as the date.

Selecting the jury that would pass on Birger's sanity took a full day. During that period the defendant made his last desperate effort to escape death. He frequently cursed the newspaper reporters who sat at a near-by table, in the vilest possible language. He cowered, rolled his head from side to side, stared wildly at the jurors and spectators. Time after time he tried to rise from his chair, only to be restrained by the guards who sat beside him.

Smith offered only one witness—the operator of a barbecue stand who had known Birger for years. The man testified that he had visited the defendant in jail two months earlier and had believed him to be insane at the time. His story convinced no one.

The state relied on several deputy sheriffs and jail guards. As they gave their opinion that the prisoner was sane Birger interrupted repeatedly, sometimes rising to his feet despite his guards.

"Aw, you're crazy yourself!" he shouted at one witness.

As another witness was about to take the oath he said in a voice audible throughout the room: "Let him swear. That's the way he makes his living."

Once he burst out to Judge Miller: "Hey, Judge, I want to take a smoke and you can't stop me. You've done all you can to me."

There was laughter when one jailer testified that Birger had told him he wanted to be buried in a Catholic cemetery. That was the last place, the gangster had explained, the Devil would ever look for a Jew.

The jury took twelve minutes to find the defendant sane. With the verdict in, the court ordered the original sentence to be carried out on April 19.° As Birger was led from the courtroom that he would never see again, he walked with a quick step, his body erect, his eyes straight ahead. But his hands trembled so violently that the handcuffs rattled.

All through the night of April 18, while thousands crowded into Benton in the hope that they might see the execution, Birger talked—to his jailers, to newspapermen, to his lawyer, to the rabbi whom he had refused to see until these last hours of his life. He talked of everything that came into his mind—of his boyhood; of his years in the army; of his first wife who, he said, was the best of the four he had had, though he didn't have sense enough to know it when he was married to her; of the crimes he had committed and of those he was charged with. He prayed with the rabbi, and told him he wanted to do what was "right toward God" for the sake of his sister and children.

"Good-bye, Bob, old boy," he said to Smith when the lawyer finally left his cell. "I know you have done all you can, and I thank you from the bottom of my heart."

To the last he denied that he had plotted the murder for which he was to die. Yet he spoke with no resentment. "They've accused me of a lot of things I was never guilty of, but I was guilty of a lot of things of which they never accused me, so I guess we're about even."

At seven o'clock on the morning of the 19th he ate a hearty breakfast. When a doctor offered him a hypodermic he refused it.† The barber entered his cell to shave him, but the man's

---

° *Reliable evidence indicates that Birger was suffering from general paresis. There is no reason to believe, however, that the malady had progressed to the stage of mental or moral irresponsibility.*

† *One of Birger's lawyers writes me: "He didn't need a shot. I have*

hand shook so badly that he could not continue. Birger took the razor and carefully went over his face himself. Then he dressed in a gray suit, tan shirt, and dark striped tie.

At nine thirty, surrounded by guards, he left his cell. As he passed other guards in the corridor he called out in a voice that carried no hint of nervousness: "Good-bye, boys, be good!" When he stepped into the jail yard and saw the mounted machine-guns he remarked: "Looks like the western front here."

Smiling, he walked briskly to the scaffold and mounted the steps. He looked at the crowd in the enclosure and at the other hundreds at windows and on rooftops outside the stockade. The spring sun came out from behind a cloud, and he turned his head to the sky.

"It *is* a beautiful world," he said.

Looking down again he waved to an acquaintance. Then he spoke to the faces before him in a quiet, even voice.

"I have nothing against anybody. I have forgiven everybody, all because of this wonderful Jewish rabbi. I have nothing to say. Let her go."

Those near the scaffold saw that he was still smiling when the black hood came down over his face. The hangman fastened the noose, and the sheriff sprang the trap.

In a few minutes life left the body of the man who had sworn that he would kill Joe Adams and that there was nothing "the God-damned Franklin County law" could do about it.

---

always understood that he was hopped up to the limit. I suspect that he had dope at any and all times during his imprisonment. He always was able to win the complete acquiescence of some of the jailers to permit him to do whatever he wished, including sleeping occasionally with his wife."

15

JUSTICE

August 1928–August 1930

■■

The final chapter of a bloody book. . . .
    Marion Republican, May 26, 1930.
Come to the church in the wildwood, O
come to the church in the dale.
                    Revival hymn.

L A T E in August 1928, Oldham Paisley, editor of the *Marion Republican,* put into print some pointed questions that had been disturbing people in Williamson County and southern Illinois for many months.

In an editorial entitled, "Somebody Has Quit," Paisley recited that Highway Patrolman Lory Price and his wife Ethel Price had lost their lives on January 17, 1927, in "one of the most brutal murders in the history of Williamson County."

"Since then," he continued, ". . . confessions have been made by two of the principals in the killing. One of the leaders is now serving a life term for another murder, while another awaits trial in the county jail and a third is in a federal prison. The leader has already been executed for another crime."

Paisley recalled that on June 11, 1927, a grand jury in Washington County, where Price was believed to have died, indicted five Birger gangsters for his murder; and that on June 15, 1927, a Williamson County grand jury returned indictments for the murder of both victims.

"What has been done about those indictments?" he asked. "Nothing yet."

"Murdered in January, 1927," Paisley summarized. "Indicted in two different counties in June, 1927, and now it is August, 1928, almost September—twenty months after the murder, fourteen months after the indictments—and still no trial."

To be sure, several of the men charged with the crime were still at large, but was that any reason for not proceeding against the three who were serving other prison sentences—Art Newman, Freddie Wooten, and Riley Simmons?

"Why wait," Paisley asked, "for the capture of others that may never be caught and who may be tried at any time they are caught? When will Washington or Williamson County start action?"

One reason for the delay came out three weeks later when a telegraphic dispatch from New York announced that State's Attorney Boswell and Coroner Bell had arrested Leslie Simpson, one of the men under indictment, when his ship docked there. Boswell, it was reported, had been working for months on a tip that Simpson, Connie Ritter, and Ernest Blue, all fugitives, were members of the crew of the Roosevelt Line S.S. *Stanley.* For several days he and Bell had been in New York waiting for the ship to reach port. Simpson, who had taken an alias and had grown a mustache by way of disguise, was readily identified. The other two men were not on board.

As soon as Simpson was behind the bars in Williamson County, Boswell announced that he planned to bring the Price murderers to trial at once: his term in office would end in early December, and before that time he was determined to prove the falsity of rumors and insinuations linking him to the Birger gang. Not until the middle of October, however, did he ask Judge Hartwell to set the trial—a lapse of time that the judge characterized publicly as "an awful delay." Before the prosecution and the attorneys for the defendants could agree on a date, Freddie Wooten forced a further delay by escaping from jail.

On November 5 Simpson was brought into court for arraignment. The young man—tall, dark-haired, pleasant-faced, without a touch of a gangster's hardness about him—stood before the bench in apparent contrition and pleaded guilty to the murder of Lory Price.

"Do you know you have a right to a trial by jury?" the judge asked.

"I do."

"Have you been promised leniency, or have you any hope for leniency by throwing yourself on the mercy of the court?"

"I have not, Judge. I just want it settled."

Hartwell announced that he would reserve his decision on the plea, and also on Boswell's petition that Simpson be sentenced to life imprisonment and used as a state's witness in the impending trial. Two days later he accepted the plea, but deferred sentence indefinitely. At the same time, in spite of the fact that Wooten was still at large, he gave notice that the trial of the other men under indictment would begin on November 26.

Ten days before that date a federal grand jury, sitting at East St. Louis, indicted Arlie Boswell, Coroner George Bell, and several other city and county officials for conspiring with the late Charlie Birger, Art Newman, and others to violate the national prohibition law. Judge Hartwell immediately postponed the Price trial until December 7, when the new Williamson County State's Attorney, Roy Browning, would be in office.

Actually, it was January 7, 1929, before the alleged murderers were brought into court, for Browning had needed time for preparation. Wooten, recaptured several weeks earlier, sat with Newman, Simmons, and Simpson as the judge called four cases —one for the murder of Lory Price, one for the murder of Ethel Price, and two for conspiracy to commit murder. One by one, attorneys for the defendants entered pleas of guilty, which the judge accepted. He stated, however, that before passing sentence he would hear the evidence of the prosecution in order to ascertain the degree of guilt of the prisoners—a procedure that Illinois law made mandatory.

Art Newman, unperturbed as ever, took the stand first. A bank robbery, he related, had led ultimately to Lory Price's death. The gang—Birger, Newman, Ritter, and several others —had "pulled the job" late in November 1926. The loot included bonds to the amount of $3,400. Not knowing whether they were negotiable or not, Birger and Newman took them to Boswell.

"He told us that $2,700 worth of them were O.K. for the market," Newman asserted, "so we left them with him. I never saw them again."

Boswell also informed the gangsters—so Newman charged— that Lory Price knew that they had committed the robbery, and that the highway officer had written a letter to the bank president offering to tell what he knew. Price, confronted with Boswell's story, denied it vehemently, but Birger suspected that he lied.

Price and Boswell, Newman continued, both participated in the car-stealing that was one of Birger's activities. Birger reported the license numbers of stolen cars to Boswell, who passed back word as soon as a reward for recovery was offered. When Price "found" the car, all three divided the reward.

But Boswell distrusted the officer. Early in January 1927, he stopped at Shady Rest to pass on his suspicions. Price, he told Birger, was talking too much to Oren Coleman, the sheriff.

"Charlie, you'd better take that son-of-a-bitch out and kill him," he warned. "He's going to cause lots of trouble."

A few days later Shady Rest was destroyed. That, Newman declared, marked Price for death. Birger believed that the officer was responsible for the burning of the resort, and made up his mind to kill him.

Newman then proceeded with the story of the actual killing, repeating the same gruesome details he had made public in his confession many months earlier.

Throughout this testimony Boswell stood a few feet from the witness stand, arms folded, chewing an unlighted cigar and staring unwaveringly at his accuser.

Leslie Simpson followed Newman. On the night the Prices were killed, he related, Ritter and Blue came out of the house with Mrs. Price shortly after Birger had driven away with her husband. They proceeded to the vicinity of the abandoned Carterville mine. There Ritter, Blue, and Simmons alighted and led Mrs. Price into the darkness. In a moment Ritter returned. When they brought her back, he told Simpson, he wanted a rifle in the back seat to go off "accidentally." Simpson must make sure, however, that it killed her.

"You go to hell," Simpson replied.

"Are you yellow?" Ritter asked.

"No, but I won't kill a woman."

"You do what I tell you," Ritter threatened, "or I'll blow hell out of you."

"Go ahead," Simpson dared him.

At this moment Riley Simmons returned to the car. Ritter ordered him and Simpson to walk down the road. Before the two men had gone fifty feet they heard shots and a scream, and as they turned they saw Ethel Price fall. They lingered long enough to smoke a cigarette, then went back to the car. By that time, Ritter and Blue were throwing refuse into the mine shaft.

Wooten corroborated Newman and Simpson in general, although he maintained that he had no firsthand knowledge of several facts about which they had testified. Riley Simmons, on the stand, professed to be even more ignorant of what had happened than Wooten. His assertion that he knew neither of the Prices, that he had never heard their names mentioned, and that he had no idea where the gang was going when they started out on the night of the murder, was too much for Judge Hartwell's short patience.

"Do you mean to tell me," he broke in, "that you fellows took two cars down to Price's house with pistols strapped on you without knowing anything was going to happen?"

"Yes, sir."

"What were those pistols for, some kind of ornaments? Was there some kind of a social gathering out there by that mine with only one woman and all you men with pistols and guns? Do you want me to believe you didn't know what was going to happen?"

"Yes, sir."

"Then," the judge snapped, "you can go ahead and testify all you please."

When Simmons finished, Browning announced that the state's case was complete. After a brief recess he recommended that the court sentence the defendants to life imprisonment for the murder of Ethel Price, fifty-seven years for conspiracy to kill Ethel Price, and fifty-seven years for conspiracy to kill Lory Price.

He explained his recommendation. Until the eve of the trial he had intended to use Leslie Simpson as his witness against Newman, Wooten, and Simmons, and on the basis of his testimony to ask for the death penalty. At the last minute Simpson called him to the jail and admitted that he had not told the whole truth in their previous interviews. Browning realized that the man could not be trusted. He believed now that all four defendants were lying, at least in part. But if they should be hanged, a fate that he thought they all deserved, he would have no witnesses to use against Ritter and Blue, who were still at large. To make sure that the four defendants who had pleaded guilty would testify against the two fugitives, he was reserving the Lory Price murder case, and would ask for the death penalty in that if they failed him.

Judge Hartwell remarked that he too believed that the four confessed murderers deserved to hang, but that under the circumstances he agreed with the State's Attorney's recommendation. He then imposed the sentences, adding the provision that on the anniversary of the Price murders the prisoners should be placed in solitary confinement for five days for re-flection and for the good of their consciences. "If you have any," he added.

Millich, Birger, Hyland, Newman, Wooten, Simpson, Simmons—now it was the turn of Boswell himself. Klansman, leader of the forces of law and order, State's Attorney of Williamson County from 1924 to 1928, was he also, as Millich and Newman had charged, as Martin had insinuated, and as most of the people of the county by now believed, a confederate of Charlie Birger's? A jury in the United States District Court, sitting at East St. Louis in the fourth week of January 1929, would answer the question.

Although Boswell was only one of several defendants—the others included the former coroner and one-time police chiefs of Johnston City and Marion—it was evident from the beginning that he would be the primary target of the prosecution. When Ralph F. Lesemann, Assistant District Attorney, outlined the government's case in his opening statement he promised the evidence would show that Boswell allowed roadhouses to operate in return for protection money, that he used the Birger gang to extract payments from reluctant bootleggers, that he received a cut on all illicit liquor distributed from Shady Rest, that he delivered confiscated slot-machines and liquor to Birger, and that he prompted the murder of Lory Price.

To prove these charges Lesemann and his superior, District Attorney Harold G. Baker, put sixty-three witnesses on the stand—an incongruous procession of bootleggers, gangsters, convicts, and law officers. One of Birger's former bartenders swore that on two occasions in 1926, in Birger's absence, he paid Boswell seventy-five dollars; the bartender's brother related that he heard Birger say he paid Boswell this sum each week for protection. A convict whom Boswell had sent up on a murder charge testified that from the spring of 1926 until fall of the same year he paid the former State's Attorney thirty-five dollars a week in protection for his bootlegging establishment. Frightened by frequent visits from Birger's men, he closed up. Boswell called him in for an explanation.

"You go ahead and open up," Boswell told him when he confessed that he was afraid of trouble, "and I'll see that the Birger gang don't bother you any more and I'll cut your payments down to twenty-five dollars a week."

A Johnston City bootlegger, raided by Sheriff Coleman, went to the State's Attorney's office to plead guilty. When Boswell's assistant informed him that the fine would be one thousand dollars he refused to make the plea. Later he met the State's Attorney on the street and told him what had happened. Boswell asked whether he had fifty dollars. He hadn't, so he was instructed to obtain the money and turn it over to a man who would knock on his door that night. When the knock came the bootlegger pushed the money through a crack. He heard no more of the case against him.

Art Newman took the witness stand to testify once more against a former associate. On as many as a hundred occasions, he asserted, he and Birger paid Boswell amounts ranging from twelve to three hundred dollars in protection money either for themselves or for other bootleggers from whom they had collected. Birger paid Boswell two dollars a can on all the alcohol he handled. Mrs. Newman, also a witness, related that she had accompanied her husband and Connie Ritter "a dozen times" when they went to Boswell's office to pay off the State's Attorney.

Law officers buttressed the government's case. A Department of Justice agent described an experience he had with Boswell in 1926. When he asked the State's Attorney to accompany him to Shady Rest, where he expected to find an interstate automobile-thief, Boswell insisted on telephoning first. "You see," he explained, "I've got to be friendly with Birger because I get lots of information from him." When the agent, accompanied by Sheriff Coleman, went out to the resort no one was there.

John Ford, one of Coleman's deputies, testified that in the

spring of 1926 he accused Boswell of taking protection money from bootleggers, and named several who were paying him.

"Yes," the State's Attorney replied, "and what are you going to do about it?"

Coleman himself related a conversation he had had with Boswell in 1928, just before the primary election in which the State's Attorney was defeated. Boswell asked the sheriff why he was not supporting him in the campaign.

"I don't understand your connections with the Birger gang," Coleman replied. "You admit that you know of the crimes but the gangsters frequent your office all the time."

On one occasion, Coleman stated, he told the State's Attorney that his practice of fining bootleggers on only one count and dismissing the others was equivalent to licensing them. Boswell chewed his cigar before he answered.

"You do things I don't like and I do things you don't like," he muttered, and changed the subject.

As damaging as all the stories of witnesses were the records of the Marion State and Savings Bank, showing that in the course of his four-year term Boswell had made deposits totaling eighty-seven thousand dollars.

Boswell answered the charges against him by a detailed, explicit denial. On the stand for several hours, he denied that Birger and Newman had visited his office frequently: he could remember only three occasions when they had called on him. He denied that Mrs. Newman had ever been a visitor, or that he had ever spoken to her. He had never taken stolen cars from Birger's place; he had never accepted protection money from anyone. On the contrary, his record showed that he had been relentless in his pursuit of the Birger gang. He had prosecuted eleven of its members, sending one to the gallows and six to prison for terms ranging from ten years to life.

That, said District Attorney Baker when he made the closing argument for the prosecution, was absurd. Did Boswell ever raid Shady Rest? he asked. Of course not: it was his own rendezvous. Did he prosecute Birger gangsters even though he had abundant evidence against them? Not until the Adams case, tried in Franklin County, showed him that the goose was cooked. Then, Baker charged, he "lost his guts" and tried to divorce himself from the gang. For that reason he finally sent Rado Millich to the gallows, and tried to obtain a last-minute reprieve for Birger.

Boswell's counsel could only argue that the government, relying on "a mass of lies" from the lips of convicts, had not proved its case.

The jury took four hours to reach its verdict: Boswell and four of his five confederates were guilty as charged.

"Well, that's that," the former State's Attorney said to his wife.

A week later he stood before Judge Lindley in the federal court at Danville and heard his sentence: two years in prison and a fine of five thousand dollars. The prison sentence was the maximum, the fine half the amount he might have been assessed. On the same day he started for Leavenworth in the marshal's custody.

With Boswell convicted, only two important members of the Birger gang remained unpunished—Connie Ritter and Ernest Blue. Neither had been seen since the discovery of Lory Price's body.

In mid-October 1929, New Orleans police officers notified Sheriff Pritchard of Franklin County that they had picked up Ritter in Gulfport, Mississippi, and were holding him there. He insisted that his name was Fred Randall, but they were certain of his identity. The sheriff left at once and in four days returned with his man. In jail at Benton, the prisoner finally admitted that he was Birger's former lieutenant.

Ritter was willing enough to remain in Franklin County and face the Adams murder charge; what he must avoid was removal to Williamson County, where he would have to stand trial for the murder of Lory and Ethel Price. After several months of legal maneuvering he succeeded. On May 26, 1930, he stood in the same courtroom in which Birger had been condemned to death, pleaded guilty to the murder of Joe Adams, and heard himself sentenced to life imprisonment.

"The final chapter of the bloody book which records the gang warfare which once ravaged Southern Illinois," a local newspaper characterized the brief proceedings.

Since Ernest Blue was never apprehended, and was later reported dead, the newspaper verdict turned out to be true. But a more appropriate final commentary was implicit in a brief article that appeared in the *Marion Republican* a few weeks later.

> The old song, "Come to the church in the wildwood, O come to the church in the dale," rings out each night at Shady Rest, where Rev. Emory Allen has been conducting a revival for the past ten days. . . . The atmosphere is restful and many from Marion enjoy driving out and listening to the helpful sermons.

Funeral in Herrin of union miners killed the day before the Herrin Massacre (this and all other photographs in this book, some from *Life and Exploits of S. Glenn Young* (1989) and some from his private collection, are used courtesy of Gordon Pruett, Crossfire Press, P.O. Box 365, Herrin, Illinois 62948)

S. Glenn Young, prohibition agent and Ku Klux Klan leader

Thousands viewed the body of S. Glenn Young in January 1925.

Williamson County Jail, Marion, built in 1913 to house the sheriff and his family in front, prisoners in back

Charlie Birger's gang. *Seated in foreground, left to right:* Oral Gowen, Bert Owens, Ural Gowen; *second row:* Rado Millich, Steve George, Ernest Blue, Riley Simmons, (standing) John Renfro, Clarence Rone, unidentified, Leon Stover; *on porch:* Ward "Casey" Jones, Art Newman, Connie Ritter, unidentified, Charlie Birger

Weapons displayed on a roadster at Shady Rest

Charlie Birger's armored truck

Charlie Birger's gang. *Standing, left to right:* Riley Simmons, Rado Millich, John Renfro, Ural Gowen, unidentified, Clarence Rone, unidentified, Oral Gowen; *foreground:* Steve George, Art Newman, Connie Ritter, Ernest Blue, Ward "Casey" Jones, Leon Stover, Bert Owens, Charlie Birger

Charlie Birger on trial

"It *is* a beautiful world," said Charlie Birger on the scaffold. A rabbi carrying a Bible stands on the step at right.

CONCLUSION

1930–1951

●●

A L M O S T a quarter of a century has passed since Connie Ritter, the last of the Birger gangsters, entered an Illinois penitentiary. Throughout that period, Williamson County has lived at peace.

Prison walls gave assurance that there would be no resumption of the gang warfare by Birger followers. Ural Gowen, who had drawn the lightest sentence, was not released until 1941. (Illinois penal authorities have no knowledge of his whereabouts; presumably he has kept out of trouble.) Connie Ritter died in the hospital at Menard Penitentiary in 1948. Leslie Simpson remained in prison until 1950, when he was released on parole; Harry Thomasson and Ray Hyland were paroled a year later. Art Newman, Riley Simmons, and Freddie Wooten still serve their terms.

The Sheltons never returned to Williamson County. After the gang war they used East St. Louis as headquarters for enterprises in gambling, bootlegging, and prostitution until an honest sheriff drove them out. Peoria was more hospitable. There, in the late thirties, they established themselves; from there they dominated an illegal empire that comprised, if informed observers are correct, most of the rackets in downstate Illinois. Apparently immune to prosecution, they were unable to protect themselves permanently against personal enemies or rival racketeers. Carl, who had left Peoria to retire on his Wayne County farm, was killed there in the fall of 1947; Bernie was fatally

267

shot outside his tavern near Peoria in the summer of 1948; Earl survived a murderous attack at Fairfield, Wayne County, in the spring of 1949, and still lives. Roy, the oldest brother, was killed in early June 1950, while driving a tractor on Earl's farm. Although he had a criminal record he had never been associated with Carl, Earl, and Bernie. "Little Earl," a son of Dalta, the fifth brother, has survived two attempted assassinations.

Early in 1951 all the Sheltons except the mother of the brothers and their youngest sister, Mrs. Lulu Shelton Pennington, disappeared. In April they sold most of their Illinois land. But the feud continues. In June 1951, a young farmer was shot from ambush as he stood talking to friends on one of the Wayne County farms that Earl had retained; the next day the barn on the same farm burned to the ground. Late in the month Mrs. Pennington and her husband, a roadhouse operator, were shot by occupants of a sedan, who forced the Penningtons' car to the curb on the outskirts of Fairfield. Both Penningtons were seriously wounded. As soon as they recovered they vanished; so did Mrs. Agnes Shelton, the mother of the brothers. On the night of December 1, 1951, the old homestead, unoccupied, burned to the ground. At the same time a garage on Big Earl's farm, a mile away, went up in flames.*

All the murders of the Sheltons and assaults on members of the clan remain unsolved.

With this attempt to wipe out the entire family, Williamson County appears to be unconcerned. Where once a shot that even grazed a Shelton head would have brought quick reprisal,

---

*On March 27, 1952, after this book had gone to press, Earl Shelton asked a St. Louis newspaper reporter to appeal to Governor Adlai Stevenson of Illinois in his behalf. He told the reporter that an armed enemy patrolled his Wayne County farm, and he wanted protection from the state so that he could return and work it. Shelton's whereabouts were not revealed.

In less than twenty-four hours after this appeal was published a tenant house on the Shelton farm and a near-by home belonging to a former Shelton gangster burned to the ground. Neighbors gathered at the scene but made no effort to save either structure.

successful murder causes only mild speculation, and the peace remains unbroken.

But prosperity, which peace so often makes possible, shunned Williamson County for more than a decade after the end of the gang war. During the Klan clean-up, businessmen began to complain of hard times. It was natural that they should attribute the decline in trade to the "troubles" that beset the county, but the cause was more deep-seated and more enduring than this diagnosis indicated. For a generation coal had been the mainstay of the region. Now coal was a sick industry, and becoming sicker.

By 1925 or thereabouts, the stimulus that the first World War gave to coal mining in southern Illinois had run its course. Consumers began to turn to oil and natural gas. In the competition for a market no longer large enough to absorb full production, southern Illinois operators found themselves at a disadvantage: producers in the nonunion fields of Kentucky and West Virginia could undersell them. Mine after mine in Williamson and Franklin counties went on part-time, many closed down altogether. Those that survived did so only by taking advantage of every technical improvement, and every technical improvement meant fewer miners on the payroll.

The depression that followed the crash of 1929 accelerated the trend. As factories closed, the demand for coal shrank to a fraction of what it had been. Miners, working a day or two a week or not at all, drew on their savings until they were gone, sold their cars, mortgaged their homes. After that only the pittance that local charity could provide kept them alive.

By 1932, actual starvation threatened Williamson and Franklin counties. When Mauritz A. Hallgren, associate editor of *The Nation*, visited the region in the spring of that year he found a dozen towns in which as many as sixty per cent of the able-bodied men were unemployed. Local business came almost to a standstill. Empty storerooms dotted every business street, and half-empty shelves marked the stores that remained open.

People walked the streets, killing time. They had nothing else to do.

Hallgren noted that of forty banks in the two counties a few years earlier, only three remained. Marion and Benton, the county seats, had no banking facilities. Local utilities and chain stores cashed the checks of those fortunate enough to have them, and merchants did much of their business through postal money-orders. Lawyers and physicians, once the most prosperous class in the region, were no better off than the miners and merchants.

Without the federal relief-programs inaugurated in 1933, the people of Williamson and Franklin counties would have been subjected to suffering inconceivable in a civilized nation. Relief quickly became the region's biggest industry. Year after year, in the thirties, relief and WPA employment-quotas were three and four times as large as in average comparable communities. In fact, conditions became so bad that in 1941 the Works Progress Administration made Williamson, Franklin, and Saline counties the subject of a special study and published the findings under the title, *Seven Stranded Coal Towns: A Study of an American Depressed Area.* The authors found that three out of every four jobs the coal mines had provided had vanished, and that no new industries had appeared to fill the gap in the economy. They summed up the result in a few stark sentences:

> Intense local unemployment has become almost a normal state of things. Thousands of good workers have had no jobs for many years. Thousands of youth, blocked from entering industry, have reached their most productive years without ever having held a job. Nearly half the people are dependent on public aid year after year, and intense poverty is common.

After war broke out in 1941, conditions improved, but less than might have been expected. The mines stepped up production, the government built a thirty-eight-million-dollar ordnance plant between Herrin and Marion, the normal number of young men were drawn into the armed forces, yet the coal towns continued to be plagued by unemployment. If there could be no real revival even under the stimulus of war production, what hope did the future hold?

Near the end of the war, Herrin faced the facts. At the instance of leading citizens, the mayor called a mass meeting. Speaker after speaker took a realistic view of the future. The ordnance plant, it was obvious, would be one of the first casualties of peace. What would happen to the hundreds of Herrin residents who worked there, and what would happen to Herrin's merchants when the paychecks stopped? Unless the city secured new industries, its population would decrease, retail trade would fall off, and property values would decline. The end might well be an aggregation of boarded storefronts and deserted, dilapidated homes. Herrin could take its fate lying down, or it could try to save itself.

The people chose to mold their own future. In a short time they subscribed one hundred thousand dollars, to be used for industrial development. The Herrin Chamber of Commerce, under the leadership of its president, O. W. Lyerla, went to work. Learning that Borg-Warner intended to build a new factory for the manufacture of washing-machines under its Norge division, Lyerla and others pressed Herrin's advantages: plenty of industrial water from Crab Orchard Lake, a federal project completed in 1941, as well as adequate electric power, an abundance of high-grade labor, ample housing, and a free factory-site. The company, convinced, constructed a modern factory, and went into production in 1946.

This was only a beginning. The same advantages that induced Borg-Warner to build a plant at Herrin led a manufacturer of women's dresses to locate there a year later. In 1950 and 1951 two other industries came to the same decision. All were influenced by the community's willingness to make a substantial investment—more than eight hundred thousand dollars alto-

271

gether—in mortgage notes on the factory buildings. Most of these notes have already been retired.

At the same time that Herrin was helping itself, it bore its share in the larger job of regional rehabilitation. Other communities in Williamson and neighboring counties faced the same bleak future, and enjoyed the same basic advantages. In addition, there were the buildings of the ordnance plant—an asset that might be turned to the advantage of the entire region. Leading citizens, working through Southern Illinois, Incorporated, a sort of regional chamber of commerce, induced the federal government to make this property available for industrial leasing. The Sangamo Electric Company, of Springfield, was the first to take advantage of the opportunity, and established a plant for the manufacture of condensers and other electronic equipment. By the summer of 1951 fifteen other industries had leased space.

The benefits of high employment at Ordill, as the ordnance plant is now called, permeate the area that includes Carbondale, Carterville, Herrin, West Frankfort, Johnston City, and many other communities. None of these cities is more than twelve miles from any other, and with good roads, and cars in every family, transportation is no problem. Some, like Marion, remain true to the rural tradition and are content to keep industry at a comfortable distance. But whether factories are located within city limits or a few miles away, well-kept homes, attractive stores displaying an abundance of new merchandise, new school-buildings, and hospitals where there were none before testify to the general prosperity these factories have created.

Williamson County, proud of what it has accomplished in recent years, would like to forget its turbulent past. The eighty-four pages of a "Progress and Achievement Edition" of the *Herrin Daily Journal,* published August 30, 1937, contained no mention of the Massacre, the Klan clean-up, or the gang war. The same subjects were carefully avoided in a county centennial history, *Pioneer Folks and Places,* published in 1939.

The people of the county feel that they are being subjected to gross injustice whenever the story of the "troubles" is retold. That has happened often in the last five years. Whenever a Shelton has been shot or shot at, feature writers have jumped for their typewriters; while in 1950 and 1951 articles on the gang war appeared in *The Saturday Evening Post, Life,* and *Esquire.* Upon the publication of the *Esquire* article (February 1951) the Herrin Lions Club passed resolutions that undoubtedly reflect majority opinion. "Articles of this nature," the Lions asserted, "serve only to open old wounds; is [*sic*] in reality nothing more nor less than persecution of Southern Illinois and its people; is a definite detriment to this area in its civic efforts; molds the minds of the peoples of the whole world so this community and this area cannot attain their rightful niche in society because of the resultant prejudices." The old disorders, the Lions insisted, "should be discontinued and forgotten by our own press as un-American and undemocratic."

The press is not likely to agree. What happened in Herrin and Bloody Williamson is still news. Besides, there is a conviction on the part of many thoughtful persons that the story has a significance that goes beyond one limited geographical area. William L. Chenery sensed it as early as December 1924, when he wrote in the *Century:*

Somehow in the process of emigration from countries in which the majesty of the law was scrupulously respected, the men who made America, or a minority of them, lost the habit of enforcing the statutes without fear or favor. Herrin's petty offenses and gross crimes are part and parcel of what is done in every large American city. The spot-light happened to turn upon this isolated community, and the people seemed peculiarly supine and sinful. They are not different from other Americans, and when they solve their difficulties, as solve them they must if Herrin is to endure, they may make a contribution of significance and value to other communities which are not yet wholly law-abiding and fully tolerant of differences in custom and in opinion.

More than twenty-five years later John Bartlow Martin groped for fundamentals when he wrote of the Sheltons, and tangentially of Williamson County:

> The Shelton boys and their havoc are an American phenomenon, and one ill-understood. Why, for example, as at Herrin and Peoria, do certain forces in American life collide at a given time and point and explode? What has made Williamson County bloody so long? Perhaps if one went far enough back into the Sheltons' childhood one would find reasons for their criminality. But this would not explain the conditions that enabled them to flourish as they did. . . . In searching for the ultimate meaning of the Shelton story we are reduced to windy rhetoric—unenforceable prohibitions against gambling and liquor tend to corrupt the public conscience, and evil is nurtured; evil flourishes, corrupting whole bodies politic and tempting respectable people, who very often regret yielding.*

What *has* made Williamson County bloody so long? We cannot explain, with assurance, why explosive forces in American life have come to the flash point not once but many times in this one small region, but we can identify the forces, and thus contribute to understanding.

The Bloody Vendetta, the Massacre, the Klan crusade, the gang war—all revealed the frailty of social restraints. Conscience, it was shown, is a monitor easily disregarded, for a man can come to kill another without losing a half-hour's sleep. Against greed and other strong emotions the law is a weak barrier. Adamant adherence to principles can breed its own troubles: witness the conflicts between union labor, certain of its right to organize, and men like Brush and Leiter, equally certain that an owner had a right to conduct his business in his own way.

Witness, too, the presence of factors never openly admitted.

---

* *"The Shelton Boys," copyright 1950 by the Curtis Publishing Company, included in* Butcher's Dozen and Other Murders, *pp. 149–50. Quoted by permission.*

In the Brush mine riots, which was more important: the fact that Brush's imported miners were strikebreakers, or the fact that they were black? Who knows what mixture of motives impelled the participants in the Klan crusade? What part was played by the rigid moralist's envy of the pleasures of sin? By the Protestant's deep-seated fear of the Catholic? By the desire of the old "American" to put the newer citizen—in this instance the Italian—in his place?

And note the almost constant presence of official incompetence or official corruption.

Lack of respect for law. Venal public servants. Union labor and "free enterprise." Black man and white man. Old-fashioned morality and lax standards of conduct. Protestant and Catholic. "American" and foreigner.

Shibboleths, trite antitheses, even windy rhetorical phrases—but they stand for conflicts that have brought violent death to one American county over more than half a century.

The same conflicts are to be found in many another community. If they persist until passion displaces reason there will be other Herrins.

THE PRINCIPAL EVENTS
Chapter by Chapter

●●

1. MASSACRE

June 22, 1922. The Herrin Massacre.

2. APPROACH TO MASSACRE

September 1921. The Southern Illinois Coal Company opens a strip mine in Williamson County, Illinois.

November 1921. The company ships its first coal.

April 1, 1922. The United Mine Workers of America go on strike, but the Southern Illinois Coal Company continues to strip coal with union permission.

June 13, 1922. The company dismisses its union miners.

June 15, 1922. Fifty strikebreakers and mine guards, imported from Chicago, take over the strip mine.

June 16, 1922. The mine ships sixteen cars of coal in defiance of the strike.

June 18, 1922. Colonel Samuel N. Hunter and Major Robert W. Davis arrive in Marion.

June 19, 1922. Hunter and Davis confer with W. J. Lester, owner of the Southern Illinois Coal Company, State's Attorney Duty, Sheriff Thaxton, and others.

June 20, 1922. John L. Lewis, president of the United Mine Workers of America, wires instructions that the members of the Steam Shovelmen's Union at the mine are to be viewed as "common strikebreakers."

277

June 21, 1922. Hunter, with prominent citizens of Williamson County, tries to avert violence, but striking miners surround the mine. In the ensuing gunfire, two strikers are killed, a third fatally wounded. Hunter and his group try to effect a truce and believe they have succeeded.

June 22, 1922. The strikebreakers surrender. In the massacre that follows nineteen are killed, one fatally wounded.

3 · MASSACRE: THE AFTERMATH

June 25, 1922. The coroner's jury attributes the deaths of those killed in the Herrin Massacre to "the acts direct and indirect" of the officials of the Southern Illinois Coal Company.

August 16, 1922. The Illinois Chamber of Commerce appeals for funds to aid in the prosecution of those guilty of the June 22 murders.

August 28, 1922. A special grand jury convenes at Marion to investigate the Herrin murders.

August 30, 1922. The grand jury returns its first indictment, charging Otis Clark, farmer and miner, with murder.

September 8, 1922. Illinois miners, in convention at Peoria, pledge one per cent of their total monthly earnings for the defense of the men indicted for the Herrin murders.

September 23, 1922. The grand jury recesses after having brought in 214 indictments, including forty-four for murder.

October 23, 1922. The grand jury returns forty-eight additional indictments and adjourns.

4 · TWO TRIALS AND AN INVESTIGATION

November 8, 1922. Five men go on trial for the murder of Howard Hoffman, one of the victims of the Herrin Massacre.

December 8, 1922. After one month of interrogation, the trial jury is completed.

December 13, 1922. The lawyers make their opening statements and begin to offer testimony.

January 17, 1923. Delos Duty, State's Attorney, makes the first of the closing arguments. The defense waives.

January 18, 1923. At 11.15 a.m. the case goes to the jury.

January 19, 1923. All five defendants are acquitted.

February 12, 1923. Six men, including two of the defendants in the first case, go on trial for the murder of Antonio Molkovich, also killed in the Herrin Massacre.

March 2, 1923. The attorneys make their opening statements and begin to offer testimony.

April 6, 1923. Otis Glenn, for the state, makes the first of the closing arguments. The defense waives its right of argument, and at 4.20 p.m. the case goes to the jury. Seven hours later a verdict of not guilty is returned.

April 7, 1923. State's Attorney Duty nol-prosses all remaining indictments.

April 11, 1923. A committee of the Illinois House of Representatives, appointed to investigate the Herrin Massacre, holds its first session at Springfield.

April 26, 1923. The House Investigating Committee begins hearings at Marion.

June 30, 1923. On this, the last day of the legislative session, the House Investigating Committee presents majority and minority reports. A House Bill providing for a new investigation fails for want of Senate action.

5 . THE BLOODY VENDETTA

July 4, 1868. Several members of the Bulliner family and Felix Henderson engage in a card game that ends in a fight.

Fall 1869. A lawsuit between David Bulliner and George W. Sisney over a crop of oats is decided in Sisney's favor.

April 26, 1870. After a violent argument, four Bulliners attack Sisney at his home. Though wounded, he repulses them.

December 25, 1872. Several members of the Crain and Sisney families engage in a brawl at the general store in Carterville.

December 30, 1872. Crains, Sisneys, Hendersons, and Bulliners come together at the trial arising from the brawl of December 25 and all take part in a riotous disturbance.

December 12, 1873. "Old George" Bulliner is murdered. The crime is never solved.

March 27, 1874. David Bulliner, a son of "Old George," is shot from ambush and mortally wounded.

March 31, 1874. Thomas Russell, charged with the murder of David Bulliner, is tried and found not guilty.

May 15, 1874. James Henderson is shot from ambush and dies eight days later.

August 9, 1874. An attempt to murder George W. Sisney fails when the guns of the assailants miss fire.

October 4, 1874. Dr. Vincent Hinchcliff is murdered.

December 12, 1874. George W. Sisney is shot while playing dominoes. He is seriously wounded, but recovers.

January 22, 1875. A bill to appropriate $10,000 for the purpose of ending the "Bloody Vendetta" in Williamson County is introduced in the Illinois General Assembly but fails to pass.

Spring 1875. J. D. F. Jennings, State's Attorney of Williamson County, absconds with county funds. J. W. Hartwell, an able man, is elected in his place.

July 28, 1875. George W. Sisney is murdered at his home in Carbondale.

July 31, 1875. William Spence, Crainville storekeeper, is killed.

August 2, 1875. The Williamson County Commissioners offer a reward of $1,000 each for the arrest and conviction of the murderers of David Bulliner, James Henderson, Vincent Hinchcliff, and William Spence.

August 9, 1875. Governor John L. Beveridge of Illinois offers a reward of $400 each for the murderers of Bulliner, Henderson, Hinchcliff, and Spence, and also for the killers of George Bulliner and George W. Sisney.

August 22, 1875. The Jackson County Commissioners offer to pay

$400 each for the arrest and conviction of the men who murdered Sisney and George Bulliner.

September 9, 1875. B. F. Lowe apprehends Samuel Music at Cairo and brings him to Marion.

September 10, 1875. On the basis of Music's revelations, John Bulliner and several members of the Crain family are arrested and charged with the murder of George W. Sisney and William Spence. Marshall Crain, whom Music names as the murderer of Sisney, is still at large.

September 26, 1875. Lowe arrests Marshall Crain in Arkansas.

October 13, 1875. John Bulliner and Allen Baker, on trial at Murphysboro for conspiring to kill George W. Sisney, are convicted on the testimony of Marshall Crain and sentenced to twenty-five years in the penitentiary.

October 20, 1875. At Marion, Marshall Crain pleads guilty to the murder of William Spence and is sentenced to death by hanging.

Jauuary 21, 1876. Marshall Crain is hanged in the jailyard at Marion.

6. DOCTRINAIRE VS. UNION

1890. Samuel T. Brush organizes the St. Louis and Big Muddy Coal Company and sinks a shaft near Carterville, Illinois.

April 10, 1894. The miners' union—the United Mine Workers of America—calls a strike for April 21 in protest against subsubsistence wages.

April 21, 1894. Though unorganized, Brush's miners respond to the strike call.

June 16, 1894. The Brush miners return to work at the rates of pay prevailing before the strike.

1897. The St. Louis and Big Muddy tops all Illinois mines in production.

May 1, 1897. Illinois operators announce new reductions in miners' wages.

June 1897. The United Mine Workers of America issue a strike call for July 4.

July 4, 1897. Brush's men, unorganized, disregard the strike call.

July 15, 1897. Brush increases his pay scale, and his men promise to stay on the job for the duration of the strike.

January 1898. A U.M.W.A. local is organized at Brush's mine without his knowledge.

March 31, 1898. Most of Brush's miners strike when he refuses to meet a new pay-scale agreed upon by Illinois operators and the union. He continues to work the mine with a reduced force.

May 20, 1898. Brush imports a trainload of Negro miners.

May 30, 1898. Union miners surround the St. Louis and Big Muddy mine and try to dissuade the men from working. They fail.

May 15, 1899. A new local, recently organized, calls a strike at the Brush mine. Half his men walk out.

June 30, 1899. A contingent of Negro miners and their families, whom Brush is bringing in from Pana, is attacked at Lauder (now Cambria). One woman is killed, twenty persons are wounded.

July 2, 1899. Two companies of militia arrive at Carterville and restore order.

September 11, 1899. The troops are sent home.

September 12, 1899. Brush, in Murphysboro, is attacked and beaten by two unidentified assailants.

September 17, 1899. Five of Brush's Negro miners are killed in rioting at Carterville. Two companies of militia return to the scene.

December 4, 1899. The trial of the Lauder rioters, charged with murder, begins at Vienna, Johnson County.

January 7, 1900. The trial ends with a verdict of not guilty.

January 23, 1900. The Carterville rioters, also charged with murder, go on trial at Vienna.

March 4, 1900. A jury finds the Carterville rioters not guilty.

June 11, 1906. The Madison Coal Company takes over the Brush mine. Thereafter it is operated with union labor.

7. MILLIONAIRE VS. UNION

1901–2. Joseph Leiter and his father, Levi Z. Leiter, buy extensive coal acreage in Franklin County.

June 1, 1904. The Zeigler Coal Company, owned by the Leiters, hoists its first coal.

June 9, 1904. Levi Z. Leiter dies. His will vests the management of his coal properties in his son.

July 7, 1904. Joseph Leiter announces a reduction in miners' tonnage rates, justified, he contends, by the extensive use of mining machinery.

July 8, 1904. All Leiter's miners go out on strike. He imports guards and begins to fortify his property.

July 27, 1904. Leiter brings in the first of many contingents of non-union workmen.

November 25, 1904. Two Leiter officials are fired on from ambush. As a result of the attack several companies of militia are ordered to Zeigler.

February 8, 1905. The troops are withdrawn.

April 3, 1905. Fifty-four men lose their lives in an explosion at Leiter's mine.

November 4, 1908. Fire breaks out in the mine, and the state mining-inspector orders that the shaft be closed for ninety days.

January 10, 1909. Mine officials send a clean-up crew underground. An explosion follows, and twenty-six men are killed.

January 11, 1909. The state mining-inspector orders the Zeigler mine closed until further notice.

February 1, 1909. Disregarding the closing notice, mine officials send repair crews underground to prepare for operations.

February 9, 1909. Another explosion kills three men.

Late February 1909. Leiter closes down for good.

8. KLANSMAN AND DICTATOR

May 20, 1923. The Ku Klux Klan makes its first public appearance at revival services in Marion.

May 26, 1923. Klansmen, 2,000 strong, initiate 200 candidates in a field near Marion.

June 24, 1923. Klansmen visit the Methodist Church of Herrin and hand a contribution to the pastor.

July 26, 1923. The Klan initiates several hundred candidates at a huge meeting near Carterville.

August 20, 1923. The Klan stages a law-and-order demonstration in Marion, and that night initiates a large class.

November 1, 1923. S. Glenn Young, hired by the Klan to take charge of its law-enforcement program, arrives in Williamson County.

December 22, 1923. Klansmen, deputized by federal prohibition-agents and led by Young, raid scores of actual and alleged bootleggers.

January 5, 1924. The raiders strike again.

January 7, 1924. The Klan conducts a third raid.

January 8, 1924. Young, acquitted of an assault charge, flashes guns in the courtroom and the sheriff wires for troops. Three companies of militia are sent in.

January 15, 1924. Most of the troops are withdrawn.

January 20, 1924. Klansmen led by Young conduct another big liquor-raid.

February 1, 1924. The Klan stages the biggest raid of all. A special train is required to take those arrested to Benton for arraignment.

February 8, 1924. Caesar Cagle is killed in Herrin. Klansmen shoot up the Herrin hospital and Young takes control of the county. The militia returns.

9. THE KLAN WAR

February 12, 1924. Young yields to the regularly constituted officers of the county.

March 3, 1924. Trials of alleged bootleggers seized in the Klan raids begin in the U.S. District Court at Danville.

March 14, 1924. The grand jury of the Herrin City Court returns ninety-nine indictments in connection with the murder of Caesar Cagle and the attack on the Herrin hospital.

March 17, 1924. The Klan stages a huge parade in Herrin as a protest against the action of the grand jury. Scores rush to sign the bonds of the indicted men.

April 25, 1924. Young takes over the job of reorganizing the Klan in East St. Louis.

10. DEATH IN A CIGAR STORE

May 23, 1924. Young and his wife, driving from Marion to East St. Louis, are attacked by the occupants of a passing car and seriously wounded.

May 24, 1924. Jack Skelcher, believed to be one of the Youngs' assailants, is killed by Klan "police" on the outskirts of Herrin.

June 26, 1924. Young and Klansmen make a threatening display of weapons at Carlyle when the Shelton brothers and Charlie Briggs, accused of the assault on Young and his wife, appear for a preliminary hearing.

July 9, 1924. The Klan dismisses Young from his position in East St. Louis.

July 29, 1924. Federal Judge Walter C. Lindley rules that Young must stand trial in the state courts on indictments growing out of the liquor raids.

August 25, 1924. Judge Bowen of the Herrin City Court rules that bonds totaling $39,000 be forfeited when Young fails to appear in a larceny case in which he is a defendant.

August 28, 1924. The Klan puts on a huge demonstration at the county fairgrounds.

August 30, 1924. In a riot between Klan and anti-Klan factions at John Smith's garage in Herrin six men are killed. The militia returns.

September 13, 1924. Young is officially expelled from the Klan.

October 11, 1924. Ora Thomas, ex-bootlegger, anti-Klansman, and bitter enemy of Young's, is appointed a deputy sheriff.

January 24, 1925. Thomas, Young, and two of Young's henchmen die in a gunfight at Herrin.

11. THE KLAN LOSES

February 7, 1925. As a part of a compromise between the factions Sheriff Galligan, anti-Klansman, turns over his office to a deputy and agrees to leave the county.

May 12, 1925. Galligan returns and resumes his office.

May 24, 1925. Harold S. Williams, evangelist, begins a series of revival meetings intended to reunite the faction-torn community.

June 27, 1925. The State's Attorney moves to strike 145 cases, all originating in the Klan war, from the docket.

July 3, 1925. The *Herrin Herald,* Klan newspaper, is attached by creditors and ceases publication.

July 12, 1925. The Williams revival, its purpose apparently achieved, comes to an end.

April 13, 1926. In an election-day riot at Herrin three Klansmen and three anti-Klansmen are killed. This marks the end of the Klan in Williamson County.

12. GANG WAR

July 1926. Fights and killings in Herrin point to a war between rival gangsters.

August 22, 1926. Harry Walker and Everett Smith kill each other in a roadhouse brawl.

September 12, 1926. "Wild Bill" Holland, Mack Pulliam, and Pulliam's wife are shot as they leave a roadhouse near Herrin. Holland dies.

September 14, 1926. Gangsters attack an ambulance carrying Pulliam from Herrin to Benton and beat the wounded man into unconsciousness.

October 4, 1926. Occupants of an armored truck owned by the Shelton brothers fire on Art Newman, a gangster allied with Charlie Birger, and Newman's wife on the highway near Harrisburg.

October 14, 1926. Birger gangsters shoot up and wreck an unoccupied roadhouse owned by the Sheltons.

October 25, 1926. Birger and a gang of his followers demand that Joe Adams, mayor of West City and friend of the Sheltons, surrender the body of the Sheltons' armored truck, and threaten to kill him when he refuses.

October 26, 1926. The dead body of "High Pockets" McQuay, Birger gangster, is found near Herrin. On the same day the body of "Casey" Jones, another Birger follower, is found in a creek near Equality.

October 28, 1926. Early in the morning a roadhouse near Johnston City, said to belong to Birger, is shot up and set on fire. It burns to the ground.

November 6, 1926. John Milroy is killed in a roadhouse near Colp. Shortly afterward W. J. Stone, mayor of the town, is fatally shot and the chief of police, James C. Keith, is wounded.

November 10, 1926. A homemade bomb is tossed at Birger's roadhouse, Shady Rest, but misses its mark.

November 12, 1926. Machine-gunners fire into the home of Joe Adams, in West City, from automobiles. An airplane drops homemade bombs, which fail to explode, on Shady Rest.

November 19, 1926. A bomb damages the home of Joe Adams but the occupants escape injury.

December 12, 1926. Two young men murder Joe Adams at his front door.

287

January 9, 1927. Shady Rest is bombed and burned to the ground. Four bodies are found in the ruins.

January 19, 1927. Lory Price, state highway-patrolman and friend of Birger's, is discovered to be missing. Mrs. Price has also disappeared.

13. MURDER—AND MORE MURDER

January 31, 1927. Carl, Earl, and Bernie Shelton go on trial for mail robbery in the United States Court at Quincy.

February 4, 1927. The Sheltons are found guilty, largely on the testimony of Charlie Birger and Art Newman.

February 5, 1927. The Sheltons are sentenced to twenty-five years in the federal penitentiary. On the same day the bullet-riddled body of Lory Price is found in a field near Dubois in Washington County.

March 4, 1927. Harry Thomasson and two other Birger hangers-on are convicted of robbery at Marion, and sentenced to ten years' imprisonment.

April 29, 1927. Charlie Birger is arrested and charged with the murder of Joe Adams.

April 30, 1927. In open court at Benton, Harry Thomasson confesses that he and his brother Elmo killed Joe Adams at Birger's instigation.

May 9, 1927. The Williamson County grand jury indicts Rado Millich, Clarence Rone, and Ural Gowen, all Birger gangsters, for the murder of "Casey" Jones, also a Birger henchman.

May 23, 1927. Art Newman is arrested at Long Beach, California, on information that he is wanted for the murder of Joe Adams.

May 26, 1927. The Shelton brothers are granted a new trial and freed on bond after Harry Dungey, Birger gangster who testified against them, admits that he perjured himself.

June 11, 1927. At Nashville, Illinois, Art Newman appears in court and admits that he took part in the murder of Lory Price and his wife. He charges Birger, Connie Ritter, Ernest Blue, Leslie Simpson, and Riley Simmons with participation in the crime. All are indicted.

June 13, 1927. The body of Mrs. Price is uncovered in an abandoned mine where Newman stated it would be found.

June 24, 1927. Rado Millich and Ural Gowen go on trial at Marion for the murder of "Casey" Jones. Clarence Rone turns state's evidence and is not prosecuted.

July 7, 1927. A jury finds both defendants guilty and sets Gowen's punishment at twenty-five years in the penitentiary, Millich's at death.

14. THE HANGING OF CHARLIE BIRGER

July 6, 1927. Charlie Birger, Art Newman, and Ray Hyland go on trial at Benton for the murder of Joe Adams.

July 27, 1927. The jury finds the three defendants guilty and decrees death for Birger, life imprisonment for Newman and Hyland. Birger is sentenced to be hanged on October 25, 1927.

October 5, 1927. Birger's attorneys file a petition for a writ of error with the state Supreme Court.

October 7, 1927. The Supreme Court grants Birger a stay of execution.

October 21, 1927. Rado Millich is hanged in the jailyard at Marion.

February 24 1928. The Supreme Court denies Birger's appeal for a new trial and directs that the original sentence be carried out on April 13, 1928.

April 12, 1928. The Illinois Board of Pardons and Paroles refuses to intercede in Birger's case. On the same day his attorney files a petition for a sanity hearing. The judge orders a stay of execution until the hearing can be held.

April 16, 1928. A jury finds Birger sane, and his execution is set for April 19.

April 19, 1928. Birger is hanged in the jailyard at Benton.

15. JUSTICE

September 20, 1928. Leslie Simpson, under indictment for the murder of Lory Price, is arrested in New York.

November 5, 1928. In court at Marion, Simpson pleads guilty to the murder of Lory Price.

November 7, 1928. Simpson's plea is accepted, but the judge defers sentence.

November 16, 1928. In the U.S. District Court at East St. Louis, Arlie O. Boswell, State's Attorney of Williamson County, and several other county and city officials are indicted for conspiring to violate the national prohibition law.

January 7, 1929. The trial of Art Newman, Leslie Simpson, Riley Simmons, and Freddie Wooten for the murder of Lory Price begins at Marion. The defendants all plead guilty, but the judge orders the prosecution to present its evidence.

January 9, 1929. The four defendants are sentenced to life imprisonment under one indictment, and to fifty-seven years under two others.

January 21, 1929. Arlie O. Boswell goes on trial in the Federal Court at East St. Louis.

January 25, 1929. Boswell is found guilty of violating the national prohibition law.

February 2, 1929. Boswell is fined $5,000 and sentenced to two years in the penitentiary.

October 18, 1929. Connie Ritter, under indictment for the murder of Joe Adams, Lory Price, and Ethel Price, is arrested at Gulfport, Mississippi.

May 25, 1930. In court at Benton, Ritter pleads guilty to the Adams murder, and is sentenced to life imprisonment.

CONCLUSION

October 23, 1941. Ural Gowen is discharged from prison at the expiration of his sentence.

October 23, 1947. Carl Shelton is killed on his farm near Fairfield, Illinois.

January 6, 1948. Connie Ritter dies in Menard Penitentiary.

July 26, 1948. Bernie Shelton is killed in front of his tavern outside Peoria.

May 24, 1949. Earl Shelton is shot in the Farmers' Club at Fairfield but recovers.

June 7, 1950. Roy Shelton is shot to death while driving a tractor on his Wayne County farm.

March 13, 1950. Leslie Simpson is paroled.

January 23, 1951. Harry Thomasson is paroled.

April 17, 1951. The Sheltons sell most of their Illinois land. All except the mother of the brothers and one of their sisters disappear.

June 28, 1951. The sister—Mrs. Lulu Shelton Pennington—and her husband are machine-gunned in Fairfield. Though seriously wounded, both survive.

July 9, 1951. Ray Hyland is paroled.

December 1, 1951. The Shelton homestead, now unoccupied, is detroyed by fire.

SOURCES

∞

In General

WHEN the Herrin Massacre took place, Oldham Paisley, editor of the *Marion Republican,* began pasting his own stories of the tragedy, as well as those which came to him in exchanges, in a scrapbook. He continued the process until the last Birger gangster was sent to the penitentiary in 1930. By that time he had filled thirteen books, and had preserved an incomparable record of most of the events with which this study deals.

Today, these scrapbooks, kept in the Marion Public Library, are the only local contemporary record of what happened in Williamson County between 1922 and 1930. Except for the chapters on the Bloody Vendetta and the Brush and Leiter mining ventures (v, vi, and vii), they have been my primary reliance and may be taken as my authority where no specific sources are indicated.

I write under circumstances that compel me to have practically every source I intend to use microfilmed or photostatted. Thus, in addition to a microfilm copy of the Paisley scrapbooks, as well as a complete set of projection prints, I acquired a microfilm copy of the *Illinois Miner* from November 25, 1922 to December 28, 1929 (the only extant file is in the Department of Labor Library), a microfilm copy of the stenographic transcript of the proceedings of the Herrin Investigating Committee, hundreds of photostats of magazine articles and newspapers not represented in the Paisley scrapbooks, a large number of clippings, and many pamphlets and books relating to my subject. These have all been placed in the library of the Chicago Historical Society, where anyone who wishes to check my sources, or examine the great surplus of original material that I could not use, may consult them.

In Particular

1. MASSACRE

There is no satisfactory account of the Herrin Massacre. The longest narratives within books are to be found in Oscar Ameringer's *If You*

Don't Weaken (New York: Holt; 1940), McAlister Coleman's *Men and Coal* (New York: Farrar & Rinehart; 1943), and Saul D. Alinsky's *John L. Lewis, An Unauthorized Biography* (New York: Putnam; 1949). All are superficial, incomplete, and biased. The one full-length account—*The Herrin Massacre,* by Chatland Parker (Chicago: Parker Publishing Company; 1923)—is accurate factually, but incomplete and repellingly hortatory. Besides, copies are almost impossible to find.

My account, in this chapter, is based almost entirely upon the sworn testimony of witnesses at the two trials and the legislative investigation. For the trials, I have followed the day-to-day reports in the *Marion Republican;* the testimony before the House Investigating Committee comes from the stenographic transcript of the committee's hearings, now to be found in the Archives Division of the Illinois State Library, Springfield. Formal testimony has been supplemented by the accounts that survivors—notably Bernard Jones and Edward Rose—gave to Thoreau Cronyn of the *New York Herald* and George E. Lyndon, Jr., of the *Brooklyn Daily Eagle.* Quotations used here are from the *Herald* of July 12 and July 13, 1922; and from the *Daily Eagle* of August 15 and August 19, 1922.

Donald M. Ewing, who appears in this chapter as Don Ewing, is now associate editor of the *Shreveport Times,* Shreveport, Louisiana. In correspondence during the summer and fall of 1951 he confirmed my account of his experiences during the Massacre and added vivid details.

2. APPROACH TO MASSACRE

This chapter opens with a characterization of William J. Lester, and an interpretation of his motives in deciding to defy the striking miners, that differs considerably from all previous accounts. As far as I know, no earlier writer on this subject has even attempted to find out what kind of man Lester really was. For my information I am indebted to Mr. R. H. Sherwood of Indianapolis, who knew him intimately for twenty years, and Mr. Arthur S. Lytton of Chicago, former member of the firm of Bull, Lytton and Olson, his Chicago lawyers.

My account of the somewhat devious course followed by local mine-union officials immediately before the Massacre is based on this passage from an address that Follett W. Bull, of Lester's law firm, made before the Association of Life Insurance Counsel on May 24,

1923 (published as a pamphlet with the title, "The Herrin Massacre"):

> It was with a distinct understanding on Mr. Lester's part with the Union officials, that that being a small mine, and its output small anyway, that that coal might be placed around in southern Illinois in charitable institutions, even during the strike; and as a matter of fact . . . they did load coal with Union men, United Mine Workers men, for one day only. . . . It immediately aroused considerable opposition, and Hugh Willis, who was the National Board member of the United Mine Workers for that district, came to him and said . . . "You better lay off for a couple of days and then you go on again"—which was done. In the meantime the sentiment got so strong against the Union men loading out any coal for any purpose, charitable institution or otherwise, that Hugh Willis told him it was impossible, they could not go on with the agreement to let them run.

This accords with the recollection of Arthur S. Lytton. A. B. McLaren, of Marion, recalls that Lester intimated to him that he had the local union officials "fixed." McLaren warned him that neither he nor anyone could "fix" the rank and file, and that the rank and file would cause serious trouble.

The report of the United States Coal Commission, from which I quote, is to be found in the National Archives, Washington. Stories of the arrogance of Lester's guards rest on testimony given at the first trial. The narrative of the efforts that Hunter and his associates made to avert trouble and to effect a truce after the attack on the mine had taken place is based almost entirely upon testimony before the House Investigating Committee, principally by Hunter, Edrington, and General Black, but I have also drawn upon Hunter's personal record of events, published in the *Marion Post*, June 24, 1922.

3. MASSACRE: THE AFTERMATH

The first paragraph of this chapter is a composite of editorial opinion as expressed by the St. *Louis Globe-Democrat,* the *New York Evening World,* the *New York Times,* the *Los Angeles Times,* the *Baltimore Sun,* and the *Augusta Journal* within a day or two of the Massacre. The *Congressional Record* is, of course, the source for the strictures spoken in the Senate and House of Representatives. The *Chicago Tribune's* comment on the verdict of the coroner's jury is to be found in the issue of June 27, 1922; that of the *St. Louis Times* in its issue of June 28, 1922. Other papers quoted in this connection are the *St. Louis Globe-Democrat* for June 27, and the *Detroit Free Press* and the *New York Herald* of the same date.

A photostat of the flyer, cited in the text, of the Illinois Manufacturers' Association, a copy of the National Coal Association's pamphlet, "The Herrin Conspiracy," and a photostat of the folder, "Herrin Massacre," issued by John Price Jones (my source for the Pershing quotation), are now in the Chicago Historical Society. The appeal of the Illinois Chamber of Commerce is recorded in that organization's official publication, the *Illinois Journal of Commerce,* for September 1922. Editorial comment on the appeal is taken from the October issue of the same publication. My authority for the miners' defense fund is Carroll Binder's article, "Herrin—Murder Trial or Holy Cause?" in *The Nation,* October 11, 1922, as well as press dispatches.

In the remainder of this chapter I have relied principally on the *Marion Republican.* In addition: the *Illinois Miner* of September 16, 1922 on the anti-union motives of the employing class; Philip Kinsley in the *Chicago Tribune* for September 2 and August 29; and the *Literary Digest* of October 14, 1922, summarizing editorial reaction, including that of labor papers, to the report of the Williamson County grand jury.

4. TWO TRIALS AND AN INVESTIGATION

The first pages of this chapter—to the point, in fact, where Kerr makes the opening speech for the defense—are based upon the stories of metropolitan-newspaper correspondents, principally McAlister Coleman in the *New York World,* November 14, 1922, and the *Illinois Miner,* January 27, 1923; Philip Kinsley in the *Chicago Tribune,* November 19, 1922; Landon Laird in the *Kansas City Star* (quoted at length in the *Literary Digest,* February 10, 1923); and staff correspondent in the *St. Louis Post-Dispatch,* November 26 and December 3, 1922. Philip Kinsley's dispatches—colorful, comprehensive, balanced—seem to me to be models of reporting. The same could be said of McAlister Coleman's were it not for their strong prolabor bias.

The reports of the *Marion Republican* are my source for both trials, and provided considerable material for the account of the legislative investigation. That part of the chapter, however, is drawn in the main from the stenographic transcript of the hearings before the Herrin Investigating Committee, to which I have already referred. Both majority and minority reports were printed in the *Journal of the House of Representatives of the 53rd General Assembly* (Springfield, Ill.: 1923).

Editorial commentary on the verdict of the first trial is taken from a comprehensive summary in the *Literary Digest* for February 3, 1923. The quotations used are from the *Baltimore American*, the *Newark* (N.J.) *News*, the *New York Daily News*, the *Chicago Journal of Commerce*, the *Rockford Star*, the *New York Call*, the *Pennsylvania Labor Herald*, and the *Herrin News*.

5. THE BLOODY VENDETTA

The most complete account of the Bloody Vendetta is to be found in the incomparable book of Milo Erwin, originally published in 1876 as *The History of Williamson County, Illinois*, but reprinted in 1914 and again in 1927 with the cover title, *The Bloody Vendetta*, by which it is generally known. Erwin's narrative is verbose, tortuous, and clothed in purple prose the like of which one seldom encounters, but the man had firsthand knowledge of the feud and a high regard for accuracy. The shorter treatment by George W. Young, "The Williamson County Vendetta," in *Transactions of the Illinois State Historical Society for 1914*, is also useful.

Newspapers of the time devoted many columns to the Bloody Vendetta. Long summary accounts appeared in the *Illinois State Journal* (Springfield), February 9, 1875, which reprinted an article from the *St. Louis Democrat* which I have been unable to locate, and in the *Chicago Weekly Tribune*, August 18, 1875. My account of the effort to obtain state aid for Williamson County is based on the reports that appeared in various issues of the *Chicago Tribune* during January, February, and March, 1875. Editorial condemnation of Governor Beveridge is drawn from a "round-up" article that the *Chicago Tribune* published August 10, 1875. A file of the *Marion Monitor* for 1874 and 1875, now in the Marion Public Library, contains much useful information.

6. DOCTRINAIRE VS. UNION

No history of mining in Illinois even approaches adequacy. The best is S. O. Andros, *Coal Mining in Illinois* (Urbana: Bulletin No. 13,

Illinois Coal Mining Investigations; 1915), but even my brief account of the development of the Williamson County field and the beginnings of Brush's operation had to be chiseled from the Illinois official publication, *Statistics of Coal in Illinois: A Supplemental Report of the State Bureau of Labor Statistics,* issued annually during the 1890's. There is good local material in the *History of Gallatin, Saline, Hamilton, Franklin and Williamson Counties, Illinois* (Chicago: 1887), and in the *Historical Souvenir of Williamson County Illinois* (Effingham, Ill.: 1905).

Existing accounts of the unionization of the Illinois coalfield are unsatisfactory. McAlister Coleman deals with the subject in *Men and Coal,* but I have relied principally upon *Statistics of Coal in Illinois,* Karl Myron Scott's unpublished doctoral dissertation, "The Coal Industry and the Coal Miners' Unions in the United States Since the World War" (University of Illinois; 1931), Chris Evans, *History of United Mine Workers of America* (n.p., n.d.), and the testimony of John Mitchell and other U.M.W.A. officials before the Industrial Commission, published in Vol. XII of the Commission's Reports, *Report of the Industrial Commission on the Relations and Conditions of Capital and Labor Employed in the Mining Industry* (Washington, D.C.: 1901).

Brush's first difficulties with the union are described in summary articles in the *Marion Leader,* October 5, 1899, which reprinted a recent *Chicago Inter-Ocean* story that I have not seen in its original form, and in the *St. Louis Globe-Democrat* of December 9, 1899. Good accounts of the Virden and Pana riots, which tie into Brush's fight with the union, are included in the fourth and fifth *Annual Reports, State Board of Arbitration of Illinois,* and in John Winfield Scott's unpublished doctoral dissertation, "The Policing of Non-urban Industry" (University of Chicago; 1929). The *Marion Leader* for the period, now in the Marion Public Library, provides the local day-to-day record.

My story of the Lauder riot is taken from the *Chicago Tribune,* July 1 and 2, 1899, and from the *Marion Leader,* July 6, 1899. The account of the Carterville riot is drawn from contemporary newsdispatches in the *Chicago Tribune* and *Marion Leader,* and from testimony offered at the trial of the rioters. Both trials were reported in great detail by the *St. Louis Globe-Democrat.* The stories appeared in that paper almost daily from early December 1899 to January 8, 1900, and again from mid-February to early March, 1900.

7. MILLIONAIRE VS. UNION

The best source for Leiter's venture into coal mining and for his side of his struggle with the union is the elaborate *Brief and Argument for Joseph Leiter and Nancy Lathrop Carver Campbell, Appellees*, in the case of *Marguerite Hyde Suffolk and Berks* vs. *Joseph Leiter et al.*, Appellate Court of Illinois, First District, October Term, 1928. In this case, a celebrated one, Leiter defended himself against charges that he had mismanaged his father's estate. He and his associates are quoted at length in the brief. Their testimony, though biased, is invaluable. For a copy of the brief I am indebted to Mr. Alfred M. Rogers of Chicago, one of Leiter's counsel and now president of the Zeigler Coal & Coke Company. Through the courtesy of Judge Charles G. Briggle of the United States District Court, Southern District of Illinois, I have also used to good purpose the Amended and Supplemental Bill in the case of the *Zeigler Coal Company* vs. *William Morris et al.*, filed in the Circuit Court of the United States in and for the Southern District of Illinois, December 20, 1905. C. H. Leichleiter's article, "The War at Zeigler," in *The Reader Magazine* for February 1905, is objective, thorough, and colorful. For a running account of the strike I have depended mainly on the *St. Louis Globe-Democrat* for the months of July and August, 1904. Its coverage was excellent.

Statistics of Coal in Illinois, to which I have already referred, furnishes the best accounts of the disasters of April 3, 1905, January 10, 1909, and February 9, 1909. The *Brief and Argument*, cited in the preceding paragraph, also contains valuable material.

The whole Leiter story is well told in a feature article by Dickson Terry, "Final Shutdown for Famous Coal Mine," in the Everyday Magazine of the *St. Louis Post-Dispatch*, January 13, 1949.

8. KLANSMAN AND DICTATOR

In addition to the *Marion Republican*, I have drawn heavily on the *St. Louis Post-Dispatch*, the *St. Louis Globe-Democrat*, and the *Chicago Tribune*, all of which covered in great detail the principal events described in this chapter. Galligan's own story, *In Bloody Williamson*, written by Jack Wilkinson and published in 1927 (n.p.), is a sounder work than its lurid paper covers would indicate. On the other hand, the *Life and Exploits of S. Glenn Young* (Herrin: Mrs. S. Glenn Young; 1924), is such an egregious piece of special pleading that it is almost worthless.

SOURCES

There is valuable material, which I have used in the first part of this chapter, in two magazine articles: "Bloody Williamson County," by Edward A. Wieck, in *The Nation*, January 3, 1923, and "Ku Kluxing in the Miners' Country," by Agnes Barnes Wieck, in *The New Republic*, March 26, 1924. The S. Glenn Young File of the Department of Justice, now in the Department of Justice Files, National Archives, is rich and often, in perspective, amusing.

9. THE KLAN WAR

No part of the book has presented more problems than the sketch of S. Glenn Young with which this chapter opens. Most of the biographical material that Young inspired is sheer fiction. George B. Young (a brother) of Lisbon, Iowa, Ira C. Young (not related) of Long Island, Kansas, and Marquette University have supplied some facts; but many more came from the Young files in the Department of Justice and the Treasury Department. The Treasury file is invaluable, and I am deeply indebted to Secretary John W. Snyder for allowing me to use it. It was there that I found the report of Special Agents A. A. Young and David Nolan, April 30, 1921, which resulted in Young's dismissal from the Prohibition Unit.

The story of the events narrated here is taken almost entirely from the contemporary press—principally the *Marion Republican*, the *St. Louis Post-Dispatch*, and the *St. Louis Globe-Democrat*. I have also made use of a series of feature stories by Jack M. Williams that appeared in the *Danville Commercial News* at various times during February and March, 1924.

10. DEATH IN A CIGAR STORE—15. JUSTICE

The narrative in these six chapters is derived almost entirely from contemporary newspapers—the *Marion Republican*, the *Marion Post* (especially for the gang war and Birger), the *St. Louis Post-Dispatch*, the *St. Louis Globe-Democrat*, and the *St. Louis Star*. Dates not given explicitly in the text will be found in the Chronology (pp. 285–90), so readers who want to consult the newspapers I have used should have little difficulty in finding the specific issues.

CONCLUSION

The story of the Sheltons is told in detail by John Bartlow Martin in "The Shelton Boys," one of the chapters in his *Butcher's Dozen and*

Other Murders (New York: Harper; 1950). Mauritz A. Hallgren's article, "Bloody Williamson Is Hungry," appeared in *The Nation,* April 30, 1932. *Seven Stranded Coal Towns: A Study of an American Depressed Area,* by Malcolm Brown and John N. Webb, was published by the Government Printing Office in 1941, but is already a hard book to find.

St. Louis newspapers have printed a number of articles recently on the industrial progress of Williamson County, but I have received most of my information from those who have had a hand in the work.

INDEX

●●

Prairie State Books

Mr. Dooley in Peace
and in War
Finley Peter Dunne

Life in Prairie Land
Eliza W. Farnham

Carl Sandburg
Harry Golden

The Sangamon
Edgar Lee Masters

American Years
Harold Sinclair

The Jungle
Upton Sinclair

Twenty Years at
Hull-House
Jane Addams

They Broke the Prairie
Earnest Elmo Calkins

The Illinois
James Gray

The Valley of Shadows:
Sangamon Sketches
Francis Grierson

The Precipice
Elia W. Peattie

Across Spoon River
Edgar Lee Masters

The Rivers of Eros
Cyrus Colter

Summer on the Lakes, in 1843
Margaret Fuller

Black Hawk: An Autobiography
Edited by Donald Jackson

You Know Me Al
Ring W. Lardner

Chicago Poems
Carl Sandburg

Bloody Williamson
Paul M. Angle

City of Discontent
Mark Harris

Wau-Bun: The "Early Day"
in the North-West
Juliette M. Kinzie

UNIVERSITY OF ILLINOIS PRESS
1325 SOUTH OAK STREET
CHAMPAIGN, ILLINOIS 61820-6903
WWW.PRESS.UILLINOIS.EDU